# MELTING THE ICE

*Engaging and educational ice-breaker activities for every learning session*

---

**Jen Schneider**

**First published 2023**

by John Catt Educational Ltd,

15 Riduna Park, Station Road,
Melton, Woodbridge IP12 1QT
UK
Tel: +44 (0) 1394 389850

4500 140th Ave North,
Suite 101, Clearwater,
FL 33762-3848
US
Tel: +1 561 448 1987

Email: enquiries@johncatt.com
Website: www.johncatt.com



**ISBN: 978 1 915261 03 8**

Set and designed by John Catt Educational Limited

# Table of Contents

Jen Schneider is an educator, instructional designer, and curriculum developer passionate about creating interactive and engaged learning environments. She teaches in both online and face-to-face settings. She also mentors teaching faculty in a variety of capacities. Her active research interests include assessment, equitable grading practices, feedback for learning, and open pedagogy.

# Introduction

As learning experiences increasingly occur in synchronous and asynchronous learning environments, strategies that both welcome students to class and support student learning are increasingly important. Traditional ice breakers, while typically shared with a goal of building community and student engagement, can sometimes have unintended and even negative consequences for students (Gonzalez, 2016; Mather, 2020; Walter, 2020). This text shares a collection of opening activities that are designed to simultaneously engage students, build safe and connected classroom communities, and support student learning. All strategies can be easily adapted and personalized to fit individual course and content needs. The strategies are adaptable for face-to-face, synchronous online, and asynchronous online learning contexts. Shared activities are aligned with associated learning-science research and incorporate strategies that have been shown to promote student engagement and learning. Activities rely on strategies such as retrieval practice, active recall, spaced practice, and interleaving, among other evidence-based instructional strategies.

# The Opening Minutes

The opening minutes of a classroom experience are critical. The tone set in a session's first five-ten minutes can significantly impact and influence, in both positive and negative ways, the quality and nature of the subsequent learning experience. How a teacher begins classroom instruction can set the tone for an entire time (session, semester, year) spent with students and as a class community. How students spend that time can also have a positive impact on their learning in both the short and long term. When the opening minutes of a class are approached as an opportunity to build student connections, collaboration, and community, all learners benefit.

> "The greatness of a community is most accurately measured by the compassionate actions of its members."
>
> *Coretta Scott King*

# The Benefits of Warm-Up Activities

The term *ice breaker* refers to a broad category of activities that typically include games, activities, and/or exercises that are designed to warm-up a conversation, welcome participants, and create a learning community. These warm-up activities are often used in classrooms, meetings, trainings, team-building sessions, and other events to encourage engagement among a group of learners and session participants. Ice breakers are often used to both encourage and support the interaction of a group of individuals who may or may not have worked with one another in a prior context.

Ice breaker or warm-up activities are excellent opportunities to increase student comfort with (and within) a class as well as the associated classroom community. Research on the importance of warm-ups is extensive. When done well, warm-ups can build community, encourage and infuse a positive tone, build trust, and set a foundation for productive and positive relationship building (Baldomero Loor Ponce et al., 2020; Cotter, 2000). Effective warm-ups can also lead to a more relaxed and supportive learning environment, contribute to positive student engagement, and support student ownership in the overall classroom experience (Baldomero Loor Ponce et al., 2020; Cotter, 2000).

### Pantry/Resource List

- ☐ Icebreakers: Why are they important? See: https://swiftkickhq.com/icebreakers-why-important/
- ☐ Icebreakers. See: https://teaching.cornell.edu/teaching-resources/building-inclusive-classrooms/icebreakers
- ☐ The Three Benefits of Using Ice Breakers. See: https://drexel.edu/goodwin/professional-studies-blog/overview/2018/July/The-3-benefits-of-ising-ice-breakers/
- ☐ 20 Great Icebreakers for the Classroom. See: https://www.gpb.org/blogs/education-matters/2016/07/21/20-great-icebreakers-for-the-classroom
- ☐ 20 Classroom Icebreakers for College Professors. See: https://tophat.com/blog/classroom-icebreakers/
- ☐ Please, No More Ice-Breakers. See: https://teachingsixes.com/iste_3/please-no-more-icebreakers/
- ☐ Ice Breaker and Warm-Up Exercises. See: https://marylandcasa.org/wp-content/uploads/2013/09/icebreakers-bklt-Annual-Conference-2011.pdf

These first five (or more) minutes of class are often where connection, community, and collaboration both originate and form (Eure & Milner, 2004). Those opening minutes are also the seeds and critical ingredients from which a lesson grows. These seeds/ingredients, however, are as varied as our students. There are more than 250,000 different types of flower seeds on record. There are even more ingredients in a market and/or culinary cupboard. Recipes are similarly infinite in number. As we think about the variation, we might also consider the instructional ingredients we bring to our classrooms. In this text, we explore some of the many different types of seeds and seasonings we might use to initiate our classroom instruction and build our classroom communities.

## The Importance of Warm-Up Activities

As noted, warm-ups have long been a part of face-to-face instruction and research on the importance of warm-up activities is extensive. The first few minutes of class are incredibly important. These important first few minutes, however, are often a challenge to sustain in content-related ways in both online and face-to-face learning contexts.

### Pantry/Resource List

- ☐ Why You Should Always Start with a Warmer. See: https://busyteacher.org/7610-why-you-should-always-start-with-a-warmer.html7 Activities to Build Community and Positive Classroom Culture During Online Learning. See: https://www.nytimes.com/2020/08/27/learning/7-activities-to-build-community-and-positive-classroom-culture-during-online-learning.html
- ☐ Some like it hot: Don't forget to warm up online learning spaces. See: https://www.timeshighereducation.com/opinion/some-it-hot-dont-forget-warm-online-learning-spaces

Ice breakers are often used to help build community. They can set tone, build trust, offer opportunities for connection, and initiate relationship building (Rosegard & Wilson, 2013).

## Pantry/Resource List

**Reduce tension and anxiety**

- ☐ Icebreakers to Reduce Stress and Build Connection. See: https://it.osu.edu/news/2020/07/22/icebreakers-reduce-stress-and-build-connection
- ☐ 7 Icebreakers for Small Groups to Break the Tension. See: https://www.time-management-abilities.com/icebreaker-games-for-small-groups.html
- ☐ Debnath, B., & Jayakrishnan, K. (2017, March–April). Ice breakers to de-stress college students. *International Journal of Pharmaceutical Sciences Review and Research*, 43(2), 97–102.
- ☐ 20 Great Icebreakers for the Classroom. See: https://www.gpb.org/blogs/education-matters/2016/07/21/20-great-icebreakers-for-the-classroom

**Encourage interaction**

- ☐ The Importance of Icebreakers in Online Classes. See: https://dl.sps.northwestern.edu/blog/2015/07/the-importance-of-icebreakers-in-online-classes/
- ☐ Icebreakers, Introductions, Energizers, and other Experiential Activities. See: https://www.albany.edu/cpr/gf/resources/Icebreakers-and-Introductions.htm

**Create expectations of learning through active engagement**

- ☐ 7 Active Icebreakers to Get Your Students Up and Moving. See: https://www.weareteachers.com/active-icebreakers/

# The Challenges

Despite good intentions, ice breakers do not always achieve desired goals. In many iterations, ice breakers have the potential to create situations directly counter to those intended. For example, many icebreaker activities unintentionally pressure students to share personal information. It is important to find ways to build community, collaboration, trust, and connection without pressuring students to share in potentially uncomfortable ways. In addition to concerns regarding the impact of common warm-ups on student privacy and comfort, there are also concerns that many ice breakers have little, if any, alignment with course learning goals and objectives.

> "Act as if what you do makes a difference. It does."
>
> *William James*

# Online Learning Contexts and Community-Building Challenges

To develop and sustain supportive classroom communities in which every member feels valued requires both intentionality and care. In both face-to-face and online classrooms, community cannot be taken for granted. Rather, community and connection must be nurtured and cultivated. Cultivation, however, requires a variety of factors, many of which are contextually dependent.

# Options

So, how can instructors better connect, collaborate, and engage with, for, and alongside their students? This text offers a collection of recipes that are all adaptable, customizable, and able to be personalized to best suit the needs and dynamics of any individual classroom setting.

## A Recipe to Break/Melt the Ice

**I:** Interaction/Instruction
**C:** Community/Connection
**E:** Engagement/Energy

# The Recipe Box/What Follows

This text presents (cooks up) a collection of powerful opening activities (ice breaker recipes) that are designed to engage students, build classroom communities, and support student learning. All strategies are pedagogically grounded in educational research and can be easily adapted and personalized. Many are variations on well-loved and long-used activities. Many will seem familiar. Hopefully, you'll also find some new ideas to adapt and implement to fit individual course and content needs.

Each recipe and illustrative warm-up can be adapted and adopted in online learning experiences as well as face-to-face learning environments. All activities are aligned with research-based learning strategies. Each of the activities is presented as an item in a buffet. Sample one or more. Taste and season to suit your individual classroom needs. Adapt and refine over time.

# A Learning Buffet

Why a buffet? Easy! There is no one recipe for optimal learning experiences. Buffets have been a staple of the food industry for decades. In traditional buffets, large bowls of nutritious—and often delicious—treats are placed on ice for cooling and freshness. Hungry guests dig in, sample, and taste a plethora of foods. Buffets are as varied as the individuals who enjoy them. Buffets and the individuals who enjoy them are also as varied as our learners.

Think of this collection of activities as a buffet of ice breaker options for you and your learners. Select one, select several. Create platters. Mix, adapt, and season as desired. Curate the perfect plate of instruction as you work to break the ice and build learning communities that strengthen learning and connection for all students. Dig in to learn more! Season as desired. Enjoy! Share!

# Test Kitchen Structure & Recipe Tidbits

## Buffet of Ice Breaker Activities

- Educational focus
- Content alignment
- Avoid personal/private questions
- Adaptable to any course content or discipline
- How-tos
- Links to supporting materials

## Buffet Style

- Open access
- Select, mix, and adapt
- Make a platter
- Garden style—pick several, make a salad, toss

## How Activities are Presented and Organized

- Aligned with one or more associated learning strategies
- Pairable activities (stack, mix, adapt)
- Anticipated time to prep
- Anticipated time to consume

## Best Practices when Introducing an Activity

- Explain how the activity is related to content
- Explain how the activity is important for learning
- Explain the learning science behind each activity

## Tools Needed (to Break the Ice)

- A positive attitude, enthusiasm
- Pencil and paper/writing instrument
- Tech tools—web browsers

## How Activities Are Coded

- Learning strategy (illustrative strategies include retrieval practice, active recall, spaced practice, interleaving practice, elaboration, visualizations, inquiry-based instruction, student-led inquiry, kinesthetic activities)
- Duration: Varies
- Time in semester/term/year (beginning/middle/end)

## Pantry/Resource List

- ☐ AAC&U. (n.d.). *High-Impact Educational Practices.* https://www.aacu.org/sites/default/files/files/LEAP/HIP_tables.pdf
- ☐ Brame, C. J. (2016). *Active Learning.* Vanderbilt University Center for Teaching. https://cft.vanderbilt.edu/active-learning/
- ☐ Bonwell, C. C., & Eison, J. A. (1991). *Active Learning: Creating Excitement in the Classroom*. ASHE-ERIC Higher Education Reports. https://files.eric.ed.gov/fulltext/ED336049.pdf
- ☐ Cornell University Center for Teaching Innovation. (n.d.). *Getting Started with Active Learning Techniques.* https://teaching.cornell.edu/getting-started-active-learning-techniques
- ☐ Dwyer, F. (2010). Edgar Dale's Cone of Experience: A quasi-experimental analysis. *International Journal of Instructional Media,* 37(4), 431–437.
- ☐ eduXpert, (n.d.). *6 Effective Learning Strategies for Effective Learning.* 6 Effective Learning Strategies for Effective Learning | EduxpertThe e-Learning Network. (2017). *The Cone of Experience by Edgar Dale.* https://www.eln.co.uk/blog/experience-cone-dale
- ☐ Handelsman, J., Miller, S., & Pfund, C. (2007). *Scientific Teaching.* Macmillan.
- ☐ Kuh, G. D. (2008). *High-Impact Educational Practices: What They Are, Who Has Access to Them, and Why They Matter.* https://provost.tufts.edu/celt/files/High-Impact-Ed-Practices1.pdf
- ☐ Janoska, L. (2017, August 28). *What Really is the Cone of Experience?* https://elearningindustry.com/cone-of-experience-what-really-is
- ☐ Teaching and Learning Commons. (n.d.). *Getting Started with Active Learning Guide.* https://engagedteaching.ucsd.edu/_files/resources/active-learning-guide.pdf

# What's on the Menu/Ice Breaker Buffet

## Organized by Category (Activities Served on a Bowl of Ice)

**A.** Hors d'oeuvres—single serve, individual, bite size, teasers

**B.** Appetizers—content and lesson teasers to share in groups

**C.** Main Courses/Entrées—substantive, sustainable activities and aligned content

**D.** Sides/Fruits/Vegetables—not necessarily aligned with content but healthy, "good for you" activities that add educational nutrition

**E.** Sweet Treats/Desserts—fun, not closely aligned with content, but easy to share

**F.** Half-Baked Snacks and Seasonings/Samplers

*Note:* These are loosely defined categories. As with most buffets, anything goes. Take a lot. Take a little. Swap. Mix. Share. Experiment. Re-imagine. Re-invent.

# The Activity Buffet

## Hors d'oeuvres

A collection of single-serve activities that are well-suited for individual use. Each of these activities is bite-sized and helpful as an introduction or teaser for an upcoming substantive lesson.

## Appetizers

A collection of smaller, teaser-type activities in which content for a lesson is previewed. These activities are often most effective when shared and "consumed" in small-group settings.

## Main Courses/Entrées

A collection of substantive exercises and activities intentionally designed to reinforce and strengthen student understanding and mastery of course content.

## Sides/Fruits/Vegetables

A collection of educational warm-up activities that may not be closely aligned with substantive course content. These activities reinforce transferable soft skills that are full of educational nutrition.

## Sweet Treats/Desserts

A collection of fun and educational warm-ups that are typically not closely aligned with substantive course content. These activities are intentionally light and easy to share.

## Half-Baked/Samplers

A collection of bite-sized sampler activities that can be used in a variety of ways, either independently or alongside other ice breaker activities. No time for a full ice breaker? Class momentum starting to melt? No problem! Grab and adapt a half-baked activity from the buffet. You might also look to these short, bite-sized activities as seasoning for an existing activity or for a mid-session snack break.

Importantly, these are all loosely defined categories. As with most buffets, anything goes. Take a lot, take a little. Swap. Mix. Share.

> "Cookery is not chemistry. It is an art. It requires instinct and taste rather than exact measurements."
>
> *Marcel Boulestin*

# Hors d'oeuvres

"...no one is born a great cook, one learns by doing."

*Julia Child*

## Grab One from the Shelf (This or That)

**Hors d'oeuvres**

**Ice Breaker Title: Grab One from the Shelf (This or That)**

"Either-Or (This or That)" activities as a tool to promote critical thinking and analysis

### Activity Description

"Grab One from the Shelf" and "This or That" activities offer opportunities for students to explore a specific topic from a variety of perspectives. Students are prompted to distinguish concepts and compare/contrast key characteristics. Students are also encouraged to prioritize and develop critical thinking and decision-making skills.

This activity works well with a range of topics (a minimum of two related concepts, as many as desired). Modify list content and length to fit lesson focus. Work to identify concepts with similarities and unique relative strengths to increase activity depth. One of the goals (or possibilities) of this exercise is the ability to highlight nuances and gray areas.

This activity works well as an introductory warm-up for a substantive lesson that involves core concepts and previously explored vocabulary terms.

### Recipe

Step 1: Define and explain "This or That" activities.

Step 2: Introduce and explain how the activity works. Clarify content focus and type of resource to be used for the activity.

Step 3: Create pairs and/or small groups (as applicable).

Step 4: Share a link or copy of paired terms/concepts to be used for purposes of the activity.

Step 5: Share student response options.

- Students might share responses privately in writing, anonymously (using polling software such as Poll Everywhere, Padlet, and Google Jamboard), or out loud.
- Google Docs and other collaborative tools also work well.

Step 6: Present initial paired concepts/topics.

Step 7: Explain that students must select one of the two items and develop an argument in support of their choice.

Step 8: Provide active work time for students to construct arguments related to the presented pairs and their selected item/concept.

- Offer support as needed.
- Share directional reminders about the activity, as applicable.

Step 9: Class Vote. Conduct a poll.

Step 10: Once responses are collected, debate and discuss (either anonymously, in pairs, or out loud).

- Vary time. 30, 60, 90 seconds, 2+ minutes

Step 11: Open discussion and reflection (out loud or independent journaling).

Sample prompts:

- How has this activity changed the way you feel about the item/concept?
- How has this activity changed the way you feel about the related topic?

Step 12: Repeat (as applicable).

## The Secret Sauce (Why It Works)

This content-aligned and **focused** activity breaks down complex material into **discrete chunks and concepts** that reduce **cognitive load** on students. Students draw on and **actively recall** prior learning and knowledge related to a specific pairing/concept. The activity promotes hands-on **active learning** that requires students to do something (identify and describe key characteristics) with a presented pairing. Goals include increased **student comfort** with a particular concept, the development of associated **analysis** skills, as well as increased **confidence** applying a particular concept (and articulating its potential applications).

The activity also promotes **critical thinking** and problem solving. Students practice **transferable skills**, such as argument construction, public speaking (as applicable), and conflict resolution. This activity works well for any concept where a teacher wants to help students explore multiple sides, perspectives, and use cases.

The activity offers many opportunities for **reflection** (both individual and group). The activity also offers many opportunities for **formative assessment**.

## Ingredients

- ☐ A list of paired items or concepts aligned with a prior course lesson or learning objective
- ☐ Clock/Timer (as applicable)

## Activity Prep

- A list of paired items or concepts aligned with a prior course lesson or learning objective.
- Optional: Students share items and/or generate lists of paired items/concepts to use for this activity.

## Activity Adaptations/Toppings

Depending on the instructional goals and objectives, this activity can be used and adapted in a variety of ways. A few examples follow:

- Conduct the activity using characters from an assigned novel or story.
    - Which character would you choose to be?
    - Which character is most ____?
    - Which character is least/most developed?
- Introduce the activity with a discussion question/reflection prompt that revisits a broader topic most closely associated with the list of paired terms.
- Introduce and/or extend the activity with discussion questions related to the paired items/concepts and that promote active recall of associated terms.
    - Examples:
        - What items are most like this one?
        - What related roles are most different from this one?
        - Create a scenario in which this item would be indispensable.
- Introduce the activity using a current event/news article related to the lesson topic and from which students identify items/concepts for use in this activity.
- Use the activity as a collaborative learning exercise where one student is responsible for generating a list of course concepts and another student is responsible for identifying possible pairings to complement each term on the list. Lists might then be swapped across groups for ongoing "This or That" interactions. Depending on desired group size, additional roles can be developed.
- Students create lists of paired items/concepts on a course topic of choice.
- Students create lists of paired items/concepts on a course theme (assigned by instructor).
- Conduct class-wide polls and facilitate a guided discussion (easy choice, difficult choice, associated reasons). Expand pairings to three or more items/concepts.
- Assign sides (one student/group "Takes" a list item, another "Leaves" a list item). Conduct 30/60/90—second debates.
- After conducting mini-debates, swap and switch. Students construct arguments for an opposing perspective ("Take" or "Leave", respectively).
- Instead of a "This or That"/"Grab One from the Shelf" activity, adapt as a "Soulmate" or "Can't Have One Without the Other" activity.
    - Sample prompt:
        - If you have this item, what else must you have (one or more items) and why?

- Alternatively, prepare a list of paired items that typically go together. Discuss why. Debate whether both are needed.
    - Examples from a "Participants in a Courtroom" activity:
        - Prosecutors and Defense Attorneys
        - Judges and Juries
        - Court Reporters and Laptops
        - Notepads and Pencils
        - Translators and Cameras
    - Students generate lists of "Soulmates" in specific contexts (e.g., office applications, courtrooms, lab settings).
        - Share lists with a missing "Soulmate". Students fill in what's missing.
        - Use guided debates and questions to support this activity.
    - Use lists of paired "Soulmates" for Either-Or discussions.
        - Sample prompt: You can keep only one. Which would you keep and why?

## Activity Extensions

- Provide opportunities for students to share arguments. Students might post arguments for or against a particular item to a class bulletin board or gallery. A Padlet board, class Google Site, or Pinterest board are examples of free options that work well.
- Students create and generate original lists of "must-have" items for a particular task (e.g., career-related, research-related). In a subsequent lesson, these must-have items serve as content for "This or That" activities.
- Read/Review: McCoy, C. (2017). Are We Teaching Political Divisiveness in English Class? See: https://www.mccoywriting.com/post/2017/04/08/are-we-teaching-political-divisiveness-in-english-class
    - This exercise is in some ways a reflection of the argument presented in the above-referenced article.
    - Conduct a related discussion on how to temper bias when evaluating topics and sources.

### Law-Based Example (Office Software, Office Tools)

Example terms/concepts from a legal technology course:

- Automated billing software
- Word
- Excel
- eDiscovery
- PDF converters
- PDF annotators
- Office products
- Google products
- Business casual
- Email forwarding
- Out-of-office replies
- Paper
- Pens
- Pencils
- Stapler
- Electronic databases
- Lexis Nexis
- Westlaw
- Case citations
- Citation generators

### Research- and Writing-Themed Concepts/Topics

- Primary sources
- Scholarly sources
- Popular sources
- Secondary sources
- Expository writing
- Narrative writing
- Memo format
- Five-paragraph essays

## Portion Type and Size

Single (independent work), pairs, small group, or whole class

Time: Variable

- As few as five minutes.
- No maximum length.
- Time will vary depending on the adopted approach to implementation.

Online and/or face to face

## Web Resources

See: "This or That: Paralegal/Law Style" https://docs.google.com/document/d/1u3LRELdmxgAy1RlehNGrowXrtEF_emjlhMh5Vv13oeg/edit?usp=sharing

Related discussion prompts:

- Reflect: How might this activity impact choices of technologies going forward?
- Guide: Think about how choices might present when working in a law firm, agency, or office setting.

## I Tried This and This Is What I Learned

| DATE USED/LESSON TOPIC | REFLECTIONS/WHAT I MIGHT DO DIFFERENTLY NEXT TIME |
|---|---|
| | |
| | |
| | |

Have a "Grab One from the Shelf" activity adaptation to share?

Submit your tweaks and experiences here: Survey Link: https://forms.gle/G7JS4RPADQK8ykp89

# I'll Take a Pass

**Hors d'oeuvres**

**Ice Breaker Title: I'll Take a Pass**

"Least favorite" inquiries as a way to practice active recall, idea construction, and reinforcement of course concepts

## Activity Description

"I'll Take a Pass" is an active identification, recall, and elaboration activity that provides opportunities for both reflection and application.

Students identify a "least favorite" or "least favored" example of a shared topic or category. The activity provides opportunities for students to reflect and retrieve prior learning. The activity also promotes application and elaboration, with students encouraged to consider a wide range of contexts in which a specific selection/item might be applied.

This activity is designed to support and sustain increased student comfort and confidence with both concept selection and application. The activity is also designed to encourage creative thinking, critical analysis, and honest discussion.

This activity works well as an introductory warm-up and/or review activity for a substantive lesson associated with the core course concept.

## Recipe

Step 1: Define and explain "I'll Take a Pass" (least favorite) activities.

Step 2: Explain how the activity will work. Clarify content focus to be used for the activity.

Step 3: Create pairs/groups (if applicable).

Step 4: Share the topic for the activity.

- This activity works well with a range of options (as few as one, as many as desired).
- Modify language to fit lesson focus.
- Avoid categories with few options or choices. One of the goals (and possibilities) of this exercise is the ability to highlight complexity, nuances, and gray areas.

Step 5: Provide time for students to reflect and identify their "favorites".

- Encourage students to explain the reasons for their selection.
- Encourage a minimum of three supporting reasons (e.g., attributes, features, applications).
- Offer support as needed.
- Share directional reminders about the activity, as applicable.

Step 6: Share student response options.

Step 7: Students might journal privately, share anonymously (Padlet, Google Docs, Jamboard, Poll Everywhere), and/or out loud (pairs, small groups, whole class).

Step 8: Discuss. Once responses are collected, debate (either anonymously, in pairs, or out loud).

- Compare and contrast shared responses.
- Explore more popular choices, least popular choices, etc.

Step 9: Open discussion and reflection on the exercise (out loud or independent journaling).

Sample prompts:

- How has this activity changed the way you feel about the topic?
- How has this activity changed the way you feel about your selection?

Step 10: Create class-specific "least favorites"/"favorites" boards. Padlet, Google Sites, Pinterest, Instagram all work well.

## The Secret Sauce (Why It Works)

This **focused** activity breaks down broad topics into **manageable chunks** that reduce **cognitive load** on students. Students draw on and **actively recall** prior learning and knowledge. The activity promotes **elaboration** and hands-on **active learning** that requires students to do something (interact) with an assigned topic. The activity promotes both **critical thinking** and **application** of course concepts to real-world scenarios. Goals include increased **student comfort** with a particular course concept as well as increased **confidence** and deeper understanding. The activity offers many opportunities for **reflection** (both individual and group). The activity also offers many opportunities for **formative assessment**.

## Ingredients

- ☐ A content and lesson-aligned topic with a variety of examples from which students identify a "least favorite"
- ☐ Clock/Timer (as applicable)

## Activity Prep

A content and lesson-aligned topic with a variety of examples from which students identify a "least favorite".

Optional: Students generate the activity topic.

## Activity Adaptations/Toppings

Depending on the instructional goals and objectives, this activity can be used and adapted in a variety of ways. A few examples follow:

- Conduct the activity using a novel or course text. Students identify "least favorite" words, phrases, sentences, or other writing elements. Students might also identify "least favored" craft elements (e.g., character, dialogue, setting).
  - This activity provides a safe space for students to critically analyze a work and express reactions to portions of a work they did not find particularly engaging, compelling, effective, etc.
- Conduct the activity using a course concept related to current events. Students conduct research and identify a "least favorite" or "least favored" article that reports on the event. Students explain the reasons why they do not favor/favorite the article (e.g., relevancy, currency, writing style, objectivity, comprehensiveness).
- Introduce the activity with a discussion question related to the topic and that promotes active recall. Questions can range from knowledge- and comprehension-related activities to analysis- and synthesis-related prompts.
  - Examples:
    - Describe and explain
    - Define
    - Distinguish
    - Choose
    - Compare
    - Contrast
    - Categorize
    - Evaluate

- Students create a collection of "least favorite" tools, resources, terms, etc., on a course theme of choice.
- Students create a collection of "least favorite" tools, resources, terms, etc., on an assigned theme.

## Activity Extensions

- Provide opportunities for students to share their "least favorite" items and reasoning. Students might post "un-favorites" to a class bulletin board or gallery. A Padlet board, class Google Site, class Instagram, Google Jamboard, or Pinterest board are examples of free options that work well.
- Students conduct research and identify competitors or alternatives to their un-favorites. Students construct compare/contrast charts to highlight similarities and differences.
- Either individually, in pairs or small groups, or as a whole-class exercise, students create lists of possible choices for an assigned course topic. Lists are swapped and then ranked according to a variety of characteristics, factors, and/or preferences.

### Law-Based Examples

Least favorite time-tracking software

Least favorite legal billing software

Least favorite eDiscovery software

Least favorite course management software

Least favorite presentation software

Least favorite legal research software

Least favorite legal technology

Least favorite case ruling

Least favorite vocabulary term

Least favorite aspect of a paralegal's job

Least favorite aspect of law

Least favorite legal database

Least favorite application

Least favorite piece of technology

Least favorite web browser

Least favorite search engine

Least favorite legal book

Least favorite legal movie

Least favorite professional YouTube channel

Least favorite legal blog

Least favorite fictional legal character

Least favorite legal villain

Least favorite course reading to date

Least favorite course assignment to date

### Workplace Examples

Least favorite email greeting

Least favorite way to sign a letter

Least favorite way to sign an email

Least favorite research database

Least favorite search engine

Least favorite place to work

Least favorite place to write

Least favorite office-based sitcom or movie

Least favorite office supply

### Political Science/History Examples

Least favorite world or country leader

Least favorite judicial decision

Least favorite Supreme Court ruling

Least favorite nonfiction book

Least favorite educational YouTube channel

Least favorite historical figure

Least favorite historical movie

### Neutral/Content-Agnostic Examples (Just for Fun)

Least favorite school-day snack

Least favorite movie

Least favorite book

Least favorite day of the week

### Customizable Templates

Templates. See: https://docs.google.com/document/d/15ziPGa-Cjao_i3sobEp-Npsglreo61kxQ0pBBv5mONg/edit?usp=sharing

## Portion Type and Size

Single (independent work), pairs, small groups, or whole class

Time: Variable

- As few as five minutes.
- No maximum length.

Online and/or face to face

## Web Resources

- The Ultimate Favorites List. See: https://www.ranker.com/list/the-ultimate-favorites-list/stevo200
- Questions Lists: Favorites. See: https://questionslisting.tumblr.com/post/137028466905/favorites
- Liz Henwood, Favorites Questions. See: https://twitter.com/MissHenwood1/status/1417998836971282437?s=09

## I Tried This and This Is What I Learned

| DATE USED/LESSON TOPIC | REFLECTIONS/WHAT I MIGHT DO DIFFERENTLY NEXT TIME |
|---|---|
| | |
| | |
| | |

Have an "I'll Take a Pass" (least favorite) activity adaptation to share?

Submit your tweaks and experiences here: Survey Link: https://forms.gle/G7JS4RPADQK8ykp89

## "Name a Number" Word Stories

**Hors d'oeuvres**

**Ice Breaker Title: "Name a Number" Word Stories**

Story construction as a tool to help students solidify understanding and support long-term learning

## Activity Description

Story drafting provides opportunities to explore creative ideas related to a specific topic. In this activity, students create original 6/9/12 (any number)-word stories on an assigned concept or topic. See the Six-Word Memoirs site and project, as well as other materials to get involved, here: https://sixinschools.com/pages/book-options. To subscribe to "Say Less by Larry Smith" and the Six-Word Memoir Project, see: https://sixwordmemoirs.substack.com/. For ongoing contest opportunities, see: https://www.sixwordmemoirs.com/story/?did=1280141.

Creative storytelling presents opportunities for students to become familiar with complicated and/or unfamiliar texts in a stress-free environment. Creating an original story on an assigned subtopic or concept is also a way to proactively mitigate the increased cognitive load (drain on working memory) and anxiety that often emerges when a student interacts with a complex resource or topic.

To create a numbered word story, student writers confine themselves to a specified number of words when writing.

## Recipe

Step 1: Define and explain "Name a Number"-word stories. Share the Six-Word Memoirs weblink with students.

Step 2: Introduce the activity. Clarify content focus, type of resource, and word count to be used for the drafting activity.

Step 3: Create groups (if applicable).

Step 4: Share a link or copy of associated resources (if applicable).

Step 5: Explain the nature of the topic, text, or resource (material to use for the "Name a Number" word story activity) (if applicable).

Step 6: Provide active work time for students to create and generate an original "Name a Number"-word story using the identified topic/concept.

- Offer support as needed.
- Share directional reminders about the activity, as applicable.

Step 7: Open discussion and reflection on the exercise (out loud or independent journaling).

Sample prompts:

- How has this activity changed the way you feel about the related topic?

Step 8: Share "Name a Number" word stories (either out loud or on digital bulletin board) (if applicable).

## The Secret Sauce (Why It Works)

This **creative writing** activity breaks down complex material into manageable chunks that reduce **cognitive load** on students. Students exercise **creative thinking** and draw on and actively **recall** prior learning and knowledge. The activity promotes hands-on **active learning** that requires students to do something (create an original story) associated with an assigned topic or concept. Goals include increased student **comfort** with a particular type of writing as well as increased **confidence** reading about a particular topic or concept. The activity offers many opportunities for **reflection** (both individual and group). The activity also offers many opportunities for **formative assessment**.

## Ingredients

- ☐ A concept or topic related to a class learning objective or lesson
- ☐ Clock/Timer (as applicable)

## Activity Prep

- A concept or topic related to a lesson topic.
- Optional: Students identify a concept or topic for this activity.

## Activity Adaptations/Toppings

Depending on the instructional goals and objectives, this activity can be used and adapted in a variety of ways.

- Vary the number of words to be used (e.g., six, 10, 15, 20).
- Students select a vocabulary term and write a story to illustrate its meaning.
- Select a passage (several paragraphs, a page of text) from a current reading, assigned book, or related news article. Students create a story based on the contents of the passage.
- Introduce the activity with a discussion question/reflection prompt that explores different types of writing (e.g., expository versus narrative).
- Share tips and strategies for writing an original story.
- Introduce a current event/news article related to the lesson topic and from which students will create (some number) word stories.
- Vary time permitted to work on story construction.

## Activity Extensions

- Provide opportunities for students to share their stories. Students might post stories to a class bulletin board or gallery. A Padlet board, class Google Site, Google Jamboard, or Pinterest board are examples of free options that would work well.

### Law-Based Example (Criminal Law)

Students are provided a list of common crimes along with definitions. Students select one crime and create an original 6/9/12-word story to illustrate the meaning of the crime. Alternatively, students are tasked with writing a 6/9/12-word story involving an assigned crime.

Sample Sources:

- Law 101: Fundamentals of Law. Author(s): Michael H. Martella. See: https://courses.lumenlearning.com/suny-monroe-law101/chapter/comparing-and-contrasting-civil-and-criminal-law/
- Inchoate crimes key terms. See: https://www.remnote.com/a/inchoate-crimes-key-terms/Nc9aaWemwQvKWXzWY
- Common legal words and terms. See: https://courses.lumenlearning.com/suny-monroe-law101/chapter/appendix-f-common-legal-words-and-terms/
- Glossary of Terms, U.S. Courts. See: https://www.remnote.com/a/qEuMmP6qR9Hyg3pkN

Students write a 6/9/12-word story that summarizes or responds to a criminal law case. For sample cases, see: https://open.lib.umn.edu/criminallaw/part/chapter-14-appendix-a-case-listings/

### Legal Context/Judicial Opinions

Judicial opinions often require multiple readings to support understanding. In this activity, students draft a 6/9/12-word story relating to an assigned case.

Many students come to legal materials fearful of the complex language. Creating a "any number"-word story is a way for students to actively engage with a complex text in a low-stakes way that is designed to help minimize the fear associated in higher-stakes settings. (Note: Judicial opinions can be swapped with any piece of writing and any primary or secondary source.)

- To reinforce research skills, students might conduct research and select a case of choice (e.g., by jurisdiction, topic) for use in this activity.

## Portion Type and Size

Single (independent work), pairs, small groups, or whole class

Time: Variable

- As short as one minute
- No maximum length
- *Note*: The activity takes less time when the instructor pre-selects the topic for story construction.

Online and/or face to face

## Web Resources

- Get involved with the Six-Word Memoirs Project. See: https://sixinschools.com/pages/book-options
- In Six Words, These Writers Tell You an Entire Story. See: https://www.huffpost.com/entry/six-word-story_n_5332833
- Six Word Stories. See: http://www.sixwordstories.net/
- Six Word Memoirs. See: https://writing.upenn.edu/wh/archival/documents/sixwords/
- Submit six-word stories. See http://www.sixwordstories.net/2009/07/submit-a-story/
- Submit six-word stories. See: https://www.narrativemagazine.com/sixwords

## Additional Resources/Readings

- Storytelling as an Instructional Method: Descriptions and Research Questions. See: https://www.academia.edu/23391039/Storytelling_as_an_Instructional_Method_Descriptions_and_Research_Questions?email_work_card=title
- Storytelling as a Learning Tool for Adults. See: https://www.academia.edu/34773068/Storytelling_as_a_Learning_Tool_for_Adults?email_work_card=interaction-paper

## I Tried This and This Is What I Learned

| DATE USED/LESSON TOPIC | REFLECTIONS/WHAT I MIGHT DO DIFFERENTLY NEXT TIME |
|---|---|
| | |
| | |
| | |

Have a "Name a Number" Word Story activity adaptation to share?

Submit your tweaks and experiences here:

Survey Link: https://forms.gle/G7JS4RPADQK8ykp89

# Haiku Generator

**Hors d'oeuvres**

**Ice Breaker Title: Haiku Generator**

Haiku construction as a tool to help students solidify understanding and support long-term learning

## Activity Description

Poetry provides opportunities for students to explore creative ideas related to course topics. In this activity, students create original haiku.

To create a haiku, student writers confine themselves to a 5-7-5-syllable, three-line construction format. This activity works well as an introductory warm-up and/or review activity for a substantive lesson associated with the term, concept, or event assigned as a topic for the haiku-writing activity.

## Recipe

Step 1: Define and explain haiku.

Step 2: Explain how the haiku drafting activity works. Clarify content focus for the activity.

Step 3: Create groups (if applicable).

Step 4: Share a link or copy of associated resources (if applicable).

Step 5: Explain the topic, text, or resource (material to use for haiku writing) (if applicable).

Step 6: Provide active work time for students to create and generate an original haiku (one or more) using the identified topic/concept.

- Offer support as needed.
- Share directional reminders about the activity, as applicable.

Step 7: Open discussion and reflection on the exercise (out loud or independent journaling)

Sample prompts:

- How has this activity changed the way you feel about the related topic?

Step 8: Share haiku (either out loud or on digital bulletin boards).

## The Secret Sauce (Why It Works)

This **creative writing** activity provides an opportunity to interact with complex material in stress-free and open-ended ways. Students exercise **creative thinking** and practice **brainstorming** to generate new writing out of existing content and knowledge. The activity promotes hands-on **active learning** that requires students to do something (create an original haiku) associated with an assigned topic or concept. Goals include increased student **comfort** with a particular type of creative writing as well as increased **confidence** regarding their understanding of a particular topic or concept. The activity offers many opportunities for **reflection** (both individual and group) and **creative thinking**. The activity offers many opportunities for **formative assessment**.

## Ingredients

- ☐ A concept or topic related to a class learning objective or lesson
- ☐ Clock/Timer (as applicable)

## Activity Prep

A concept or topic related to a lesson topic.

Optional: Students identify a concept or topic to use for this activity.

## Activity Adaptations/Toppings

- Vary the number of lines and recommended syllables per line for the haiku writing process (modify the original 5-7-5 format).
- Students select a course vocabulary term and write a haiku to illustrate its meaning.
- Conduct the activity using a passage (several paragraphs, a page of text) from a current reading, assigned book, or related news article. Students create a haiku based on the contents of the passage.

- Introduce the activity with a discussion question/reflection prompt that explores different types of creative writing and poetry.
- Introduce haibun. Students write haibun instead of haiku.

## Activity Extensions

Provide opportunities to publicly share haiku. Students might post their writing to a class bulletin board or gallery. A Padlet board, class Google Site, Google Jamboard, or Pinterest board are examples of free options that work well.

### History-Based Example (Conflict and War)

Students are provided a list of historical conflicts and wars along with timelines, key players, and related definitions. Students select one war or conflict and create an original haiku to illustrate some aspect of the war, historical time period, conflict, etc.

List of major American wars:

- List of Major American Wars. See: https://www.gettysburgflag.com/history-of-american-wars
- Wars and Battles Throughout History. See: https://www.thoughtco.com/famous-wars-and-battles-4140297

### English Example

Students select a common grammatical term and write a haiku to illustrate its meaning.

- Glossary of Grammatical Terms. See: https://public.oed.com/how-to-use-the-oed/glossary-grammatical-terms/
- 100 Key Terms Used in the Study of Grammar. See: https://www.thoughtco.com/key-grammatical-terms-1692364

## Portion Type and Size

Single (independent work), pairs, small groups, or whole class

Time: Variable

- As short as one minute.
- No maximum length.
- *Note*: The activity takes less time when the instructor pre-selects the topic for haiku construction.

Online and/or face to face

## Web Resources

- What are haiku? See: https://literaryterms.net/haiku/
- Poets.org, Haiku. See: https://poets.org/glossary/haiku
- Haiku Journal. See: https://haikujournal.org/submit/
- Modern Haiku. See: https://www.modernhaiku.org/submissions.html
- The Haiku Foundation. See: https://thehaikufoundation.org/new-to-haiku-preparing-your-first-submission/
- How to Write Haibun Poetry. See: https://www.masterclass.com/articles/how-to-write-haibun-poetry#what-is-haibun-poetry

- More Than the Birds, Bees, and Trees. A Closer Look at Writing Haibun. See: https://poets.org/text/more-birds-bees-and-trees-closer-look-writing-haibun
- Haibun Poems: Poetic Forms. See: https://www.writersdigest.com/write-better-poetry/haibun-poems-poetic-form
- You've Written Haiku, Not Try Haibun. See: https://ypn.poetrysociety.org.uk/workshop/youve-written-haiku-now-try-haibun/
- Where to submit haibun:
    - The Haibun Journal. See: https://www.poetryireland.ie/writers/opportunities/the-haibun-journal
    - Contemporary Haibun Online. See: https://contemporaryhaibunonline.com/submissions/
    - Drifting Sands Haibun. See: https://drifting-sands-haibun.org/submissions/
    - Under the Basho. See: https://www.underthebasho.com/submission/haibun-submissions.html

## Additional Resources/Readings

- Let's Do Haiku. See: https://teachmag.com/archives/7894
- Haiku in the Classroom. More than Counting Syllables. See: https://www.jstor.org/stable/24484126
- Haiku Starter. See: https://www.readwritethink.org/classroom-resources/printouts/haiku-starter

## I Tried This and This Is What I Learned

| DATE USED/LESSON TOPIC | REFLECTIONS/WHAT I MIGHT DO DIFFERENTLY NEXT TIME |
|---|---|
| | |
| | |
| | |

Have a "Haiku Generator" activity adaptation to share?

Submit your tweaks and experiences here:

Survey Link: https://forms.gle/G7JS4RPADQK8ykp89

## Kitchen Aromas: How Does It Taste?

**Hors d'oeuvres**

**Ice Breaker Title: Kitchen Aromas: How Does It Taste (Smell, Feel, Sound, Look)?**

Reflection, discussion, and term generation as a tool to promote active recall, critical thinking, and heightened awareness

## Activity Description

"How Does It Taste?" activities offer opportunities for students to explore a topic from a variety of perspectives. The activity is well suited for increasing depth of understanding and promoting reflection on a topic and/or proposition.

This activity works well with a range of course topics and concepts. One of the goals (or possibilities) of this exercise is the ability to highlight variations in perception and experience.

This activity is also designed to support and sustain increased student comfort and confidence when reviewing course topics, processes, and/or problems.

## Recipe

Step 1: Define and explain "How Does It Taste?" activities.

Step 2: Explain how the activity will work. Clarify content focus and resources to be used for the activity.

Step 3: Share student response options.

- Students might share responses privately in writing, anonymously (polling software such as Poll Everywhere, Padlet, and Google Jamboard work well), or out loud.

Step 4: Present concept/topic. Prompt students to write four words that best capture their current feelings about the topic. Sample questions follow:

- When you read or hear the term ____, what do you feel?
- When asked to ____, what do you feel?
- In four words or less, share how you feel when you start to work on a ____ problem.

Step 5: Provide active work time for students to reflect and document their responses (10–30 seconds).

- Offer support as needed.
- Share directional reminders about the activity, as applicable.
- Vary time based on the complexity and number of shared question prompts.
    - Examples: 30, 60, 90 seconds, 2+ minutes

Step 6: Once responses are shared, discuss.

Step 7: Repeat (as applicable).

## The Secret Sauce (Why It Works)

This content-aligned and **focused** activity breaks down complex material into **discrete chunks** that reduce **cognitive load** on students. Students draw on and **actively recall** prior learning and knowledge related to a specific concept. The activity promotes hands-on, **active learning** that requires students to do something (identify and generate words associated with a topic) for an identified concept. Goals include increased **student comfort** with a particular concept as well as increased **confidence** applying a particular concept (and articulating its potential applications).

The activity also promotes **critical thinking**, problem-solving, and application of course concepts. Students practice **transferable skills**, including communication and public speaking (as applicable).

The activity offers many opportunities for **reflection** (both individual and group). The activity also offers many opportunities for **formative assessment**.

## Ingredients

- ☐ A list of items or concepts aligned with a prior course lesson or learning objective
- ☐ Clock/Timer (as applicable)

## Activity Prep

A list of items or concepts aligned with a prior course lesson or learning objective.

Optional: Students share topics and/or generate lists of topics/concepts for this activity.

## Activity Adaptations/Toppings

This activity can be used and adapted in a variety of ways.

- Modify prompts to explore different senses. Example prompts follow:
  - How does it smell?
  - How does it taste?
  - How does it sound?
  - How does it feel?
- Use drawings and quick doodles. Rather than generating words associated with the topic, students draw their reactions and associated feelings.
- Use characters from an assigned novel or story.
  - How might this character feel if ___?
  - What are four words that come to mind when you think about this character?
- Introduce the activity with discussion questions related to associated course topic(s) and which promote active recall of associated concepts.

## Activity Extensions

Provide opportunities for students to share their word and phrase collections. Students might post their responses to a class bulletin board or gallery. A Padlet board, class Google Site, or Pinterest board are examples of free options that work well.

### Mathematics Example (Algebraic Equations)

In four words or less, describe how you feel when asked to solve a ____ equation.

Repeat with a different different equation.

Discuss why responses might differ.

### English/Language Arts Example

In four words or less, describe how you feel when asked to read a text in the ____ genre.

Repeat with a different question genre.

Discuss why responses might differ.

### Group Work Example (Content Agnostic)

In four words or less, describe how you feel when asked to participate in a group activity as part of a course assignment.

Repeat with a different question (focusing on a different sense).

Group projects, in four words or less:

- How do they smell?
- How do they sound?
- How do they feel?
- How do they taste?

Discuss.

Being a good group/team member, in four words or less:

- How does it smell?
- How does it sound?
- How does it feel?
- How does it taste?

Discuss.

### Communication-Based Example (Giving a Presentation, Content Agnostic)

In four words or less, describe how you feel when asked to give a presentation as part of a course assignment.

Repeat with a different question (focusing on a different sense).

Presentations, in four words or less:

- How do they smell?
- How do they sound?
- How do they feel?
- How do they taste?

Discuss.

Being a good audience member, in four words or less:

- How does it smell?
- How does it sound?
- How does it feel?
- How does it taste?

Discuss.

## Portion Type and Size

Single (independent work), pairs, small groups, or whole class

Time: Variable

- As few as five minutes
- No maximum length

Online and/or face to face

## I Tried This and This Is What I Learned

| DATE USED/LESSON TOPIC | REFLECTIONS/WHAT I MIGHT DO DIFFERENTLY NEXT TIME |
|---|---|
| | |
| | |
| | |

Have a "How Does It Taste?" activity adaptation to share?

Submit your tweaks and experiences here:

Survey Link: https://forms.gle/G7JS4RPADQK8ykp89

# Cookie & Concept Swap

**Hors d'oeuvres**

**Ice Breaker Title: Cookie & Concept Swap**

Topic generation, swaps, and ranking to promote critical thinking, analysis, and understanding

## Activity Description

"Cookie & Concept Swap" activities offer opportunities for students to explore a topic from a variety of perspectives. The activity promotes focused analysis of the utility, use, value, and application of course concepts. The activity also presents opportunities for students to review prior concepts and reinforce understanding. This activity is designed to support and sustain increased student comfort and confidence when reviewing course topics and key terms. This activity works well as an introductory warm-up for a substantive lesson that involves core concepts and previously explored vocabulary terms.

## Recipe

Step 1: Define and explain "Cookie & Concept Swap" activities.

Step 2: Introduce the activity. Clarify content focus and type of resource to be used for the activity.

Step 3: Create pairs and/or small groups (if applicable).

Step 4: Present initial concept/topic.

Step 5: Share student response options.

Step 6: Provide active work time for students to generate six (or some other number) key terms and concepts related to a presented concept/topic. Students might rank items on some identified characteristic and/or include definitions.

Offer support as needed.

- Share directional reminders about the activity, as applicable.

Step 7: After lists are generated, students swap. Students define listed concepts, explain relationships, and/or rank associated comfort levels.

Step 8: Open discussion and reflection on the exercise (out loud or independent journaling).

## The Secret Sauce (Why It Works)

This content-aligned and **focused** activity breaks down complex material into **discrete chunks** that reduce **cognitive load** on students. Students draw on and **actively recall** prior learning and knowledge related to a specific concept. The activity promotes hands-on, **active learning** that requires students to do something (generate a list of terms, concepts, characteristics, and/or features) with an identified concept. Goals include increased **student comfort** as well as increased **confidence** applying a particular concept.

The activity promotes **critical thinking**, problem solving, and application of course concepts. Students practice **transferable skills** such as negotiation, communication, and conflict resolution. This activity works well for any concept where a teacher wants to help students explore prioritization, ranking, and negotiation techniques.

The activity offers opportunities for **reflection** (both individual and group). The activity also offers opportunities for **formative assessment**.

## Ingredients

- ☐ A topic or concept aligned with a prior course lesson or learning objective
- ☐ Clock/Timer (as applicable)

## Activity Prep

A topic or concept aligned with a prior course lesson or learning objective.

Optional: Students share topics for this activity.

## Activity Adaptations/Toppings

This activity can be used and adapted in a variety of ways.

- Students list all items needed to complete a course-related activity, skill, or process. After students generate lists, provide opportunities for 1:1 swaps. Students practice barter and negotiation skills as they swap for items/ingredients they may have initially forgotten to add to their list.

    Science-Based Example: Generate a list of six items needed to conduct a specific experiment.

    Culinary Example: Generate a list of six items needed to prepare an identified food item or dish.

- Conduct the activity using characters from an assigned novel or story.
    - Students generate a list of six characteristics or features of an assigned character.
    - Students generate character profiles for a character from a course novel or a primary actor in a course topic.

- Students create and generate their own lists of "must-have" items for a particular task (e.g., career-related, research-related). These must-have items serve as content for cookie swap (barter) activities.

### Writing/English-Based Example (Story Construction)

Prompt: Generate a list of six key craft elements/components of every story.

- Modify number: eight, ten, etc.
- Examples:
    - Character
    - Plot
    - Setting
    - Dialogue
    - Voice
    - Point of View
    - Conflict
- How might you prioritize this list?
- Student swaps. Explain why you might swap each element.

### Research and Writing Themed Examples

Prompt: Generate a list of five types of sources/research databases.

- Prioritize, then swap
- Samples:
    - Primary Sources
    - Scholarly Sources
    - Popular Sources
    - Secondary Sources
    - Field Notes

Prompt: Generate a list of four types of writing.

- Prioritize, discuss, then swap (swaps might be tied to a specific context).
- Samples:
    - Expository Writing
    - Narrative Writing
    - Memo Format
    - Five-Paragraph Essays

## Portion Type and Size

Single (independent work), Pairs, Small Groups, or Whole Class

Time: Variable

- As few as five minutes
- No maximum length

Online and/or face to face

## I Tried This and This Is What I Learned

| DATE USED/LESSON TOPIC | REFLECTIONS/WHAT I MIGHT DO DIFFERENTLY NEXT TIME |
|---|---|
| | |
| | |
| | |

Have a "Cookie & Concept Swap" activity adaptation to share?

Submit your tweaks and experiences here:

Survey Link: https://forms.gle/G7JS4RPADQK8ykp89

## 10-Word Summaries

**Hors d'oeuvres**

**Ice Breaker Title: 10-Word Summaries**

Summary drafting to help students practice active recall, solidify understanding, and support long-term learning

## Activity Description

Students create original 10-word summaries on an assigned concept or topic. Summary drafting helps students practice active recall and engage with complex concepts in reflective ways. Summarizing also presents instructional opportunities for students to become familiar with complicated and/or unfamiliar texts in a stress-free environment. Summarizing an assigned topic or concept can help proactively mitigate the increased cognitive load (drain on working memory) and anxiety that often emerges when a student interacts with a complex resource.

To create a 10-word summary, student writers confine themselves to 10 words when writing.

This activity works well as an introductory warm-up and/or review activity for a substantive lesson associated with the topic assigned for summary writing.

## Recipe

Step 1: Define and explain "10-Word Summaries."

Step 2: Introduce the activity. Explain how the 10-word summary drafting activity works. Clarify content focus and type of resource to be used for the activity.

Step 3: Create groups (if applicable).

Step 4: Share a link or copy of associated resources (if applicable).

Step 5: Provide active work time for students to create and generate an original 10-word summary of an identified topic/concept (recommended minimum five minutes).

- Offer support as needed.
- Share directional reminders about the activity, as applicable.

Step 6: Open discussion and reflection on the exercise (out loud or independent journaling).

Sample prompts:

- How has this activity changed the way you feel about the related topic?

Step 7: Share 10-word summaries (either out loud or on digital bulletin board) (if applicable).

## The Secret Sauce (Why It Works)

This **scaffolded** activity breaks down complex material into manageable chunks that reduce **cognitive load** on students. Students practice **retrieval** and draw on and actively **recall** prior learning and knowledge. The activity promotes hands-on, **active learning** that requires students to do something (create an original summary) associated with an assigned topic or concept. Goals include increased student **comfort** with a particular type of writing as well as increased **confidence** related to a particular topic or concept. The activity offers opportunities for reflection (both individual and group). The activity also offers opportunities for **formative assessment**.

## Ingredients

- ☐ A concept or topic related to a class learning objective or lesson
- ☐ Clock/Timer (as applicable)

## Activity Prep

A concept or topic related to a lesson topic.

Optional: Students identify a concept or topic for this activity.

## Activity Adaptations/Toppings

This activity can be used and adapted in a variety of ways. A few examples follow:

- Vary the number of words to be used for the summary (e.g., 10, 15, 20, 30, 50).
- Students select a course vocabulary term and write a 10-word summary to illustrate its meaning.
- Select a passage (several paragraphs, a page of text) from a current reading, assigned book, or related news article. Students create an original summary based on the contents of the passage.
- Introduce the activity with a discussion question or reflection prompt that explores different types of writing. Share tips and strategies for summarizing.
- Introduce the activity using a current event or news article related to the lesson topic and from which students create 10-word summaries.
- Students create a 10-word summary on a course topic of choice.
- Students create a 10-word summary on an assigned course topic.
- Vary time permitted to work on the summary drafting.

## Activity Extensions

- Provide opportunities for students to publicly share 10-word summaries. Students might post summaries to a class bulletin board or gallery. A Padlet board, Google Site, or Pinterest board are free options that work well.
- Variations

  - Questions
  - Stories
  - Length
  - Number of characters
  - Summary swaps. Guess the summarized topic or term

### Law-Based Examples (Criminal Law)

Provide students a list of common crimes along with definitions. Students select one crime and create an original 10-word summary to illustrate its meaning.

Sample Resources:

- Law 101: Fundamentals of Law. Author(s): Michael H. Martella. See: https://courses.lumenlearning.com/suny-monroe-law101/chapter/comparing-and-contrasting-civil-and-criminal-law/
- Inchoate Crimes, Key Terms. See: https://www.remnote.com/a/inchoate-crimes-key-terms/Nc9aaWemwQvKWXzWY
- Common legal terms. See: https://courses.lumenlearning.com/suny-monroe-law101/chapter/appendix-f-common-legal-words-and-terms/
- U.S. Courts, Glossary of Terms. See: https://www.remnote.com/a/qEuMmP6qR9Hyg3pkN

Students write a 10-word summary that summarizes a criminal law case.

- For a list of possible cases, see: https://open.lib.umn.edu/criminallaw/part/chapter-14-appendix-a-case-listings/

### Legal Context/Judicial Opinions

Judicial opinions often require multiple readings to support understanding. Students write a 10-word summary of an assigned case.

Many students come to legal materials fearful of the complex language. Creating a 10-word summary helps students actively engage with and approach a complex text in a low-stakes setting.

(*Note*: Judicial opinions can be swapped with any piece of writing and any primary or secondary source.)

- If an instructor wants to reinforce research skills, students might conduct research and select a case of choice (e.g., by jurisdiction, topic) to summarize.
- Variation: Either individually, in pairs, small groups, or as a whole-class exercise, students create an original 10/15/20/30/50-word story from an identified judicial opinion.

## Portion Type and Size

Single (independent work), pairs, small group, or whole class

Time: Variable

- No maximum length.
- Time will vary depending on the adopted approach to implementation.
- *Note*: The activity takes less time when the instructor pre-selects a topic for summary construction.

Online and/or face to face

## Web Resources

- Six-Word Memoirs. See: https://www.sixwordmemoirs.com/story/?did=1280141
- In Six-Words, These Writers Tell You an Entire Story. See: https://www.huffpost.com/entry/six-word-story_n_5332833
- Six-Word Stories. See: http://www.sixwordstories.net/
- Six-Word Memoirs. See: https://writing.upenn.edu/wh/archival/documents/sixwords/

## I Tried This and This Is What I Learned

| DATE USED/LESSON TOPIC | REFLECTIONS/WHAT I MIGHT DO DIFFERENTLY NEXT TIME |
|---|---|
| | |
| | |
| | |

Have a "10-Word Summary" activity adaptation to share?

Submit your tweaks and experiences here

Survey Link: https://forms.gle/G7JS4RPADQK8ykp89

# Name That Pantry Staple: A Variation on 20 Questions

**Hors d'oeuvres**

**Ice Breaker Title: Name That Pantry Staple: A Variation on 20 Questions**

Clue and/or question construction to promote critical thinking, active inquiry, and creativity. Question-and-answer activities to activate recall, deepen long-term memory of core concepts, and engage in retrieval practice

## Activity Description

20 Questions is a traditional spoken-word game where one player guesses a word or phrase by asking targeted questions. The game was first introduced in America by former British Prime Minister George Canning (Selin, 2016). Its origins date back as far as 1829 when William Fordyce Marvor (a Scottish teacher) recommended a "Game of Twenty" to pass time (Selin, 2016).

Question-and-answer activities offer opportunities to engage in collaborative review and active recall. In this "Name That Pantry Staple" activity, students ask yes/no questions of the Pantry Keeper (the student who "sees" the pantry staple item and answers the identification/discovery questions).

Question-and-answer activities provide opportunities for students to engage (and re-engage) with core concepts in creative ways. The activity supports skills such as deductive reasoning and creativity.

Providing opportunities for students to create their own questions for a "Name That Pantry Staple" activity is also a way to proactively mitigate the increased cognitive load (drain on working memory) and anxiety that often emerges when a student interacts with complex or new concepts (or series/list of items).

Relatedly, providing opportunities to students to generate and draft clues associated with a designated resource or concept promotes critical thinking, creativity, and higher-order thinking skills.

This activity works well as an introductory warm-up and/or review. This activity works well with a range of topics and activities.

## Recipe

Step 1: Define and explain "Name That Pantry Staple" (and 20 Questions type) activities.

Step 2: Introduce the activity. Clarify content, focus, and type of resource to be used.

Step 3: Create pairs or small groups (as applicable).

Step 4: Choose a core concept that is associated with a lesson, discipline, and/or field. Think of a pantry staple. Share a link or copy of the focus resource (if applicable). Provide time for students to research and locate a text-based resource (if applicable).

Sample Topics:

- Bill of Rights
- U.S. Presidents
- List or Series of Items
- Historical Dates
- Human Anatomy
- A Role in the Courts Process
- A State, Country, or Location of Interest

Step 5: Explain the nature of the text or resource (the material to be used for the "Name That Pantry Staple" activity) (if applicable).

Step 6: Provide active work time for students to review assigned resources (if desired).

Step 7: Provide active game time for students to ask questions in yes/no format about the assigned resource/topic.

## Example

First student selects a topic/item and provides clues, examples, or hypotheticals that illustrate the topic/item without identifying it by name.

Student provides one clue at a time.

Clues can be shared with the whole class, in small groups, in pairs, or in a line-type formation (e.g., alphabetically, by student ID, by seat).

Pass down the line. If a student gets it right, they then select a new topic/item and play continues.

Provide a new clue.

If a student guesses wrong, play continues. Either continue down the line, wait for another response, and/or share another clue if no one guesses correctly.

- Offer support as needed.
- Share directional reminders about the activity, as applicable.

Step 8: Open discussion and reflection on the exercise (out loud or independent journaling).

Sample prompts:

- How has this activity changed the way you feel about the resource?
- How has this activity changed the way you feel about the related topic?

Step 9: Share question collections (either out loud or on digital bulletin board).

## The Secret Sauce (Why It Works)

This interactive activity breaks down course material into manageable chunks that reduce cognitive load on students. Clue and/or question construction promotes **elaboration, creativity, critical thinking, and higher orders of thinking**. Students draw on and **actively recall** prior learning and knowledge. The activity promotes hands-on, active learning that requires students to do something (clue construction, active recall, and guessing) with a course topic. Goals include increased student comfort, understanding, and **confidence** with a particular concept or topic. The activity offers many opportunities for reflection (both individual and group). The activity also offers many opportunities for formative assessment.

## Ingredients

- ☐ A primary or secondary resource related to a class learning objective or lesson
- ☐ Clock/Timer (as applicable)

## Activity Prep

A primary or secondary resource related to a lesson or course concept.

Optional: Students identify a topic to use for this activity.

## Activity Adaptations/Toppings

Depending on the instructional goals and objectives, this activity can be used and adapted in a variety of ways. A few examples follow:

- Conduct the activity in pairs (or grouped pairs). Each student or pair creates a list of questions to be shared with the opposing partner. Once questions (or clues) are created, pairs swap, provide yes/no responses to all questions. Then, each group reviews responses and has 60 seconds to share their guess.
- Conduct the activity using a chapter from a current reading, assigned book, or related news article. Tasks might include identifying a character, concept, or date.
- Introduce the activity with a discussion question/reflection prompt that explores the general topic area at a high level.
- Vary time permitted for concept/resource review.
- Provide a question limit/cap (e.g., five, 10, 15, 20) before a guess is required.
- One student may share clues about resource/topic. Rather than asking questions, a defined number of clues are provided to the student "guesser."

## Activity Extensions

- Provide opportunities for students to create question-and-answer resources as preparation and review for summative assessments. Resources might be collected and shared on a class Google Site.
- If student research leads to supplemental resources on a particular course topic, students can share their resources in a class-wide library (Google Docs, Google Sites, Padlet board). Source identification can be used as research reinforcement and also as library building.
- Students conduct research and identify a resource on an assigned topic. Students then create five yes/no questions, with an associated answer sheet, associated with the resource. Questions and resources are swapped amongst pairs/groups.

### Paralegal/Law-Based Example (NALA Canons)

The NALA Code of Ethics and Professional Responsibility is one of infinite examples. This activity works well for any topic or concept where a teacher wants to help students solidify memory and practice active inquiry. This activity might be used as a warm-up on a lesson exploring ethics and ethical responsibilities in the paralegal context. (*Note*: NALA Canons can be swapped with any associated body of ethical rules and professional guidelines.)

- If an instructor wants to reinforce research skills, students might conduct research and identify applicable rules and guidelines (e.g., by jurisdiction, career field).
- Alternatively, an instructor can share a pre-selected body of guidelines or content.
- In paired groups, students select roles (Questioner/Answerer). First player selects a canon and provides clues, examples, or hypotheticals that illustrate the canon without identifying it by number.

**Canon 1**: A paralegal must not perform any of the duties that attorneys only may perform nor take any actions that attorneys may not take.

### Sample Clue Examples

- Paralegal may not perform duties that attorneys only may perform.
- Paralegal may not take actions that attorneys may not take.

**Answer/Topic:** NALA Canon 1

Provide one clue at a time. Alternatively, ask one question at a time.

Clues can be shared with a whole class, in small groups, in pairs, or in a line-type formation (e.g., alphabetically, by student ID, by seat).

Pass down the line. If a student guesses correctly, they then select a new canon and play continues.

If a student guesses incorrectly, play continues. Either continue down the line, wait for another response, and/or share another clue.

**Canon 2:** A paralegal may perform any task which is properly delegated and supervised by an attorney, as long as the attorney is ultimately responsible to the client, maintains a direct relationship with the client, and assumes professional responsibility for the work product.

### Sample Clue Examples

- Paralegal may perform any properly delegated task, as long as attorney is ultimately responsible.
- Attorney must maintain a direct relationship with client.

**Answer/Topic:** NALA Canon 2

**Canon 3:** A paralegal must not: (a) engage in, encourage, or contribute to any act which could constitute the unauthorized practice of law; and (b) establish attorney-client relationships, set fees, give legal opinions or advice or represent a client before a court or agency unless so authorized by that court or agency; and (c) engage in conduct or take any action which would assist or involve the attorney in a violation of professional ethics or give the appearance of professional impropriety.

### Sample Clue Examples

- Must not contribute to any act which could constitute the unauthorized practice of law.
- Must not establish attorney-client relationships.
- Must not take any action which would assist or involve a violation of professional ethics.

**Answer/Topic:** NALA Canon 3

**Canon 4:** A paralegal must use discretion and professional judgment commensurate with knowledge and experience but must not render independent legal judgment in place of an attorney. The services of an attorney are essential in the public interest whenever such legal judgment is required.

### Sample Clue Examples

- Must use discretion and professional knowledge commensurate with experience.
- Must not render independent legal judgment in place of an attorney.

## Portion Type and Size

Single (independent work), Pairs, Small Group, or Whole Class

Time: Variable

- As few as five minutes
- No maximum length
- Time will vary depending on the adopted approach to implementation.

Online and/or face to face

## Web Resources

**Play Classic 20 Questions**

- 20Q. See: http://20q.net/

## Reference

Selin, S. (2016). *How the 20 questions game came to America.* Shannon Selin: Imagining the bounds of history. Retrieved from https://shannonselin.com/2016/08/20-questions-game/#:~:text=Though%20it%20has%20been%20said,game%20he%20played%20in%201823.

## I Tried This and This Is What I Learned

| DATE USED/LESSON TOPIC | REFLECTIONS/WHAT I MIGHT DO DIFFERENTLY NEXT TIME |
|---|---|
| | |
| | |
| | |

Have a "Name That Pantry Staple" activity adaptation to share?

Submit your tweaks and experiences here:

Survey Link: https://forms.gle/G7JS4RPADQK8ykp89

# I'll Take Seconds

**Hors d'oeuvres**

**Ice Breaker Title: I'll Take Seconds**

"Favorite" inquiries as a tool to practice active recall and reinforcement of course concepts

## Activity Description

"I'll Take Seconds" is an active identification, recall, and elaboration activity that provides opportunities for both reflection and application.

Students identify a "favorite" or "favored" example of a shared topic or category. The activity provides opportunities for students to reflect and retrieve prior learning. The activity also promotes application and elaboration, with students encouraged to consider a wide range of contexts in which a specific selection/item might be applied.

This activity is designed to support and sustain increased student comfort and confidence with both concept selection and application.

This activity works well as an introductory warm-up and/or review activity for a substantive lesson associated with a core course concept.

## Recipe

Step 1: Define and explain "I'll Take Seconds (Favorites)" activities.

Step 2: Introduce the activity. Clarify content focus to be used for the activity.

Step 3: Create pairs/groups (if applicable).

Step 4: Share the activity topic.

- This activity works well with a range of potential "favorites" (as few as one, as many as desired).
- Work to avoid categories with few options/choices. One of the goals (or possibilities) of this exercise is to highlight complexity, nuances, and gray areas.

Step 5: Provide time for students to reflect and identify their favorite.

- Encourage students to explain the reasons for their selection.
- Encourage a minimum of three reasons (e.g., attributes, features, applications).
- Offer support as needed.
- Share directional reminders about the activity, as applicable.

Step 6: Share student response options.

Step 7: Students might journal privately, share anonymously (Padlet, Google Docs, Poll Everywhere), and/or share out loud (pairs, small groups, whole class).

Step 8: Discuss. Once responses are collected, debate (either anonymously, in pairs, or out loud).

- Compare and contrast shared responses.
- Explore most popular choice, least popular choice, etc.

Step 9: Open discussion and reflection on the exercise (out loud or independent journaling).

Sample prompts:

- How has this activity changed the way you feel about the topic?
- How has this activity changed the way you feel about your selection?

Step 10: Create a class-specific "favorites" board. Padlet, Google Sites, Pinterest, and Instagram all work well.

## The Secret Sauce (Why It Works)

This **focused** activity breaks down broad topics into **manageable chunks** that reduce **cognitive load** on students. Students draw on and **actively recall** prior learning and knowledge. The activity promotes **elaboration** and hands-on, **active learning** that requires students to do something with (interact with) an assigned topic. The activity promotes both **critical thinking** and **application** of course concepts to real-world scenarios. Goals include increased **student comfort** with a particular course concept. The activity offers many opportunities for **reflection** (both individual and group). The activity also offers many opportunities for **formative assessment**.

## Ingredients

- ☐ A content and lesson-aligned topic that has a variety of examples from which students can identify a "favorite"
- ☐ Clock/Timer (as applicable)

## Activity Prep

A content and lesson-aligned topic that has a variety of examples from which students can identify a "favorite".

Optional: Students generate a topic for this activity.

## Activity Adaptations/Toppings

- Conduct the activity using a novel or course text. Students might identify favorite words, phrases, sentences, or other writing elements. Students might also identify favorite craft elements (e.g., character, dialogue, setting).

- Conduct the activity using a course concept related to current events. Students might conduct research and identify a "favorite" or "favored" article that reports on the event. Students explain the reasons why they favor/favorited the article (e.g., relevancy, currency, writing style, objectivity, comprehensiveness).
- Introduce the activity with a discussion question related to the topic and which promotes active recall. Questions can range from knowledge and comprehension activities to analysis and synthesis related prompts. Then, transition to the "favorites" selection.
    - Examples:
        - Describe and explain...
        - Define...
        - Distinguish...
        - Choose...
        - Compare...
        - Contrast...
        - Categorize...
        - Evaluate...
- Students create a collection of "favorite" tools, resources, terms, etc., on a course topic of choice.
- Students create a collection of "favorite" tools, resources, terms, etc., on an assigned topic.

## Activity Extensions

- Provide opportunities for students to publicly share their favored items and reasoning. Students might post favorites to a class bulletin board or gallery. A Padlet board, class Google Site, class Instagram account, or Pinterest board are examples of free options that work well.
- Students conduct research and identify competitors or alternatives to their "favorites." Students construct compare/contrast charts to highlight similarities and differences.
- Either individually, in pairs, in small groups, or as a whole-class exercise, students create lists of possible choices for an assigned course topic. Lists are swapped and then ranked according to a variety of characteristics, factors, or preferences.

### Law-Based Examples

Favorite time-tracking software

Favorite legal billing software

Favorite eDiscovery software

Favorite course management software

Favorite presentation software

Favorite legal research software

Favorite legal technology

Favorite case ruling

Favorite vocabulary term

Favorite aspect of a paralegal's job

Favorite aspect of our law

Favorite legal database

Favorite application

Favorite piece of technology

Favorite web browser

Favorite search engine

Favorite legal book

Favorite legal movie

Favorite law-related YouTube Channel

Favorite legal blog

Favorite fictional legal character

Favorite legal villain

Favorite course reading to date

Favorite course assignment to date

### Workplace Examples

Favorite email greeting

Favorite way to sign a letter

Favorite way to sign an email

Favorite research database

Favorite search engine

Favorite place to work

Favorite place to write

Favorite office-based sitcom or movie

Favorite office supply

### Political Science/History Examples

Favorite president

Favorite judicial decision

Favorite Supreme Court rulings

Favorite nonfiction book

Favorite educational YouTube channel

Favorite historical figure

Favorite historical movie

### Neutral/Content Agnostic Examples (Just for Fun)

Favorite school-day snack

Favorite movie

Favorite book

Favorite day of the week

## Portion Type and Size

Single (independent work), Pairs, Small Group, or Whole Class

Time: Variable

- As few as five minutes
- No maximum length

Online and/or face to face

**Customizable Templates.** See: https://docs.google.com/document/d/15ziPGa-Cjao_i3sobEp-Npsglreo61kxQ0pBBv5mONg/edit?usp=sharing

## Web Resources

- The Ultimate Favorites List. See: https://www.ranker.com/list/the-ultimate-favorites-list/stevo200

- Questions Lists, Favorites. See: https://questionslisting.tumblr.com/post/137028466905/favorites
- Liz Henwood, Favorites Questions. See: https://twitter.com/MissHenwood1/status/1417998836971282437?s=09

## I Tried This and This Is What I Learned

| DATE USED/LESSON TOPIC | REFLECTIONS/WHAT I MIGHT DO DIFFERENTLY NEXT TIME |
| --- | --- |
| | |
| | |
| | |

Have an "I'll Take Seconds/Favorites" activity adaptation to share?

Submit your tweaks and experiences here: Survey Link: https://forms.gle/G7JS4RPADQK8ykp89

# Taste Tests

**Hors d'oeuvres**

**Ice Breaker Title: Taste Tests**

Problem-posing and questioning to promote active recall, critical thinking, and analysis

## Activity Description

"Taste Tests" are designed to promote visible thinking and out-loud problem solving. Students work together to identify a term, phrase, or extended concept.

This activity provides opportunities for students to review prior learning and activate recall. The activity also presents review opportunities for students to prepare for formal/summative assessments.

Creating clues can promote critical thinking and creativity. This activity is designed to support and sustain increased student comfort and confidence when interacting with a variety of course concepts and terms.

The activity works well with any collection of key terms or course concepts, especially core concepts that are fundamental to an area of study. Concepts that are sometimes intimidating for students (because of vocabulary, complexity, unfamiliarity, or otherwise) are especially well suited to this activity. Concepts that benefit from repetition and reinforcement are also well suited for this activity.

## Recipe

Step 1: Describe and explain the "Taste Tests" activity.

Step 2: Clarify content focus. Identify and describe the topic or lesson objective that is the focus of the exercise.

Step 3: Create groups (if applicable).

Step 4: Explain how the activity will work.

- Assign roles. Roles include clue creator, clue sharer, and concept guesser.
- Clue sharer states, writes, or presents three (this number can vary) clues about a word, phrase, or provision.
- Concept guesser attempts to identify (guess) the word, phrase, or provision.
- Once a guess is made, students give a variety of responses. Options include:
    - Yes/No
    - Hot/Warm/Cold
    - Additional Clues

Step 5: Share a link or copy of a resource, terms document, or clues document (if applicable). Provide time for students to draft clues associated with an assigned topic (if applicable).

Step 6: Students guess in pairs, small groups, or as a whole class. Guessing can be done anonymously (e.g., via Google Docs, Padlet, Poll Everywhere).

Step 7: Activity can be conducted as a whole class, in small groups, and/or in pairs.

- Offer support as needed.
- Share directional reminders about the activity, as applicable.

Step 8: Open discussion and reflection on the exercise (out loud or independent journaling)

Sample prompts:

- How has this activity changed the way you feel about the shared terms?
- How has this activity changed the way you feel about the related topic?

## The Secret Sauce (Why It Works)

This targeted activity promotes **active recall** by requiring students to generate possible responses based on provided clues. Focusing on a single topic pulled from related, complex material helps break down course concepts into **manageable chunks** that reduce **cognitive load** on students. Students draw on, **actively recall**, and **reinforce** prior learning and knowledge. The activity is well-suited for content from a variety of topics and, as such, can support **interleaving**. The activity promotes hands-on, **active learning** that requires students to do something (create clues) with a course concept. Goals include increased **understanding** of a particular concept as well as increased **confidence**. The activity offers opportunities for **reflection** (both individual and group). The activity also offers opportunities for **formative assessment**.

## Ingredients

- ☐ A collection of clues related to a course topic, concept, or vocabulary term (and aligned with a class learning objective or lesson)
- ☐ Clock/Timer (as applicable)

## Activity Prep

A collection of clues related to a course topic, concept, or vocabulary term (and aligned with a class learning objective or lesson).

Optional: Students create clues (individually, in pairs, or in small groups) to use for this activity.

## Activity Adaptations/Toppings

Depending on the instructional goals and objectives, this activity can be used and adapted in a variety of ways.

- Change the number of clues provided (any number of clues would work).
- Students (either individual, in pairs, or small groups) create clues, then swap with a peer or small group.
- Conduct the activity in team or game format. Teams/players take turns providing clues (rotating). Students earn points for each successful guess. Points are tallied after a certain number of rounds.
- Conduct the activity using a passage (several paragraphs, a page of text) or chapter from a current reading, assigned book, or related news article.
- Introduce the activity with a discussion question/reflection prompt that explores the related concept. Then, transition to the "Taste Tests" guessing activity.
- Introduce the activity using a current event/news article related to the lesson topic and from which students create clues for covered concepts or vocabulary terms.
- Use the activity as a collaborative learning exercise where one student is responsible for defining unfamiliar vocabulary in a shared resource, another is responsible for generating associated clues, and another is responsible for documenting the group's process. Groups then swap and conduct the activity as described above. Depending on desired group size, additional roles can be developed.
- Students create collections of "Taste Tests" with key terms and associated clues. Students post the newly created collections on a class-wide resource as study resources.
- Students create a collection (some assigned number) of clues on a course topic of choice.
- Students create a collection (some assigned number) of clues on an assigned topic.
- Vary time permitted to work on clue construction and/or guessing.

## Activity Extensions

- Students create collections of clues for terms associated with a specific topic. Students might post clues to a class bulletin board or gallery. A Padlet board, class Google Site, or Pinterest board are examples of free options that work well.
- Continue the activity with discussion questions related to the topic and which promote active recall.
    - Examples:
        - Where might we locate more information on ___?
        - When did we discuss ___ ?
        - What additional terms and/or concepts might we add to this list of terms?

### Law-Based Example (ABA Model Rules of Professional Conduct)

Samples for ABA Model Rules of Professional Conduct

- ABA Model Rule 1.1 Competence
    - Sample Clues
        - Continuing legal education
        - Up-to-date knowledge and skill
        - Thoroughness and preparation

- ABA Model Rule 1.4 Communication with Client
    - Sample Clues
        - Responsiveness
        - Clarity
        - Consistency

### Law-Based Example (Judicial Opinions)

Creating "Taste Tests" for judicial opinions is a way for students to actively engage with complex text in a low-stakes, fun way.

This activity might be used as a warm-up on a lesson for how to read and/or brief a judicial opinion.

- If an instructor wants to reinforce research skills, students might conduct research and select a case brief of choice (e.g., by jurisdiction, topic). Then, clues might be created for unfamiliar terms used in the opinion.
- Alternatively, an instructor can share a pre-selected judicial opinion (perhaps one that students will later read and brief as part of a graded activity).
- Either individually, in pairs, in small groups, or as a whole-class exercise, students create clues for terms used in an identified judicial opinion.
- Extension: Develop clues for elements of a case brief.
    - Example terms: Procedural History, Facts, Legal Issues, Concurring Opinion, Dissenting Opinion, Majority Opinion

## Portion Type and Size

Single (independent work), pairs, small groups, or whole class

Time: Variable

- As short as one minute
- No maximum length
- Time will vary depending on the adopted approach to implementation

Online and/or face to face

## I Tried This and This Is What I Learned

| DATE USED/LESSON TOPIC | REFLECTIONS/WHAT I MIGHT DO DIFFERENTLY NEXT TIME |
|---|---|
| | |
| | |
| | |

Have a "Taste Tests" activity adaptation to share?

Submit your tweaks and experiences here:

Survey Link: https://forms.gle/G7JS4RPADQK8ykp89

## The Daily Special (Facts of the Day/Content-Driven Trivia)

**Hors d'oeuvres**

**Ice Breaker Title: The Daily Special (Facts of the Day/Content-Driven Trivia)**

Trivia as tool to increase familiarity, promote connections, and practice active recall

## Activity Description

Content-aligned trivia and randomly presented facts of the day offer opportunities for students to re-engage with previously learned content. Doing so can strengthen memory, deepen long-term retention, and promote connections to new content. Content-aligned trivia questions also present instructional opportunities to introduce new concepts in a fun and stress-free environment.

In this "Facts of the Day" or trivia activity, students respond to a series (one or more) of randomized questions related to course and learning objectives. The activity works well with any type of content.

## Recipe

Step 1: Introduce the activity. Explain how the question prompt and response process will work. Clarify content focus and type of resource to be used for the activity.

Step 2: Create groups (if applicable).

Step 3: Share a link or copy of the presented question (or series of questions, if applicable).

Step 4: Share a short question or series of questions that are presented in a low-stakes way. Questions might include random facts aligned with a module or lesson.

Step 5: Provide a defined amount of time to respond.

Step 6: Open discussion and reflection on the presented question(s) and/or topic (out loud or independent journaling).

Sample prompts:

- What else might you want to know about this topic?
- What new questions do you now have about this topic?
- What topics related to the question might you want to review?

## The Secret Sauce (Why It Works)

This **scaffolded** activity breaks down complex material into **manageable chunks** that reduce **cognitive load** on students. Students draw on and **actively recall** prior learning and knowledge. The activity promotes hands-on, **active learning** that requires students to do something with (interact with) course concepts. Goals include increased **student comfort** with a particular type of course content as well as increased **confidence** associated with such content. The activity offers opportunities for **reflection** (both individual and group). The activity also offers opportunities for **formative assessment**.

## Ingredients

- ☐ A question or collection of questions (trivia/facts of the day) that are related to a class learning objective or lesson
- ☐ Clock/Timer (as applicable)

## Activity Prep

A question or collection of questions (trivia/facts of the day) that are related to a class learning objective or lesson.

Optional: Students conduct research and prepare a question (or series of questions) for this activity.

## Activity Adaptations/Toppings

Depending on the instructional goals and objectives, this activity can be used and adapted in a variety of ways.

Provide active work time for students to create original questions (one or more). Time provided for research can vary (anything from no research allowed to several minutes). Students might research online and/or look to designated resources only.

  - Offer support as needed.
  - Share directional reminders about the activity, as applicable.

- Students might create an original question (or collection of questions) prior to the course session.
- Students can work independently, in pairs, or in small groups. Students can also respond out loud or anonymously.
- A collection of questions of the day and/or trivia-type questions can be consolidated and used for interactive game play.
- A variety of free software (Google Docs, Google Jamboard, online chat functions, Poll Everywhere, and more) work well for this activity.
- Questions can be presented in open-ended, multiple choice, or true/false format. In online chat features, students might release at the count of three (or some other designated benchmark) for a simultaneous reveal.
- Students might add original questions to a class Google Doc or Padlet board. Questions might be presented via software tools and digital flashcards as well.
- Conduct the activity using a passage (e.g., several paragraphs, a page of text) from a current reading, assigned book, or related news article.
- Introduce the activity using a current event/news article related to the lesson topic and from which students create questions to share.
- Students create a collection of trivia questions on a course-related topic of choice.
- Students create a collection of trivia questions on an assigned course-related topic.
- Vary time permitted to work on question responses.

## Activity Extensions

- Students publicly share original questions. Students post questions to a class bulletin board or gallery. A Padlet board, class Google Site, or Pinterest board are examples of free options that work well.
- If student research leads to course and topic-relevant resources, students might share their resources in a class-wide library (Google Docs, Google Sites, Padlet board). Source identification can be used as research reinforcement and library building.

### Legal Technology Examples

- What is the origin of the term spreadsheet?
- On what date did the first computer come onto the market in the United States?
- On what date did a certain technology first hit the market?
- What does the "i" in iPhone stand for?

### Law-Based Example (Judicial Opinions)

Students might be assigned a judicial opinion for independent and/or out-of-class reading. Questions based on the opinion might then be shared as a way of reinforcing comprehension and promoting increased familiarity and comfort with complex text.

Legal opinions are one example (although complex text is relative, of course, depending on grade, level, etc.). This activity works well for any complex text, topic, or resource.

## Portion Type and Size

Single (independent work), pairs, small groups, or whole class

Time: Variable

- As few as two minutes
- No maximum length
- Time will vary depending on the adopted approach to implementation.

Online and/or face to face

## Web Resources

Jeopardy, Law Questions. See: https://www.lawyersmutualnc.com/blog/take-this-jeopardy-law-quiz-2

Legal Trivia Questions. See: https://www.triviaplaying.com/364-legal-law-trivia.htm

Oyez! Oyez! This Trivia Question is Called to Order. See: https://abovethelaw.com/2017/03/oyez-oyez-this-trivia-question-is-called-to-order/

## I Tried This and This Is What I Learned

| DATE USED/LESSON TOPIC | REFLECTIONS/WHAT I MIGHT DO DIFFERENTLY NEXT TIME |
|---|---|
| | |
| | |
| | |

Have a "Daily Special" (Fact of the Day/Content-Aligned Trivia)" activity adaptation to share?

Submit your tweaks and experiences here:

Survey Link: https://forms.gle/G7JS4RPADQK8ykp89

# Appetizers

"I'm just someone who likes cooking and for whom sharing food is a form of expression."

*Maya Angelou*

## Collaborative Shopping Lists/Word Chains

**Appetizers**

**Ice Breaker Title: Collaborative Shopping Lists/Word Chains**

Word generation to promote reflection and collaboration

### Activity Description

"Collaborative Shopping Lists and Word Chain" activities are short exercises that ask students to generate a single word on a shared prompt or question. Students might share a feeling word related to a recent lesson or an assignment in progress. Students might also share a word associated with a course concept and/or a concept-related word that begins with a specific letter.

After sharing their word, each student then "passes the list" to another student in class.

Students might be asked to recite the list (either from notes or memory) before adding a new word. Alternatively, a student might be assigned as a record-keeper for the activity.

Students might be asked to generate words that begin with a certain letter, contain at least a certain number of letters, and/or conform to some other identified characteristic or exercise parameter. Generated words should relate to course content in some way.

Students might then be asked to rank how closely related the terms are to the provided topic.

Using "Collaborative Shopping Lists and Word Chains" activities as warm-ups provides opportunities to engage in active recall and retrieval practice with respect to previously learned vocabulary and key terms. The activity also provides opportunities for both individual and whole-class reflection.

This activity works well as reinforcement for a prior lesson in which new terms and concepts were introduced. The activity also works well as a pulse check and reflection activity to gauge student mindset and confidence levels associated with a specific topic or assignment.

### Recipe

Step 1: Define and explain "Collaborative Shopping Lists and Word Chain" activities.

Step 2: Introduce the activity. Explain how the activity will work.

Step 3: Clarify the content focus, subject-area, and/or question prompt to be used for the activity. Explain whether the content will draw on previously covered material, an upcoming assignment, etc.

Step 4: Provide parameters/prompts for the activity.

Sample parameters:

- Minimum number of letters per word
- Words that begin with a specific letter
- Nouns only
- Adjectives only
- Verbs only
- Generated words should begin with the final letter of the previously shared word

Sample feeling prompts:

One or two words

- How do you feel about last week's lesson on ___?
- How are you feeling about an upcoming assignment on ___?

Step 5: Assign a record-keeper to document shared words.

Step 6: Students take turns sharing words.

Step 7: After stating a word, each student selects another student to continue and share.

Step 8: Before sharing a new word, each student recites, recalls, or reads the word chain in progress out loud.

Step 9: Encourage students to practice active recall and include (in written or verbal format) the term's definition.

Step 10: After all students participate, students might rank the generated terms based on how closely related they are to the initial topic.

Step 11: Facilitate a discussion associated with the generated terms. Pose open-ended questions related to the terms. Share prompts that direct and promote conversation. Encourage students to elaborate on their responses and avoid yes/no answers. Avoid questions that can be answered in a yes/no format.

Step 12: Provide active work time for students to respond to shared discussion questions in writing (if applicable).

- Offer support as needed.
- Share directional reminders about the activity, as applicable.

Step 13: Open discussion and reflection on the written exercise and shared term(s).

Sample prompts:

- Which of the shared terms are you most comfortable with?
- Which of the shared terms are you least comfortable with?

## Prep (How to Create Collaborative Shopping Lists/Word Chains)

Prepare a topic to use for this exercise.

- Select topics that are aligned with a prior lesson and/or current lesson objectives.
- Alternatively, select topics that assess student confidence and mindset associated with course material.

## The Secret Sauce (Why It Works)

This collaborative activity provides a stress-free opportunity for students to **reflect** on course concepts and increase familiarity with key terms and concepts. Students draw upon and **actively recall** prior learning and knowledge. This activity promotes hands-on, **active learning** that requires students to do something (interact with) with a set of concepts or mindsets. Goals include increased **student comfort** with a particular set of key terms as well as increased **awareness** of course progress. The activity offers opportunities for **reflection** (both individual and group). The activity also offers opportunities for **formative assessment**.

## Ingredients

- ☐ A topic or question prompt to use for this exercise
- ☐ Clock/Timer (as applicable)

## Activity Prep

A topic or question prompt to use for this exercise.

Optional: Students create original lists of prompts (topics and questions) to use for this activity.

## Activity Adaptations/Toppings

Depending on instructional goals and objectives, this activity can be used and adapted in a variety of ways.

- Introduce the activity with a discussion question/reflection prompt that explores key concepts related to the associated lesson topic. Doing so promotes related recall associated with the topic and related concepts.
- Introduce the activity using a current event/news article related to the lesson topic and from which students will generate words in response to the article or event.
- Students earn points for each word in the chain that they can actively recall and recite.
- Students compete in teams to see which team can recite the most words.
- Vary parameters that define the scope of the activity and word generation.
- Conclude the activity with five minutes of independent writing. Students write a short scenario that uses all generated terms (or as many as possible). At the end of the five-minute period, conduct a whole-class or small-group discussion. Provide optional opportunities for students to share their writing and/or related thoughts.

## Activity Extensions

- Collect generated terms and definitions in a digital notebook. Create associated spaced repetition flashcards as a study resource. See RemNote in web resources below.
- Provide opportunities for students to share term lists. Students might post word lists to a class bulletin board or gallery. A Padlet board, class Google Site, or Pinterest board are examples of free options that work well.

- Students swap generated lists and practice active recall and retrieval by writing definitions for each term from memory and then discussing.

## Portion Type and Size

Single (independent work), pairs, small groups, or whole class

Time: Variable

- As few as five minutes
- No maximum length
- Time will vary depending on the adopted approach to implementation.

Online and/or face to face

## Web Resources

- Generated words might be saved in a digital notebook such as RemNote. See: https://www.remnote.com/
- Generated words might be populated in a Word Cloud.
    - Best Free Word Cloud Generators to Visualize Data. See: https://monkeylearn.com/blog/word-cloud-generator/
    - Free Word Cloud Generator. See: https://www.freewordcloudgenerator.com/
    - Free Word Cloud Creation Tools for Teachers. See: https://elearningindustry.com/the-8-best-free-word-cloud-creation-tools-for-teachers
    - Word Clouds. See: https://www.wordclouds.com/
    - Word Cloud Classroom Activities. See: https://blog.polleverywhere.com/10-word-cloud-activities-classroom/
    - Seven Good Tools for Creating Word Clouds. See: https://www.freetech4teachers.com/2019/04/seven-good-tools-for-creating-word.html

## References

Miley, F., & Read, A. (2011). Using word clouds to develop proactive learners. *Journal of the Scholarship of Teaching and Learning*, 11(2), 91–110.

## I Tried This and This Is What I Learned

| DATE USED/LESSON TOPIC | REFLECTIONS/WHAT I MIGHT DO DIFFERENTLY NEXT TIME |
|---|---|
| | |
| | |
| | |

Have a "Collaborative Shopping Lists/Word Chains" activity adaptation to share?

Submit your tweaks and experiences here

Survey Link: https://forms.gle/G7JS4RPADQK8ykp89

# Time to Double Check Our Recipes

**Appetizers**

**Ice Breaker Title: Time to Double Check Our Recipes**

True/false activities to reinforce existing knowledge and strengthen understanding

## Activity Description

In "Time to Double Check Our Recipes" activities, students work through a collection of true/false statements related to a specific course concept or topic. Students practice active recall and deepen understanding of course terms through a related question-and-answer process.

Students are encouraged to think of fundamental course concepts as ingredients in a larger application. Students are also reminded of the importance of a strong foundation (recipe and ingredients) for a final product or outcome. By reviewing targeted statements (in true/false contexts), students can solidify existing knowledge and strengthen long-term memory.

True/false activities provide opportunities for students to reinforce prior learning of key terms and concepts. The activity also creates opportunities to apply creative thinking skills and imagine (or re-imagine) the applications of key terms to real-world scenarios and situations.

This activity is designed to support and sustain increased student comfort and confidence when interacting with core concepts and vocabulary terms. The activity promotes critical thinking and analysis relating to question construction, word choice, and implications of binary approaches to analysis. The activity is also designed to improve student test-taking skills and related test-taking confidence with deeper awareness of both how to read and analyze true/false statements.

This activity works well as an introductory warm-up for a substantive lesson that relies on and/or is aligned with prior vocabulary terms and concepts.

## Recipe

Step 1: Define and explain "Time to Double Check Our Recipes" activities.

Step 2: Introduce the activity. Explain how course vocabulary and core concepts can be thought of as ingredients for rich and meaningful course-related writing or communications. Reinforce the importance of accuracy when describing core terms and concepts. Clarify content focus and type of resource to be used for the activity.

Step 3: Create groups (if applicable).

Step 4: Share a collection of true/false statements. Alternatively, provide time for students to create original lists and collections of true/false statements.

- Recommended: Share a minimum of 5 to 10 true/false statements.

Step 5: Provide instructions. Sample prompt follows:

> Review the list of true/false statements. Reflect and discuss.

Step 6: Provide active work time for students to share answers. Answers can be shared anonymously or in pairs, small groups, or whole-class scenarios. Questions might be reviewed and addressed one-by-one or as a collection.

- Offer support as needed.

- Share directional reminders about the activity, as applicable.

Step 7: Open discussion and reflection on the exercise (out loud or independent journaling)

Sample prompts:

- How has this activity changed the way you feel about your understanding of the key terms and concepts?
- How has this activity changed the way you feel about true/false scenarios and questions?

## The Secret Sauce (Why It Works)

This **targeted** activity breaks down complex material into manageable chunks that reduce **cognitive load** on students. Students draw on and actively **recall** prior learning and knowledge. The activity promotes hands-on, **active learning** that requires students to interact with a collection of true/false statements. Goals include increased student **comfort** with course content as well as increased **confidence** analyzing presented statements for accuracy, clarity, and word choice. The activity offers many opportunities for **reflection** (both individual and group). The activity also offers many opportunities for **formative assessment**.

## Ingredients

- ☐ A collection or list of true/false statements related to a current or prior class learning objective or lesson
- ☐ Clock/Timer (as applicable)

## Activity Prep

A collection or list of true/false statements related to course vocabulary concepts and/or a class learning objective or lesson.

Optional: Students conduct original research and prepare lists of true/false activities.

## Activity Adaptations/Toppings

- Conduct the activity using a passage (several paragraphs, a page of text) from a current reading, assigned book, or related news article. Create true/false statements based on content in the identified resource.
- Introduce the activity with a discussion question/reflection prompt that explores a variety of strategies for reading and analyzing statements for "truth" (e.g., accuracy, credibility, objectivity, fact checking, word choice).
- Introduce the activity with a discussion question/reflection prompt that explores different types of question/assessment writing (e.g., true/false, multiple choice, fill in the blank) and strategies for approaching each.
- Use the activity as a collaborative learning exercise. One student is responsible for defining unfamiliar vocabulary in a text-based resource. Another student is responsible for drafting associated true/false statements. Another student is responsible for creating an answer key. Depending on desired group size, additional roles can be developed.
- Vary time permitted to work on true/false statement responses and/or construction.
- Students create a collection of true/false statements by topic. Collections are swapped across small groups.

## Activity Extensions

- Provide opportunities for students to share drafted questions for ongoing review and study. Students might post true/false statement sets to a class bulletin board or gallery. A Padlet board, class Google Site, or Pinterest board are examples of free options that work well.
- Create true/false digital flashcards in a spaced repetition note-taking software. See: https://www.remnote.com/. Students can create free accounts and import notes and flashcards for ongoing review and study. The tool personalizes practice based on how well students know the presented material.

### Math Example (Basic Geometry)

- A triangle is a shape with three sides. (T)
- The measure of a triangle's three interior angles is 360°. (F, 180°)
- A square is a shape with five sides. (F, 4)
- A rectangle is shape with four sides. (T)
- The measure of the interior angles of a quadrilateral is 360°. (T)
- A pentagon is a shape with five sides. (T)
- A hexagon is a shape with seven sides. (F, 6)
- A heptagon is a shape with eight sides. (F, 7)
- An octagon is a shape with eight sides. (T)

Source: Geometry. See: https://www.splashlearn.com/math-vocabulary/geometry/geometry

### Language Arts Example (Grammar)

- Every sentence must include a noun.
- All sentences include at least one verb.
- Only some sentences include adjectives.

### Anatomy Example (Human Body)

- There are more than 100 bones in the human body.
- There are fewer than 100 muscles in the human body.

### History Example (U.S. Presidents)

- The fifth president of the United States served one four-year term.
- The tenth president of the United States declared war exactly two times.

### Test-Taking Strategies

Use as an opportunity to explore test-taking strategies for true/false questions.

### Resources:

- Five Tips for Answering True-False Questions. See: https://www.drmontedavenport.com/true-false-questions/
- True/False Test Taking Strategies. See: https://www.educationcorner.com/true-false-tests.html

- Five Quick Tips for Answering True-or-False Test Questions. See: https://www.saintleo.edu/about/stories/blog/5-quick-tips-for-answering-true-or-false-test-questions.
- Suggestions for Writing True-False Questions. See: https://www.bristol.ac.uk/esu/media/e-learning/tutorials/writing_e-assessments/page_28.htm
- Assessment: True-False Questions. See: https://camosun.libguides.com/c.php?g=711496&p=5109205.
- Critical Thinking Question Stems. See: https://www.teachthought.com/critical-thinking/28-critical-thinking-question-stems-content-area/

## Portion Type and Size

Single (independent work), pairs, small groups, or whole class

Time: Variable

- As short as one minute
- No maximum length
- Time will vary depending on the adopted approach to implementation.

Online and/or face to face

## I Tried This and This Is What I Learned

| DATE USED/LESSON TOPIC | REFLECTIONS/WHAT I MIGHT DO DIFFERENTLY NEXT TIME |
|---|---|
| | |
| | |
| | |

Have a "Time to Double Check Our Recipes" activity adaptation to share?

Submit your tweaks and experiences here:

Survey Link: https://forms.gle/G7JS4RPADQK8ykp89

# I Know That Word/Word Search

**Appetizers**

**Ice Breaker Title: I Know That Word/Word Search**

Word searches as a tool to promote active recall, reinforce vocabulary, and increase familiarity with course and lesson concepts

## Activity Description

Word searches are word puzzles that require players to search for hidden words (strings of letters) in a grid of letters. The grids are often square or rectangular, however a variety of shapes work well. Players search horizontally, vertically, and diagonally for hidden words. Some word searches are themed, with the list of words to be found all related to a specific topic. Others are random. The English version of the word search puzzle was first published by Norman E. Gibat in 1968 (Gamesver Team, n.d.).

Word searches provide opportunities for students to review course terms and concepts. Word searches also provide opportunities to increase student familiarity with vocabulary terms and meanings. Although most word searches are conducted using a list of provided terms, this activity recommends a different approach. Here, students are provided definitions and are tasked with locating the corresponding key term.

Students can work collaboratively as a group or in pairs. Students can also work independently.

This activity is designed to support student retention and recall of key terms and vocabulary words.

Students can complete word searches with either a provided list of key terms or definitions only. Students can also create original word searches to share with peers.

Terms that are sometimes confusing and unfamiliar to students work well in this activity. Terms with complex and/or unusual spellings are also well suited to this activity.

This activity works well as reinforcement for a prior lesson in which a variety of new terms were introduced. The activity also works well as an introductory warm-up for a substantive lesson in which a variety of new terms will be introduced.

## Recipe

Step 1: Define and explain vocabulary word search activities.

Step 2: Introduce the activity. Clarify the content focus and subject area to be used for the activity.

Step 3: Create work groups (if applicable).

Step 4: Share a link or copy of the word search activity (if applicable).

Step 5: Provide time for students to create their own word search (if applicable).

Step 6: Provide active work time for students to complete the assigned word search activity.

- Offer support as needed.
- Share directional reminders about the activity, as applicable.

Step 7: Open discussion and reflection on the exercise (out loud or independent journaling).

Sample prompts:

- How has this activity changed the way you feel about the key terms?
- How has this activity changed the way you feel about the related topic?

Step 8: Share reflections (out loud or on a digital bulletin board).

## Prep (How to Create a Vocabulary Word Search Activity)

Step 1: Create a list of key terms and associated definitions.

Step 2: Submit list of key terms to an online word search maker. See: https://thewordsearch.com/maker/

Step 3: Generate word search puzzle.

Step 4: Remove list of key terms from puzzle.

Step 5: Share list of vocabulary definitions and word search puzzle. Retain list of key terms.

## Variations

Words Only. See: https://thewordsearch.com/maker/

Flippity. See: https://www.flippity.net/WordSearch.htm

## The Secret Sauce (Why It Works)

This targeted activity provides a stress-free opportunity for students to increase familiarity with key terms and concepts. Students draw on and **actively recall** prior learning and knowledge. Students become more familiar with unfamiliar and/or confusing spellings. Students also strengthen skills associated with context clue fluency and related communication (Gamesver, n.d.). This activity promotes hands-on, **active learning** that requires students to do something (interact with) with a set of vocabulary terms and concepts. Goals include increased **student comfort** with a collection of key terms as well as increased **confidence** with spelling and communicating the key terms. The activity offers opportunities for **reflection** (both individual and group). The activity also offers opportunities for **formative assessment**.

## Ingredients

- ☐ A list of key terms and definitions related to a class learning objective or lesson
- ☐ An associated word search
- ☐ Clock/Timer (as applicable)

## Activity Prep

A list of key terms and definitions that is related to a class learning objective or lesson

An associated word search

- Optional: Students create their own word searches

## Activity Adaptations/Toppings

Depending on the instructional goals and objectives, this activity can be used and adapted in a variety of ways.

- Introduce the activity with a discussion question/reflection prompt that explores the related course topic/concept that is the focus of the word search activity.
- Use the activity as a collaborative learning exercise where one student is responsible for defining unfamiliar vocabulary in a course-based resource and another is responsible for creating a word search using those unfamiliar terms. Depending on desired group size, additional roles can be developed.
- Students create a word search on a course topic of choice.
- Students create a word search on an assigned course topic.
- Vary time permitted to work on the word search activity (or word search construction).
- Provide a word limit/cap on the number of words used for word search creation.

## Activity Extensions

Provide opportunities for students to share original word searches. Students might post word searches to a class bulletin board or gallery. A Padlet board, class Google Site, or Pinterest board are examples of free options that work well.

### Law-Based Example (Judicial Opinions)

Legal Terms Word Search. See: https://wordmint.com/public_puzzles/316309

Legal Terms Word Search. See: https://www.proprofsgames.com/word-search/legal-terms/

## Portion Type and Size

Single (independent work), pairs, small groups, or whole class

Time: Variable

- As few as five minutes
- No maximum length
- Initial use will be most time intensive.
- Time will vary depending on the adopted approach to implementation.
- *Note*: The activity takes significantly less time when the instructor creates a word search in advance of class.

Online and/or face to face

## Web Resources

- Make a 4th of July Word Search. See: https://alicekeeler.com/2021/07/02/make-a-4th-of-july-word-search/
- Alice Keeler Word Search Template. See: https://docs.google.com/spreadsheets/d/1ZP9hqeZ6YiajcpOmKpsVjAYlRbzl3npMRcYmiDcjvnA/edit#gid=1748333898
- Create Your Own Word Search Tools. See: https://www.flippity.net/WordSearch.htm

## References

Gamesver Team. (n.d.). *Word search: What is it? Objective, purpose, and more!* https://www.gamesver.com/word-search-what-is-it-objective-purpose-and-more/

## I Tried This and This Is What I Learned

| DATE USED/LESSON TOPIC | REFLECTIONS/WHAT I MIGHT DO DIFFERENTLY NEXT TIME |
|---|---|
| | |
| | |
| | |

Have a "I Know That Word/Word Search" activity adaptation to share?

Submit your tweaks and experiences here: Survey Link: https://forms.gle/G7JS4RPADQK8ykp89

# In the Kitchen: Hot, Cold, or Lukewarm

**Appetizers**

**Ice Breaker Title: In the Kitchen: Hot, Cold, or Lukewarm**

Student reflection to build community and confidence

## Activity Description

In "In the Kitchen: Hot, Cold, or Lukewarm" activities, students reflect and post (anonymously) words, phrases, or numbers that capture current feelings from a variety of perspectives. This activity is designed to promote trust in a learning community and a deeper appreciation of the value of each member of a learning community.

This activity works well as an introductory or review activity for a substantive lesson.

## Recipe

Step 1: Define and explain "In the Kitchen: Hot, Cold, or Lukewarm" activities.

Step 2: Introduce the activity. Explain how the "In the Kitchen: Hot, Cold, or Lukewarm" activity will work. Clarify content focus and type of resource to be used for the activity.

Step 3: Compose a question or topic for student reflection. Prompt students to consider existing comfort and confidence levels with the concept.

- Hot: I understand the topic well.
- Lukewarm: I understand the topic somewhat well, but not as well as I'd like.
- Cold: I don't understand the topic well.

Students can answer anonymously.

Step 4: Provide active work time for students to reflect on a presented topic, text, or resource and then respond in the assigned manner (Hot, Cold, Lukewarm).

- Offer support as needed.
- Share directional reminders about the activity, as applicable.

Step 5: Open discussion and reflection on the exercise

- Summarize student responses. Identify and clarify review opportunities, as applicable.

## The Secret Sauce (Why It Works)

This **targeted** activity presents complex material in discrete chunks to reduce **cognitive load** on students. Students draw on and actively **recall** prior learning and knowledge. The activity promotes hands-on, **active learning** that requires students to do something (clarify current comfort levels) with a presented topic or concept. Goals include increased awareness regarding student **comfort** and **confidence** associated with a course topic or concept. The activity offers opportunities for **reflection** (both individual and group). The activity also offers opportunities for **formative assessment**.

## Ingredients

- ☐ A concept, topic, or resource related to a class learning objective or lesson
- ☐ Clock/Timer (as applicable)

## Activity Prep

A concept, topic, or resource related to a lesson topic.

Optional: Students identify a concept or topic for this activity.

## Activity Adaptations/Toppings

This activity can be used and adapted in a variety of ways.

- Vary review options. Include additional gradients (e.g., Very Hot and Very Cold).
- Present a course vocabulary term. Students indicate their comfort level. Next, students write down as much about the term as they can recall.
- Vary the number of presented concepts.

## Activity Extensions

Students engage in additional practice (independently, in pairs, or in small groups) on presented topics for which a gradient less than "Hot" was the response.

### Mathematical-Based Example (Algebraic Formulas)

Students are provided a list of common algebraic formulas and asked to respond (Hot, Cold, Lukewarm) to each.

- Sample Resource. Algebraic Formulas. See: https://www.cuemath.com/algebra/algebraic-formulas/

### Mathematical-Based Example (Algebraic Expression)

Students are provided a list of common algebraic expressions and asked to respond (Hot, Cold, Lukewarm) to each.

- Sample Resource. Reading Algebraic Expressions. See: https://edu.gcfglobal.org/en/algebra-topics/reading-algebraic-expressions/1/

### Language Arts Example (Grammatical Terms)

Students are provided a list of common grammatical terms and asked to respond (Hot, Cold, Lukewarm) to each.

- Sample Resource. Key Grammatical Terms. See: https://www.thoughtco.com/key-grammatical-terms-1692364

## Portion Type and Size

Single (independent work)

Time: Variable

- As short as one minute
- No maximum length
- Time will vary depending on the adopted approach to implementation.

Online and/or face to face

## Web Resources

- Using Technology Tools for Formative Assessment (Answer Garden and Thumbs Up Activity). See: https://files.eric.ed.gov/fulltext/EJ1223780.pdf
- Formative Assessment Tech Tools. See: https://docs.google.com/presentation/d/1cUcPXxgbSiQDYlLHy-29vu3q0buz882uAFnrAOQc5n0/edit#slide=id.gc6f73a04f_0_0

## Additional Resources/Readings

- Answer Garden. See: https://answergarden.ch/
- Poll Everywhere. See: https://pollev.com/
- Best Free Polling Software. See: https://www.capterra.com/polling-software/s/free/

## I Tried This and This Is What I Learned

| DATE USED/LESSON TOPIC | REFLECTIONS/WHAT I MIGHT DO DIFFERENTLY NEXT TIME |
|---|---|
| | |
| | |
| | |

Have a "In the Kitchen: Hot, Cold, or Lukewarm" activity adaptation to share?

Submit your tweaks and experiences here:

Survey Link: https://forms.gle/G7JS4RPADQK8ykp89

# I've Got to Remember That Recipe!

**Appetizers**

**Ice Breaker Title: I've Got to Remember That Recipe!**

Retrieval practice and active recall to strengthen long-term memory and learning

## Activity Description

Retrieval practice and active recall are evidence-based learning activities that promote long-term learning and memory.

Instructors can introduce and reinforce course material in ways that help students keep track of new knowledge, terminology, and information. Instructors can also encourage students to be active participants in the learning process and actively consider how to hold on to new knowledge.

It is important to make sure students understand just how easy it is to forget hard-earned knowledge. Memory science shows that all of us are susceptible to forgetting information. Something called the "forgetting curve" illustrates just how quickly this happens. For more on Ebbinghaus's Forgetting Curve, see: https://www.mindtools.com/pages/article/forgetting-curve.htm However, there are strategies that can help.

Spaced retrieval practice is one such strategy and there are easy-to-use tools that can help us remember what we learn. Practicing just a few minutes a day makes a real difference in terms of what individuals can retain.

In this activity, instructors share prepared notes and flashcards (paper or digital) for students to practice. Students can practice independently, in small groups, or as a class.

This activity is designed to support and sustain deeper understanding of course concepts and stronger long-term retention.

This activity works well as an introductory and/or review warm-up. The activity works especially well as a review for upcoming assessments.

## Recipe

Step 1: Define and explain "I've Got to Remember That Recipe!"

Step 2: Define and explain: active recall, retrieval practice, spaced repetition practice, and the forgetting curve.

Step 3: Introduce and explain how the activity will work. Clarify content focus and type of resource to be used.

Step 4: Create groups (if applicable).

Step 5: Share digital or paper-based flashcards. Alternatively, provide time for students to create original flashcards.

Step 6: Clarify progress and/or journal reflection submission expectations (if applicable). Google Forms works well.

Step 7: Demonstrate active recall with sample flashcards.

Step 8: Share active recall and retrieval practice strategies. Discuss recommended thinking processes, how long to work to retrieve information, etc.

Step 9: Provide time for students to complete active review of shared cards (recommended minimum five minutes). Alternatively, cards might be presented one by one to students. Students might write down responses and/or take associated notes relating to how comfortable they feel with a presented term or concept.

- Offer support as needed.
- Share directional reminders about the activity, as applicable.

Step 10: Open discussion and reflection on the exercise (out loud or independent journaling)

Sample prompts:

- How has this activity changed the way you feel about each presented concept/term (from a substantive perspective)?
- How has this activity changed the way you feel about the related course topic?
- How has this activity changed the way you feel about memory and learning, as well as spaced repetition practice and active recall?

## The Secret Sauce (Why It Works)

This **interactive, hands-on** activity breaks down course concepts and topics into manageable chunks (unique flashcards) that reduce **cognitive load** on students. Students draw on and actively **recall** prior learning and knowledge. Students also practice **spaced repetition** and **interleaving** as they work through a variety of course concepts and practice over time. The activity promotes hands-on, **active learning** that requires students to do something (actively retrieve knowledge from memory) in response to flashcard prompts. Goals include increased student **comfort** with a particular area of course content (topics presented in shared flashcards) as well as deeper **connections** across course concepts and stronger **long-term memory** associated with presented course concepts. The activity offers opportunities for **reflection** (both individual and group). The activity also offers opportunities for **formative assessment**.

## Ingredients

- ☐ A collection of class notes and associated digital or paper-based flashcards (a few as three to five, as many as 15 to 20) that are related to a class learning objective or lesson.
- ☐ Clock/Timer (as applicable)

## Activity Prep

A collection of class notes and associated digital or paper-based flashcards (a few as three to five, as many as 15 to 20) that are related to a class learning objective or lesson.

Optional: Students draft (either independently or in groups) a collection of flashcards for activity use.

## Activity Adaptations/Toppings

Depending on instructional goals and objectives, this activity can be used and adapted in a variety of ways.

- Present cards one by one to students.
- Students might write responses and/or take associated notes relating to how comfortable they feel with a presented term or concept.
- Introduce the activity with a discussion question/reflection prompt that explores related course topic(s).
- Introduce the activity with a discussion that develops parameters (guidelines and expectations) for flashcard practice (e.g., number of cards, time spent per card).
- Introduce the activity with a discussion question related to short- and long-term memory and recommended study practices.
    - Examples:
        - Explain the Forgetting Curve
        - Explain Active Recall
        - Explain Spaced Repetition Practice
        - Explain Interleaving
- Use the activity as a collaborative learning exercise where students create notes and associated flashcards to swap and share with peers.

## Activity Extensions

- Students reflect and complete a journal exercise after flashcard practice is complete. Prompts might encourage students to identify areas of relative strength and weakness associated with course concepts. Students might develop a study plan for future and ongoing use.
- Students share original flashcards with peers. Students might post collections of cards to a class bulletin board or gallery. A Padlet board, class Google Site, or Pinterest board are examples of free options that work well.

### Sample Digital Flashcards

OpenStax Organizational Behavior, Chapter Terms

Chapter One. See: https://remnote.com/a/chapter-1-terms/CkKJFj6Rpzp3DCLup

Chapter Two. See: https://remnote.com/a/chapter-2-terms/TicsSxCcsCjP8QYu9

Chapter Three. See: https://remnote.com/a/chapter-3/Dv6nhCTRdaTzJ8pH8

Chapter Four. See: https://remnote.com/a/chapter-4-terms/Qi3bWS4xZCScns6nZ

Chapter Five. See: https://remnote.com/a/chapter-5/wBxjTh4m28wmKQbYG

Chapter Six. See: https://remnote.com/a/chapter-6/cm6cTLvquqki8rqNK

Chapter Eight. See: https://remnote.com/a/organizational-behavior-chapter-8-performance-appraisal-and-rewards-/NXD2xFvWQ8aWCmzTG

#### OpenStax Intellectual Property, Chapter Terms

Chapter One Key Terms. See: https://remnote.com/a/chapter-one-key-terms/6174942cb0bca400 35dd403c

Chapter Two Key Terms. See: https://remnote.com/a/chapter-two-key-terms/617495edb0bca400 35dd4053

Chapter Three Key Terms: See: https://remnote.com/a/chapter-three-key-terms/6174977db0bca400 35dd406b

Chapter Four Key Terms. See: https://remnote.com/a/chapter-four-key-terms/61749a45b0bca400 35dd407d

Chapter Five Key Terms. See: https://remnote.com/a/chapter-five-key-terms/61749ba7b0bca400 35dd4094

#### OpenStax Psychology, Chapter Terms

Chapter One Key Terms. See: https://remnote.com/a/openstax-cnxarticleintro-to-psychology-chapter-1-terms/LoYLr7EEyRSLZJa2N

Chapter Two Key Terms. See: https://remnote.com/a/openstax-cnx-psychological-research-chapter-2-terms/yjXzSrDuB79uKy3so

Chapter Three Key Terms. See: https://remnote.com/a/openstax-cnx-biopsychology-chapter-3-terms/gyfaJ2qmtj6QnXLA8

Chapter Four Key Terms. See: https://remnote.com/a/openstax-cnx-states-of-consciousness-chapter-4-terms/DwPqWraPhh5EyApk6

Chapter Five Key Terms. See: https://remnote.com/a/open-stax-cnx-chapter-5-sensation-and-perception-terms/Lm9DSXCudJrKGtapi

Chapter Six Key Terms. See: https://remnote.com/a/openstax-cnx-chapter-6-learning-key-terms/ANuykqFud3LbQedEi

Chapter Seven Key Terms. See: https://remnote.com/a/openstax-cnx-chapter-7-thinking-and-intelligence-key-terms/sdKXmfjweqF8oMcqY

Chapter Eight Key Terms. See: https://remnote.com/a/openstax-cnx-chapter-8-memory-key-terms/Ake66J4NGn9tM6YxP

Chapter Nine Key Terms. See: https://remnote.com/a/openstax-cnx-chapter-9-lifespan-development-key-terms/my9n8hQtmqbi3LWCN

Chapter Ten Key Terms. See: https://remnote.com/a/openstax-cnx-chapter-10-emotion-and-motivation-key-terms/KaGCtidNCndEM4ier

Chapter Eleven Key Terms. See: https://remnote.com/a/openstax-cnx-psychology-chapter-11-personality-key-terms-/QDKagBhbHHxSZpYQQ

Chapter Twelve Key Terms. See: https://remnote.com/a/openstax-cnx-chapter-12-social-psychology-key-terms/2vbFdsrcvKfvFkoDr

## Portion Type and Size

Single (independent work), pairs, small group, or whole class

Time: Variable

- As few as five minutes
- No maximum length
- Time will vary depending on the adopted approach to implementation.
- *Note*: The activity takes significantly less time when the instructor creates digital notes and associated flashcards in advance of use.

## Web Resources

RemNote. See: https://www.remnote.com/homepage

For more on Retrieval Practice, see:

- Retrieval Practice. See: https://www.retrievalpractice.org/
- Retrieval Practice. See: http://www.learningscientists.org/retrieval-practice/
- Learn How to Study Using Retrieval Practice. See: http://www.learningscientists.org/blog/2016/6/23-1
- Retrieval Practice: The Most Powerful Learning Strategy You're Not Using. See: https://www.cultofpedagogy.com/retrieval-practice/

For more on Spaced Practice, see:

- Learn How to Study Using Spaced Practice. See: http://www.learningscientists.org/blog/2016/7/21-1
- Learn to Study Using Spaced Practice (Poster). See: http://www.learningscientists.org/spaced-practice/

For more on The Forgetting Curve, see:

- Combat the Forgetting Curve. See: https://elearningindustry.com/forgetting-curve-combat

## I Tried This and This Is What I Learned

| DATE USED/LESSON TOPIC | REFLECTIONS/WHAT I MIGHT DO DIFFERENTLY NEXT TIME |
|---|---|
| | |
| | |
| | |

Have an "I've Got to Remember That Recipe!" activity adaptation to share?

Submit your tweaks and experiences here:

Survey Link: https://forms.gle/G7JS4RPADQK8ykp89

# Let's Add a Visual to the Recipe

**Appetizers**

**Ice Breaker Title: Let's Add a Visual to the Recipe**

Word cloud activities to promote active recall, reflection, and collaboration

## Activity Description

"Let's Add a Visual to the Recipe" activities are short exercises that utilize free word cloud software to incorporate a variety of experiences that provide visual representations of course content.

There are many ways to utilize word clouds in instruction. Simple questions relating to course content and/or student experiences with concepts work well. As students share responses to a prompt, word cloud generator software populates a visual using student-generated input.

Students might reflect on the word cloud visual and participate in an associated discussion.

"Let's Add a Visual to the Recipe" activities provide opportunities to engage in active recall and retrieval practice with respect to previously learned vocabulary and key terms. The activity also provides opportunities for both individual and whole-class reflection.

This activity works well as reinforcement for a prior lesson in which new terms and concepts were introduced. The activity also works well as a reflective exercise.

## Recipe

Step 1: Define and explain "Let's Add a Visual to the Recipe" activities.

Step 2: Introduce the activity. Explain how the activity will work.

Step 3: Clarify the content focus and subject area and/or question prompt to be used for the activity.

Step 4: Provide parameters that will apply to the activity.

Sample Parameters

- One word or phrase per student
- Multiple words or phrases permitted

Step 5: Students take turns sharing and/or inputting responses. Input procedures will vary based on the tool used. Many free polling software include word cloud options.

Step 6: Once contributions are complete (set a time), generate and/or share the word cloud.

Step 7: Facilitate a discussion associated with the generated image. Pose open-ended questions related to the terms and visual. Share prompts that direct and promote conversation. Encourage students to elaborate on their responses and avoid yes/no answers. Avoid questions that can be answered in a yes/no format.

Step 8: Open discussion and reflection on the exercise and shared term(s).

Sample prompts:

- Which of the shared terms are you most comfortable with?
- Which of the shared terms are you least comfortable with?

## Prep (Let's Add a Visual to the Recipe)

Prepare a prompt (or series of prompts) for use in this exercise.

- Select topics that are aligned with a prior lesson and/or current lesson objectives.
- Alternatively, select topics that assess student confidence and mindset associated with course material.

## The Secret Sauce (Why It Works)

This collaborative activity provides a stress-free opportunity for students to **reflect** on course concepts and increase their familiarity with key terms and topics. Students might draw on and **actively recall** prior learning and knowledge. This activity promotes hands-on, **active learning** that requires students to do something (interact with) with a set of concepts or mindsets. Goals include increased **student comfort** with a particular set of key terms as well as increased **awareness** of course progress and associated mindsets. The activity offers opportunities for **reflection** (both individual and group). The activity also offers opportunities for **formative assessment**.

## Ingredients

- ☐ A prompt (or series of questions)
- ☐ Clock/Timer (as applicable)

## Activity Prep

A question (or series of questions) to use for this exercise

Optional: Students create original lists of prompts (topics and questions) to use for this activity.

## Activity Adaptations/Toppings

Depending on instructional goals and objectives, this activity can be used and adapted in a variety of ways.

- Introduce the activity with a discussion question/reflection prompt that explores related course concepts. Doing so promotes related recall associated with the topic and related concepts.

- Introduce the activity using a current event/news article related to the lesson topic and from which students generate words in responses to the article or event.
- Vary prompt coverage to extend beyond substantive responses where students offer one- or two-word responses to a reflection question related to course content.
    - Examples include:
        - How do you feel about last week's lesson on ___?
        - How are you feeling about an upcoming assignment on ___ ?
        - On a scale of 1–10, how comfortable are you with ____?
- Conclude the activity with two to three minutes of independent writing. Students reflect on the generated word cloud(s) and spend independent time writing (a) a short scenario that uses all of the generated terms (or as many as possible) and/or (b) a reaction to the visual. At the end of the writing period, conduct a whole-class or small-group discussion. Provide optional opportunities for students to share their writing and/or related thoughts.

## Activity Extensions

- Import generated terms and definitions to a digital notebook and create spaced repetition flashcards as a study resource. For example, RemNote. See: https://www.remnote.com/
- Provide additional opportunities for students to explore generated word clouds. Word clouds might be posted to a classroom image gallery and/or used for future reflection assignments. A Padlet board, class Google Site, or Pinterest board are examples of free options that work well.
- Use generated word clouds as prompts for future written assignments, journaling, or reflections.

## Portion Type and Size

Single (independent work), Pairs, Small Groups, or Whole Class

Time: Variable

- As few as five minutes
- No maximum length
- Time will vary depending on the adopted approach to implementation.

Online and/or face to face

## Web Resources

- Word Cloud Software and Activities.
    - Best Free Word Cloud Generators to Visualize Data.
        - Word Cloud Generators. See: https://monkeylearn.com/blog/word-cloud-generator/
    - Free Word Cloud Generators.
        - Free Word Cloud Generator. See: https://www.freewordcloudgenerator.com/
        - Free Word Cloud Creation Tools for Teachers. See: https://elearningindustry.com/the-8-best-free-word-cloud-creation-tools-for-teachers

- Word Clouds.
  - Word Clouds. See: https://www.wordclouds.com/
  - Word Cloud Activities for the Classroom. See: https://blog.polleverywhere.com/10-word-cloud-activities-classroom/
- Seven Good Tools for Creating Word Clouds.
  - Seven Good Tools for Creating Word Clouds. See: https://www.freetech4teachers.com/2019/04/seven-good-tools-for-creating-word.html
  - Ten Active Learning Stratehies for Using Word Clouds. See: https://community.macmillanlearning.com/t5/bits-blog/ten-active-learning-strategies-using-word-clouds/ba-p/6010
- Consider additional visualization-based activities using web-based visualizations.
  - Visualizations. See: https://www.visualcapitalist.com/

## References

Miley, F., & Read, A. (2011). Using word clouds to develop proactive learners. *Journal of the Scholarship of Teaching and Learning*, 11(2), 91–110.

## I Tried This and This Is What I Learned

| DATE USED/LESSON TOPIC | REFLECTIONS/WHAT I MIGHT DO DIFFERENTLY NEXT TIME |
|---|---|
| | |
| | |
| | |

Have a "Let's Add a Visual to the Recipe" activity adaptation to share?

Submit your tweaks and experiences here:

Survey Link: https://forms.gle/G7JS4RPADQK8ykp89

# Lots of Letters

**Appetizers**

**Ice Breaker Title: Lots of Letters**

Word generation to promote active recall

## Activity Description

"Lots of Letters" activities are short exercises that ask students to generate as many words as they can on a given topic. Students might be asked to generate words that begin with a certain letter, contain at least a certain number of letters, and/or conform to some other identified characteristic or exercise parameter.

Students might next rank how closely related the generated terms are to the initial topic. Students might also scramble their generated list and then swap with peers.

Using "Lots of Letters" activities as warm-ups provide opportunities to engage in active recall and retrieval practice with respect to previously learned vocabulary and key terms.

Selected topics might serve as a review of past lessons, with opportunities for active recall and retrieval practice. Alternatively, selected topics might serve as a preview of a new lesson topic or content area with students prompted to brainstorm what the topic might involve (and/or explore what they already know).

Students can work collaboratively as a group or in pairs. Students can also work independently.

This activity works well as reinforcement for a prior lesson in which new terms and concepts were introduced. The activity also works well as an introductory warm-up for a substantive lesson in which a new topic, theory, or idea will be introduced.

## Recipe

Step 1: Define and explain "Lots of Letters" activities.

Step 2: Introduce the activity. Explain how the activity will work.

Step 3: Clarify content focus and subject area to be used for the activity. Explain whether the activity will draw on previously covered material or new material.

Step 4: Create work groups (if applicable).

Step 5: Share the selected topic.

Step 6: Provide parameters that apply to the activity.

Sample parameters:

- Minimum number of letters per word
- Words that begin with a specific letter
- Nouns only
- Adjectives only
- Verbs only

Step 7: Students generate as many terms as possible.

Step 8: Provide active work time for students to generate lists. Offer support as needed.

- Share directional reminders about the activity, as applicable.

Step 9: Encourage students to practice active recall. Students might also include (in written or verbal format) term definitions.

Step 10: Students might rank generated terms based on how closely related they are to the initial topic.

Step 11: Facilitate a discussion associated with the generated terms. Pose open-ended questions. Share prompts that direct and promote conversation. Encourage students to elaborate on their responses and avoid yes and no answers. Avoid questions that can be answered in a yes or no format.

Step 12: Provide active work time for students to respond to discussion questions in writing (if applicable).

- Offer support as needed.
- Share directional reminders about the activity, as applicable.

Step 13: Open discussion and reflection on the written exercise and shared term(s)

Sample prompts:

- Which of the shared terms are you most comfortable with?
- Which of the shared terms are you least comfortable with?

## The Secret Sauce (Why It Works)

This targeted activity provides a stress-free opportunity for students to increase their familiarity with key terms and concepts. Students draw on and **actively recall** prior learning and knowledge. Students become more familiar with unfamiliar and/or confusing spellings and terms. Students can work collaboratively and thereby strengthen communication and problem-solving skills. This activity promotes hands-on, **active learning** that requires students to do something (interact with) with a set of vocabulary terms and concepts. Goals include increased **student comfort** with a particular set of key terms as well as increased **confidence** spelling and communicating with key terms. The activity offers opportunities for **reflection** (both individual and group). The activity also offers opportunities for **formative assessment**.

## Ingredients

- ☐ A list of key terms related to a class learning objective or lesson
- ☐ Clock/Timer (as applicable)

## Activity Prep

A list of key terms related to a prior or current lesson topic

Optional: Students create original lists of key terms for this activity.

## Activity Adaptations/Toppings

Depending on instructional goals and objectives, this activity can be used and adapted in a variety of ways.

- Introduce the activity with a discussion question/reflection prompt that explores key concepts related to the topic.
- Introduce the activity using a current event/news article related to the lesson topic and from which students create lists of key terms.
- Use the activity as a collaborative learning exercise where one student is responsible for generating terms and another is responsible for defining the terms. Depending on group sizes, additional roles can be developed.
- Vary time permitted to work on the term list construction.

- Students earn points for each generated word that is unlike those generated by other students. Additional points might be earned based on word length. For example, four letter words earn 1 point, five letter words earn 2 points, etc.
- Students compete in teams to see which team generates the most relevant and original words.
- Vary parameters that define the scope of the activity and word generation.
- Conclude the activity with five minutes of independent writing. Students write a short scenario using the generated terms (as many as possible). At the end of the five-minute period, conduct a whole-class or small-group discussion. Provide optional opportunities for students to share their writing and/or related thoughts.

## Activity Extensions

- Upload generated terms and definitions to a digital notebook. Create spaced repetition flashcards as a study resource. See RemNote: https://www.remnote.com/
- Provide opportunities for students to share term lists. Students might post word lists to a class bulletin board or gallery. A Padlet board, class Google Site, or Pinterest board are free options that work well.
- Students swap generated lists and practice active recall and retrieval by writing definitions for each term from memory and then discussing.

Law-Based Examples

- Roles and Participants in a Courtroom
- Environmental Laws
- Ethical Responsibilities
- Legal Billing Technologies
- Case Management Software
- eDiscovery Software
- Legal Research Databases

## Portion Type and Size

Single (independent work), Pairs, Small Group, or Whole Class

Time: Variable

- As few as five minutes
- No maximum length
- Time will vary depending on approach to implementation.

Online and/or face to face

## Web Resources

- Active Recall Study Technique. See: https://aliabdaal.com/activerecallstudytechnique/
- RemNote. See: https://www.remnote.com/

## I Tried This and This Is What I Learned

| DATE USED/LESSON TOPIC | REFLECTIONS/WHAT I MIGHT DO DIFFERENTLY NEXT TIME |
|---|---|
| | |
| | |
| | |

# Name that Culinary Dish and/or Role (Kitchen Jeopardy)

**Appetizers**

**Ice Breaker Title: Name that Culinary Dish and/or Role (Kitchen Jeopardy)**

"Name That Culinary Dish and/or Role (Kitchen Jeopardy)" activities to promote critical thinking, analysis, and active recall

## Activity Description

"Kitchen Jeopardy" and "Name That Culinary Dish and/or Role" activities offer opportunities for students to apply knowledge in career-specific contexts and simultaneously practice active recall. Students are presented with characteristics or clues associated with a specific role aligned with course concepts and content. Students are tasked with generating a question that best fits the presented clue.

Students practice active recall and interleaving (with a variety of concepts presented in random orders and/or by category). Students also distinguish concepts and compare/contrast key characteristics.

This activity works well as a tool to emphasize and highlight real-world applications of course skills and processes. The activity is also well-suited for promoting recall of prior course content.

This activity works well with a range of concepts/items. Concepts/items can be presented as themes or in random order.

This activity works well as an introductory warm-up for a substantive lesson that involves core concepts and previously explored vocabulary terms.

## Recipe

Step 1: Define and explain "Kitchen Jeopardy" (and Jeopardy-type) activities.

Step 2: Introduce the "Kitchen Jeopardy" and "Name That Culinary Dish or Role" activity. Explain how the activity will work. Clarify content focus and type of resource to be used for the activity.

Step 3: Create pairs and/or small groups (if applicable).

Step 4: Share a link or copy of clues (themed or general) to be used for the activity.

Step 5: Share student response options.

- Students might share responses privately in writing, anonymously (polling software such as Poll Everywhere, Padlet, and Google Jamboard work well), or out loud.

Step 6: Present initial clue and the associated concept/topic.

Step 7: Explain that students must construct a question related to the clue (with the clue being the answer to their generated question).

Step 8: Provide active work time for students to draft questions, especially if presenting a series of clues at once.

- Vary time allocated per question: 30, 60, 90 seconds, 2+ minutes
- Offer support as needed.
- Share directional reminders as applicable.

Step 9: Once responses are collected, discuss (either anonymously, in pairs, or out loud).

Step 10: Open discussion and reflection on the exercise (out loud or independent journaling).

Sample prompts:

- How has this activity changed the way you feel about presented clues?
- How has this activity changed the way you feel about related course topics?

Step 11: Repeat (as applicable).

## The Secret Sauce (Why It Works)

This content-aligned and **focused** activity breaks down complex material into **discrete chunks and concepts** that reduce **cognitive load** on students. Students draw on and **actively recall** prior learning and knowledge (presented either by theme or in a random manner that promotes **interleaving**). The activity promotes hands-on, **active learning** that requires students to do something (generate questions that identify and describe key characteristics of a course concept). Goals include increased **student comfort** with a particular concept, the development of associated **analysis** skills, and increased **confidence** explaining a particular concept.

The activity also promotes **critical thinking** and problem solving. Students practice **transferable skills** such as argument construction and public speaking (as applicable).

The activity offers opportunities for **reflection** (both individual and group). The activity also offers opportunities for **formative assessment**.

## Ingredients

- ☐ A list of clues aligned with a course topic, lesson, or learning objective
- ☐ Clock/Timer (as applicable)

## Activity Prep

A list of clues aligned with a course topic, lesson, or learning objective

Optional: Students generate clues for this activity.

## Activity Adaptations/Toppings

Depending on instructional goals and objectives, this activity can be adapted in a variety of ways.

- Structure as a game, with team  points earned for each properly drafted question.
- Conduct the activity using characters from an assigned novel or story.
  - Who is ________?
  - Which character was guilty of ______?
  - Which character completed ____?
  - Which character said _______?
- Introduce and/or extend the activity with discussion questions related to the themed collection of clues and which promote active recall of associated concepts.
  - Examples
    - What additional concepts/examples are most like the ones shared in this list?
- Introduce the activity using a current event/news article related to the lesson topic and from which students identify items/concepts for use in the "Kitchen Jeopardy" activity.
- Use the activity as a collaborative learning exercise where students collaborate and draft collections of clues on an assigned course topic.
- Students create lists of clues on a course topic of choice.
- Students create lists of clues on an assigned course topic.

## Activity Extensions

- Provide opportunities for students to publicly share clue sets. A Padlet board, class Google Site, or Pinterest board are free options that work well.

### Courtroom and Courtroom Role Examples

#### Roles

- Police
- Prosecutor
- Defense attorney
- Witness
- Judge
- Jury
- Bailiff
- Court reporter

### Functions

- Makes arrests
- Writes reports
- Collects evidence
- Presents reports at trial
- Representative for the state/government
- Represents a defendant
- Provides an opening statement
- Presents evidence to a jury
- Rules on motions
- Provides a verdict
- Drafts complaints
- Prepares appeals
- Provides testimony
- Files an appeal
- Overrules a verdict
- Overrules a motion

- Presents arguments to a judge
- Conducts direct examination
- Conducts cross examination
- Presents a closing statement
- Drafts legal briefs
- Drafts motions
- Listens to evidence
- Evaluates evidence
- Evaluates motions
- Grants a new trial
- Conducts interrogations
- Maintains order in a courtroom
- Administers oaths
- Assists judges
- Issues ruling
- Maintains order in a courtroom
- Records trial proceedings
- Determines punishments

Example Questions

Who is ____?

### Legal Technology Examples (Office Software, Office Tools)

Collections of features from a variety of tools, including:

- Automated billing software
- Word
- Excel
- eDiscovery software
- PDF converters
- PDF annotators
- Office products
- Google products
- Electronic databases
- Lexis Nexis
- Westlaw
- Citation generators

### Research- and Writing-Themed Concepts/Topics

Types of research and/or writing concepts:

- Primary sources
- Scholarly sources
- Popular sources
- Secondary sources
- Expository writing
- Narrative writing
- Memo format
- Five-paragraph essays

## Portion Type and Size

Single (independent work), pairs, small groups, or whole class

Time: Variable

- As few as five minutes
- No maximum length
- Time will vary depending on the adopted approach to implementation.

Online and/or face to face

## I Tried This and This Is What I Learned

| DATE USED/LESSON TOPIC | REFLECTIONS/WHAT I MIGHT DO DIFFERENTLY NEXT TIME |
|---|---|
| | |
| | |
| | |

Have a "Name That Culinary Dish or Role (Kitchen Jeopardy)" activity adaptation to share?

Submit your tweaks and experiences here: Survey Link: https://forms.gle/G7JS4RPADQK8ykp89

## Name That Time, Place, Person, Tune, Provision

**Appetizers**

**Ice Breaker Title: Name That Time, Place, Person, Tune, Provision**

Concept/Term identification and guessing to promote active recall and long-term learning

## Activity Description

This activity is a word guessing activity similar to games like *Taboo* and *Catch Phrase*. Players work to guess as many words per round as possible. Game cards include target words along with related words that cannot be shared during game play.

One player acts as the guesser. Another player provides clues with the hopes that their partner guesses the game-play word. Words listed on the card cannot be shared.

Game objective: Players attempt to guess the word from provided clues. The player providing clues may not state any "off-limit" clues. If an off-limit clue is stated, the word/card becomes off limits and out of play.

Players rotate so that all players have a chance to be a "guesser" and a "clue giver."

All clues must be spoken. Hand motions and sketches are not permitted.

Players can guess as often as possible within the allotted time. Each time a player correctly guesses a word, game play continues onto the next card in the deck. Round time can vary (60 seconds, 120 seconds).

Points can be allotted for all correctly guessed words (1 point per word).

Term guessing and associated clue construction offer opportunities for students to engage with course concepts in creative ways. Term guessing and associated clue construction activities also present instructional opportunities for students to deepen long-term learning and associated understanding of complicated terms in a stress-free environment.

Creating a game environment in which students describe and guess key words is also a way to proactively mitigate the increased cognitive load (drain on working memory) and anxiety that often emerges when a student interacts with many complex terms and concepts at once. This activity is designed to support and sustain increased student comfort and confidence when interacting with course concepts and terminology.

This activity works well as an introductory warm-up and/or review activity for a substantive lesson associated with the text(s) and materials used for the exercise.

## Recipe

Step 1: Define and explain how *Taboo* and *Catch Phrase*-type games are typically played.

Step 2: Introduce the activity. Explain how "Name That Time, Place, Person, Tune, Provision" activities work. Clarify content focus and resources to be used for the activity.

Step 3: Clarify rules of game and numbers of rounds.

Step 4: Create groups (if applicable).

Step 5: Provide time for card creation (if applicable, see options and adaptations). Collect all cards before game play.

Step 6: Game play (see Activity description on previous page). Select a category.

Step 7: Share a link or copy of the cards/resources (if applicable).

Step 8: Provide active work time for students to play game rounds (recommended minimum five minutes).

- Offer support as needed.
- Share directional reminders about the activity, as applicable.

Step 9: Open discussion and reflection on the exercise (out loud or independent journaling).

Sample prompts:

- How has this activity changed the way you feel about your learning?
- How has this activity changed the way you feel about the related topic?

## The Secret Sauce (Why It Works)

This **interactive** activity breaks down complex material into **manageable chunks** that reduce **cognitive load** on students. Students draw on and **actively recall** prior learning and knowledge as they work to **retrieve** course concepts from memory. The activity promotes hands-on, **active learning** that requires students to do something (interact with peers and engage in a clue-guessing activity) associated with course content. Goals include increased **student comfort** with a particular topic as well as increased **confidence** with current levels of learning and memory. The activity offers opportunities for **reflection** (both individual and group). The activity also offers opportunities for **formative assessment**.

## Ingredients

- ☐ A collection of game play cards (key terms and associated words) related to a course topic
- ☐ Clock/Timer (as applicable)

## Activity Prep

Create a collection of game play cards (key terms and associated words) related to a course topic.

Optional: Students create card decks for this activity.

Create card decks using index cards for in-person use.

Create card decks using PowerPoint or Google Slides for virtual and/or in-person use.

On each card, include a category (a course topic or learning objective) and an associated key word (to be guessed). In addition to the key word, include several (three to five) related words. The related words will be off limits to students when sharing clues.

## Activity Adaptations/Toppings

Depending on instructional goals and objectives, this activity can be adapted in a variety of ways.

- Students create cards for use in this activity. For example, all students create three (or more) game cards. Each game card includes a category (course topic or learning objective), a key word/term, and three to five words or phrases that describe the key term.
    - Legal technology category example. Students conduct research on popular case management software, five clues/words per card.
- In small groups or pairs, students create decks of card sets for use in a later session.
- Vary time permitted to work on card construction.
- Vary number of rounds and/or time permitted per round of game play.
- Sprints. In five minutes, students create three cards within an assigned category (term and five off-limit words or phrases that describe the term). Collect all cards. Begin game play.

## Activity Extensions

- Students create and trade decks/sets of cards for game play.

### Law-Based Examples

Category: Bill of Rights

Category: Legal Technology

Word

- Documents
- Resume
- Memorandum

Excel

Legal Billing Software

- TimeSolv
- Time tracker
- Increments
- Hours
- Minutes

Category: Crimes by State

Robbery

Burglary

Arson

### History Examples

Category: U.S. Presidents

- Sample Digital Flashcards
    - RemNote U.S. President Flashcards. See: https://remnote.com/a/list-of-presidents-first-ten-names-only-/j8iKMxesEx255wQpt

Category: Wars

Category: Geographic Locations

### Mathematics Examples

Category: Formulas and Applications

## Portion Type and Size

Single (independent work), pairs, small group, or whole class

Time: Variable

- As few as five minutes
- No maximum length
- Time will vary depending on the adopted approach to implementation.
- *Note*: The activity takes significantly less time when the instructor prepares game cards in advance of use.

Online and/or face to face

## I Tried This and This Is What I Learned

| DATE USED/LESSON TOPIC | REFLECTIONS/WHAT I MIGHT DO DIFFERENTLY NEXT TIME |
|---|---|
| | |
| | |
| | |

Have a "Name That Time, Place, Person, Tune, Provision" activity adaptation to share?

Submit your tweaks and experiences here:

Survey Link: https://forms.gle/G7JS4RPADQK8ykp89

# The Most Important Ingredient: Prioritization and Debate

**Appetizers**

**Ice Breaker Title: The Most Important Ingredient: Prioritization and Debate**

Identification of argument elements to promote active recall, reinforce vocabulary, and deepen understanding of course concepts

## Activity Description

Debates are useful exercises for developing argument construction skills as well as critical thinking and analysis skills. Not all debates need to be conducted in an A versus B format. Students can generate reasons for an argument and prioritize their reasoning and/or points in support of or opposed to an issue.

Modified debate structures provide opportunities for students to review key terms and course concepts. Modified debates and associated reflections also provide an opportunity to increase student familiarity with vocabulary terms and meanings. Doing so supports brainstorming and elaboration, as well as recall and critical thinking.

In this activity, students evaluate and identify components of an argument for strengths and weaknesses. Students focus on a single side of an argument and rank elements.

Students can work collaboratively in groups or pairs. Students can also work independently.

This activity is designed to support depth of analysis and understanding, as well as strengthen retention, recall, and interactions between key terms and concepts.

Students can analyze existing arguments. Students can also create original arguments to share with peers.

## Recipe

Step 1: Define and explain argument review and prioritization activities.

Step 2: Introduce the activity. Explain how "The Most Important Ingredient" activities work.

Step 3: Clarify content focus and subject area to be used for the activity.

Step 4: Create work groups (if applicable).

Step 5: Share a link or copy of a brief article that takes a position on a course topic.

Step 6: Provide time for students to read the article (three to five minutes, although times can vary).

Step 7: After reading, students "brain dump" what they recall from the article. This serves to reinforce and strengthen connections. This can be done in writing or out loud. This can be done privately or collaboratively.

Step 8: In pairs, small groups, or as a whole class, students identify the reasons shared in support of an article's main argument/position.

Step 9: In pairs, small groups, or as a whole class, students prioritize the reasons in writing or out loud. Work can be done independently, in pairs, small groups, or as a whole class.
Prompts:

- What is the strongest reason shared in support of the argument?
- What is the weakest reason shared in support of the argument?
- What is missing from the article?
- Should any additional reasons/factors be added?

Step 10: Open discussion and reflection on the exercise (out loud or independent journaling).

Sample prompts:

- How has this activity changed the way you feel about the article/argument?
- How has this activity changed the way you feel about the related topic?

## The Secret Sauce (Why It Works)

This targeted activity provides a stress-free opportunity for students to increase familiarity with key course concepts as well as argument construction. Students draw on and **actively recall** prior learning and knowledge. Students become more familiar with arguments shared in connection with an identified course topic. Students also strengthen skills associated with argument analysis. This activity promotes hands-on, **active learning** that requires students to do something (interact) with a collection of premises and an associated argument. Goals include increased **student comfort** with a particular course topic as well as increased **confidence** analyzing associated arguments. The activity offers opportunities for **reflection** (both individual and group). The activity also offers opportunities for **formative assessment**.

## Ingredients

- ☐ A collection of brief articles that are related to a class learning objective or lesson
- ☐ Clock/Timer (as applicable)

## Activity Prep

A primary or secondary article (electronic or paper) related to a lesson topic

Optional: Students identify a resource to use for this activity.

Curate a collection of articles on a topic related to a prior or current course topic. Selected articles should take a position on the topic. Selected articles should be relatively brief (reading time three to five minutes).

## Activity Adaptations/Toppings

This activity can be used and adapted in a variety of ways.

- Students locate an argument article in preparation for the class.
- Provide an article that takes a side on a topic. Then, share (or encourage students to find) an article that shows another side of the topic.
- Introduce the activity with a discussion question/reflection prompt that reviews the associated course topic.
- Introduce the activity using a current event/news article related to the lesson topic. Students analyze the article's argument.
- Vary time permitted to work on argument analysis.
- Vary time permitted to identify an argument article.
- Vary student focus when evaluating an article. Identify ten (some identified number) key terms used in the article. Define each. Prioritize the terms for importance when developing the article's related argument.

## Activity Extensions

- If student research leads to credible sources related to a course topic/concept, ask students to share resources in a class-wide library (Google Docs, Google Sites, Padlet board). Source identification can be used as research reinforcement and also as library building.
- Article identification can be assigned as independent work.

### Law-Based Example (Billing Automation)

Sample Article: “Five Ways Billing Automation Saves Time and Money”.

See: https://www.lawtechnologytoday.org/2021/07/five-ways-billing-automation-saves-time-and-money/

Students read for three to five minutes.

Then, students brain dump what they recall from the article. This serves to reinforce and strengthen connections.

Discuss reasons in support of automation.

Ask students to prioritize reasons. What do they believe is the strongest reason?

Discuss as a class, in small groups, and/or pairs.

What is missing from the article? Should any new factors be added?

## Portion Type and Size

Single (independent work), pairs, small groups, or whole class

Time: Variable

- As few as five minutes
- No maximum length
- Time will vary depending on the adopted approach to implementation.
- *Note*: The activity takes significantly less time when the instructor selects articles for use in the activity.

Online and/or face to face

## Web Resources

- For a tool that estimates reading times based on article length and word choice, see Read-O-Meter, at: https://niram.org/read/.
- For tips on calculating reading time, see “How to Calculate Reading Time, at: https://infusion.media/content-marketing/how-to-calculate-reading-time/.

## I Tried This and This Is What I Learned

| DATE USED/LESSON TOPIC | REFLECTIONS/WHAT I MIGHT DO DIFFERENTLY NEXT TIME |
|---|---|
| | |
| | |
| | |

Have a “The Most Important Ingredient: Prioritization and Debate” activity adaptation to share?

Submit your tweaks and experiences here:

Survey Link: https://forms.gle/G7JS4RPADQK8ykp89

# What's in the Pantry? (Hidden Word Finds)

**Appetizers**

**Ice Breaker Title: What's in the Pantry? (Hidden Word Finds)**

Word Finds as a tool for active reading, retrieval practice, and engaged discussion

## Activity Description

"What's in the Pantry? (Hidden Word Finds)" are short activities that ask players to reuse letters from a presented word or collection of words to form new words.

The word search puzzle (also sometimes referred to as a Seek and Circle, WordSeek, Search a Word, WordFind, and/or WonderWord puzzles, among other names) was originally designed and published by Norman E. Gibat in the Selenby Digest on March 1, 1968 (Lovattspuzzles, n.d.; Wordsearch 365, n.d.). A Spanish puzzle creator by the name of Pedro Ocón de Oro published a similar word puzzle (called "Sopas de letras") before that date (Wordsearch 365, n.d.). Boggle is another similar word game, with randomly presented rows and columns of letters from which words are created.

Using hidden word finds as warm-ups provides opportunities to review past vocabulary and/or introduce new key terms.

Selected words might serve as a review of past lessons, with opportunities for active recall and retrieval practice. Alternatively, selected words might preview a new lesson topic or content area.

Students can work collaboratively as a group or in pairs. Students can also work independently.

## Recipe

Step 1: Define and explain "What's in the Pantry?" (Hidden Word Find) activities.

Step 2: Introduce the activity. Explain how the hidden word activity will work.

Step 3: Clarify content focus and subject area to be used for the activity. Explain whether content will draw on previously covered material or new material.

Step 4: Create work groups (if applicable).

Step 5: Instructor provides a definition (either in writing or on a presentation slide). Avoid verbal presentations, if possible.

Step 6: Class responds with the word.

Step 7: Write word on a visible space (e.g., classroom whiteboard, presentation slide). Share a link, slide, or Google Doc with a copy of the selected term (or collection of terms).

Step 8: Students identify as many course-related words as possible using the letters in the provided word.

Step 9: Facilitate a discussion associated with the key terms. Share prompts that direct and promote conversation. Avoid questions that can be answered in a yes/no format.

Step 10: Provide active work time for students to respond to related discussion questions in writing (if applicable).

- Offer support as needed.
- Share directional reminders about the activity, as applicable.

Step 11: Open discussion and reflection on the written exercise and shared term(s).

Sample prompts:

- Which of the shared terms are you most comfortable with?
- Which of the shared terms are you least comfortable with?

## Variations

- Initiate the activity with five minutes of independent writing. Students write a short scenario that uses provided terms (or as many as possible). At the end of the five-minute period, conduct a whole-class or small-group discussion. Provide optional opportunities for students to share writing and/or related thoughts.
- Allow use of letters multiple times.
- Limit words to a minimum number of letters.
- Present more than one word (two, three, etc.) for hunting for new words.
- Provide points for the length of all found words.
- Create teams with leader boards for earned points.

## The Secret Sauce (Why It Works)

This targeted activity provides a stress-free opportunity for students to increase familiarity with key terms and concepts. Students draw on and **actively recall** prior learning and knowledge. Students become more familiar with unfamiliar and/or confusing spellings and terms. Students can work collaboratively and thereby strengthen communication and problem-solving skills. This activity promotes hands-on, **active learning** that requires students to do something (interact) with a set of vocabulary terms and concepts. Goals include increased **student comfort** with a set of key terms, as well as increased **confidence** spelling and discussing the terms. The activity offers opportunities for **reflection** (both individual and group). The activity also offers opportunities for **formative assessment**.

## Ingredients

- ☐ List of definitions and key terms related to a class learning objective or lesson
- ☐ Clock/Timer (as applicable)

## Activity Prep

A collection of key terms related to a prior or current lesson topic.

Optional: Students create lists of key terms and associated definitions.

## Activity Adaptations/Toppings

This activity can be used and adapted in a variety of ways.

- Conduct the activity using key terms from an assigned reading or book.
- Conduct the activity using key terms from a current event or news article.
- Use the activity as a collaborative learning exercise where students take on different roles (list construction, definitions, etc.).
- Vary time permitted to work on term list construction.

## Activity Extensions

- Students create original term lists for use in the activity.
- Students post terms lists to a class bulletin board or gallery. A Padlet board, Google Site, or Pinterest board are free options that work well.
- Students swap generated lists and practice active recall and retrieval by writing definitions for each term from memory.
- Students swap lists and then prioritize the shared terms in order of importance, relevance, utility, or some other identified characteristic. Students share associated reasoning (either orally or in writing).

### Law-Based Example (Roles and Participants in a Courtroom)

Roles in a courtroom (present any collection of the following words):

- Judge
- Jury
- Prosecutor
- Defense counsel
- Court reporter
- Court interpreter
- Clerk
- Bailiff
- Attorney

### English Example

- This activity might be used as a warm-up on a lesson requiring students to draw on pre-existing knowledge of certain key terms (e.g., craft elements—plot, character, descriptive detail, dialogue, theme—and/or writing elements).

## Portion Type and Size

Single (independent work), pairs, small group, or whole class

Time: Variable

- As few as five minutes
- No maximum length
- Time will vary depending on the adopted approach to implementation.
- *Note*: The activity takes significantly less time when the instructor prepares word lists.

Online and/or face to face

## References

Lovatt's Puzzles. (n.d.). About word search puzzles. https://lovattspuzzles.com/online-puzzles-competitions/play-daily-word-search-puzzle-online/

Wordsearch 365. (n.d.). The origin and history of word search. https://www.wordsearch365.com/tips/history-of-word-search

## I Tried This and This Is What I Learned

| DATE USED/LESSON TOPIC | REFLECTIONS/WHAT I MIGHT DO DIFFERENTLY NEXT TIME |
|---|---|
| | |
| | |
| | |

Have a "What's in the Pantry? (Hidden Word Finds)" activity adaptation to share?

Submit your tweaks and experiences here:

Survey Link: https://forms.gle/G7JS4RPADQK8ykp89

# What's Cooking? (Word Scramble)

**Appetizers**

**Ice Breaker Title: What's Cooking? (Word Scramble)**

Word scrambles to promote active recall

## Activity Description

Word scrambles are short activities that ask players to rearrange randomly mixed/jumbled letters (a collection of both consonants and vowels) to form a familiar and meaningful word. Scrambles were originally invented by Martin Naydel in 1954 (with a variation called Jumble).

Word scrambles provide excellent opportunities to review past vocabulary and/or introduce new key terms. Selected words might serve as a review of past lessons, with opportunities for active recall and retrieval practice. Alternatively, selected words might serve as a preview of a new lesson topic or content area.

Students can work collaboratively as a group or in pairs. Students can also work independently.

## Recipe

Step 1: Define and explain word scramble (mixed letters) activities.

Step 2: Introduce the activity. Explain how the word scramble activity will work.

Step 3: Clarify the content focus and subject area to be used for the activity. Explain whether the content will draw on previously covered material or new material.

Step 4: Create work groups (if applicable).

Step 5: Share a link, slide, Google Doc, or copy of scrambled vocabulary terms.

Step 6: Students work to unscramble the list of terms.

Step 7: Encourage students to recall and then share (in written or verbal format) term definitions.

Step 8: Facilitate a discussion associated with key terms. Avoid questions that can be answered in a yes/no format.

Step 9: Provide active work time for students to respond to discussion questions in writing (if applicable).

- Offer support as needed.
- Share directional reminders about the activity, as applicable.

Step 10: Open discussion and reflection on the written exercise and shared term(s).

Sample prompts:

- Which of the shared terms are you most comfortable with?
- Which of the shared terms are you least comfortable with?

## Prep (How to Create a "What's Cooking? Word Scramble")

Step 1: Prepare a list of vocabulary terms to use for this exercise.

Step 2: Create a new list of the same terms, with scrambled letters.

Step 3: Present the list of scrambled terms on a prepared slide, visible presentation board, or other written format (e.g., Google Doc, paper). Avoid relying on verbal presentation formats only. It is important that students can read and reflect on the scrambled text as a part of their thinking process.

Step 4: Pose open-ended questions related to the terms. Encourage students to elaborate on their responses and avoid yes and no answers.

## Variations

Initiate the activity with five minutes of independent writing. Students spend independent time writing a short scenario that uses all provided terms (or as many as possible). At the end of the five-minute period, conduct a whole-class or small-group discussion. Provide optional opportunities for students to share their writing and/or related thoughts.

## The Secret Sauce (Why It Works)

This targeted activity provides a stress-free opportunity for students to increase familiarity with key terms and concepts. Students draw on and **actively recall** prior learning and knowledge. Students become more familiar with unfamiliar and/or confusing spellings and terms. Students can work collaboratively and thereby strengthen communication and problem-solving skills. This activity promotes hands-on, **active learning** that requires students to do something (interact) with a set of vocabulary terms and concepts. Goals include increased **student comfort** with key terms as well as increased **confidence** associated with such terms. The activity offers opportunities for **reflection** (both individual and group). The activity also offers opportunities for **formative assessment**.

## Ingredients

- ☐ A list of key terms related to a class learning objective or lesson
- ☐ An associated list of those same key terms in scrambled format
- ☐ Clock/Timer (as applicable)

## Activity Prep

A collection of key terms related to a prior or current lesson topic.

Optional: Students create lists of key terms and associated word scrambles to swap for this activity.

## Activity Adaptations/Toppings

This activity can be used and adapted in a variety of ways.

- Use key terms from an assigned reading or book.
- Use key terms from a current event or news article.
- Introduce the activity using a current event/news article related to the lesson topic and from which students create lists of key terms for the scramble activity.
- Use the activity as a collaborative learning exercise where one student is responsible for defining unfamiliar vocabulary in a text-based resource, another is responsible for documenting the group's process, another is responsible for putting together a list of terms for scrambling. Depending on desired group size, additional roles can be developed. Groups then swap scrambles.
- Vary time permitted to work on term list construction and/or scramble activity.

## Activity Extensions

- Provide opportunities for students to create original term lists and scrambles. See EZ Word Scramble at: https://ezwordscramble.glitch.me/. Students might post scrambles to a class bulletin board or gallery. A Padlet board, class Google Site, or Pinterest board are free options that work well.
- Students swap generated lists and practice active recall and retrieval by writing definitions for each term from memory and then discussing.

### Law-Based Example (Roles and Participants in a Courtroom)

#### Roles in a Courtroom (Unscrambled)

- Judge
- Jury
- Prosecutor
- Defense counsel
- Court reporter
- Court interpreter
- Clerk
- Bailiff
- Attorney

#### Roles in a Courtroom (Scrambled)

- UJEDG
- UJYR
- SEPROTROCU
- DNEEEFS CUOLESN
- TCRUO PROERERT
- ORCTU PRREEEINRTT
- RKLEC
- FABIILF
- TATYNERO

## Portion Type and Size

Single (independent work), pairs, small groups, or whole class

Time: Variable

- As few as five minutes.
- No maximum length.
- Time will vary depending on the adopted approach to implementation.
- *Note*: The activity takes significantly less time when the instructor provides pre-scrambled word lists.

Online and/or face to face

## Web Resources

- Auto-Scrambler. See: https://ezwordscramble.glitch.me/
  - The auto-scrambler generates new scrambles each time, thereby encouraging reuse and replay.
  - To use, copy and paste a list of terms into the left-hand panel. Press Enter. Scrambled terms will appear on the right-hand panel.

## Sample Templates

- Electronic Discovery Term Scramble. See: https://docs.google.com/presentation/d/1gJM2QdCZwQ8Y5pnYytACIY16P4SGQmMqOD3v5amp36Y/edit?usp=sharing
- Roles in a Court Room. See: https://docs.google.com/document/d/12c7OouAB-uPcrVO-zgOFHAEdjuc7-euK10ERSoV23Z0/edit?usp=sharing
- Craft Elements. See: https://docs.google.com/document/d/1a6tUVe9NbsFIKYDcJUKRBgdqjfkurSJhz1pweyG0reE/edit?usp=sharing
- Writing Elements. See: https://docs.google.com/document/d/1KkIWQ8v22lhwu5c82pVdsFvN7w2MXoYydCaaY5U404Y/edit?usp=sharing

## References

Education. (n.d.). *Word scrambler.* https://www.education.com/worksheet-generator/reading/word-scramble/

Jumble. (n.d.). *About the jumble.* https://www.jumble.com/about

Word Tips. (n.d.). *Word scramble—word finder.* https://word.tips/word-scramble/

## I Tried This and This Is What I Learned

| DATE USED/LESSON TOPIC | REFLECTIONS/WHAT I MIGHT DO DIFFERENTLY NEXT TIME |
|---|---|
| | |
| | |
| | |

Have a “What’s Cooking? (Word Scramble)” activity adaptation to share?

Submit your tweaks and experiences here:

Survey Link: https://forms.gle/G7JS4RPADQK8ykp89

# Word Soup: Quotable Text

**Appetizers**

**Ice Breaker Title: Word Soup (Quotable Text and Words Worth Savoring)**

Quotations as open-ended discussion prompts and a tool to promote reflection, creative thinking, and connected thought

## Activity Description

Quotations are words or phrases that are taken directly from another source and shared in either written or oral form. Using quotations as prompts for discussion provides opportunities for deeper learning, critical thinking, connected thoughts, and reflection.

Selected quotations might align with a variety of learning objectives and course goals. Shared quotes can be closely or loosely aligned with a specific course topic or content area.

Quotes might highlight the work and thinking of an influential researcher or scholar. Quotes might also highlight controversial ideas, opposing perspectives, or novel ways of thinking about and/or describing a topic.

Quotations often provide opportunities for students to explore and analyze complex ideas in a low-stakes, safe environment.

Students can work collaboratively as a group or in pairs. Students can also work independently.

This activity works well as reinforcement for a prior lesson in which a new topic, theory, or idea was introduced. The activity also works well as an introductory warm-up for a substantive lesson in which a new topic, theory, or idea will be introduced.

## Recipe

Step 1: Define and explain "Word Soup" (Quotable Text) activities.

Step 2: Introduce the activity. Explain how the quotation activity will work.

Step 3: Clarify the content focus and subject area to be used for the activity.

Step 4: Create work groups (if applicable).

Step 5: Share a link, slide, or copy of a selected quotation.

Step 6: Facilitate a discussion associated with the quotation. Share prompts that direct and promote conversation. Avoid questions that can be answered in a yes and no format.

Step 7: Provide active work time for students to respond to shared quotations in writing (if applicable).

- Offer support as needed.
- Share directional reminders about the activity, as applicable.

Step 8: Open discussion and reflection on the written exercise and shared quotation(s).

Sample prompts:

- How has this quotation changed the way you feel about associated key terms?
- How has this quotation changed the way you feel about the related topic?

Step 9: Share reflections (either out loud or on digital bulletin board) (optional/if applicable).

## Prep (How to Create a "Word Soup"/Quotable Text Activity)

Step 1: Prepare a quotation (or collection of quotations). Selected quotations should be related to and aligned with course content and lesson objectives.

Step 2: Present a quotation on a prepared slide, visible presentation board, or other written format. Avoid relying on verbal presentation formats. It is important that students can read and refer back to the quotation as a part of their thinking process.

Step 3: Pose open-ended questions related to the quotation. Encourage students to elaborate on their responses and avoid yes and no answers.

## Variations

- Initiate the activity with five minutes of independent writing. Students spend independent time responding to the quotation in writing. At the end of the five-minute period, conduct a whole-class or small-group discussion. Provide optional opportunities for students to share their writing and/or related thoughts.
- Students locate quotations of interest on an assigned topic and then lead a related discussion.
- Students locate quotations of interest on an assigned topic and then draft associated open-ended, guided questions as discussion prompts.

## The Secret Sauce (Why It Works)

This targeted activity provides a stress-free opportunity for students to increase their familiarity and deepen their **critical thinking** with key terms and concepts. This activity promotes hands-on, **active learning** that requires students to do something (interact with) a thought-provoking quotation and related discussion prompts. Students are encouraged to **elaborate** on a topic, explore ideas in a **low-stakes, safe environment**, and respond to guided questions. Goals include increased student comfort with complex and ambiguous topics, as well as increased confidence in original thought and inquiry. The activity offers opportunities for **reflection** (both individual and group). The activity also offers opportunities for **formative assessment**.

## Ingredients

- ☐ A quotation (or collection of quotations) related to a class learning objective or lesson
- ☐ Clock/Timer (as applicable)

## Activity Prep

A quotation (or collection of quotations) from a primary or secondary resource (web-based or paper) related to a lesson topic

Optional: Students identify quotations for this activity.

## Activity Adaptations/Toppings

This activity can be used and adapted in a variety of ways.

- Use a quotation from a current reading, assigned book, or related news article.
- Present a quotation related to a lesson topic. Provide five minutes for students to draft related discussion prompts to be shared in small-group or whole-class discussion.

## Activity Extensions

- Students curate quotations related to course topics. Students might post quotations to a class bulletin board or gallery. A Padlet board, class Google Site, or Pinterest board are free options that work well.

### Entrepreneurship and Observation-Based Examples

Sample quotations used in an innovation and creativity course:

- "Whatever you can do, or dream you can, begin it. Boldness has genius, power and magic in it." - Goethe
- "Whether or not you can observe a thing depends on the theory you use. It is the theory which decides what can be observed." - Albert Einstein
- "Discovery is seeing what everybody else has seen, and thinking what nobody else has thought." - Albert Szent-Gyorgyi
- "A pile of rocks ceases to be a rock pile when somebody contemplates it with the idea of a cathedral in mind." - Antoine Saint-Exupery
- "The silly question is the first intimation of some totally new development." - Alfred North Whitehead
- "The meaning of life is to see." - Hui Neng
- "Be confident, don't doubt yourself, and go for it. If you are sure there is an opportunity, you need to believe wholeheartedly in it—your team won't be driven to succeed unless you are." - Kellee Khalil

### Legal Technology/Ethics-Based Examples

Sample quotations used in a legal technology course:

- "It's still magic even if you know how it's done." - Terry Pratchett, A Hat Full of Sky
- "We are stuck with technology when what we really want is just stuff that works." - Douglas Adams, The Salmon of Doubt
- "It has become appallingly obvious that our technology has exceeded our humanity." - Albert Einstein
- "#ALTAwards2020 judge @imokx: "Technology isn't a silver bullet. What really moves the needle is a culture change within the people and processes."
- "If I have seen further than others, it is by standing on the shoulders of giants." - Isaac Newton
- (While this quotation is often attributed to Isaac Newtown in 1675, it can be traced back to Bernard of Chartres in 1159.)
- "The advance of technology is based on making it fit in so that you don't really even notice it, so it's part of everyday life." - Bill Gates
- "If you can't explain it simply, you don't understand it well enough." - Albert Einstein

Sample quotations to promote collaboration:

- "If you hear a voice within you say 'you cannot paint,' then by all means paint, and that voice will be silenced." - Vincent Van Gogh
- "When you pick up one end of the stick, you also pick up the other." - African Prove

Sample quotations to promote a growth mindset:

- "Impossible spells I'm possible" – Audrey Hepburn
- "You got to be careful if you don't know where you're going, because you might not get there." – Yogi Berra

Sample Quotation Libraries:

- Feedback Quotations. See: https://www.thefeedbackbank.com/ (Click on Feedback Quotations)
- Quotations that Inspire a Growth Mindset. See: https://www.remnote.com/a/quotations-that-inspire-a-growth-mindset/Hn44x9AxAumM5qPdX
- Quotations that Encourage Questions. See: https://www.remnote.com/a/quotations-to-encourage-questions/kuz7SKXPes6MA3692
- Quotations that Inspire. See: https://www.remnote.com/a/quotations-to-inspire/6TeocZ7wEkBSbPYWW
- Quotations on Feedback. See: https://www.remnote.com/a/quotations-on-feedback/fNQzAkPRu7ahwbrHK

Sample Technology-Related Quotations:

- "If you automate a process that has errors, all you've done is automate the generation of those errors." – W.L.W. Borowiecki
- "Automation is cost cutting by tightening the corners and not cutting them." – Haresh Sippy
- "Technology is best when it brings people together." – Matt Mullenweg, Social Media Entrepreneur
- "Technology offers us a unique opportunity, though rarely welcome, to practice patience." – Allan Lokos, Patience: The Art of Peaceful Living
- "Innovation is the outcome of a habit, not a random act." – Sukant Ratnakar
- "The technology you use impresses no one. The experience you create with it is everything." – Sean Gerety

## Presentation Preparation Examples

- "Five minutes of planning are worth fifteen minutes of just looking." – E.L. Konigsburg, *From the Mixed-Up Files of Mrs. Basil E. Frankweiler*

## Additional Quotation Category Examples

- Writing and Word Choice
    - "The difference between the almost-right word & the right word is really a large matter—it's the difference between the lightning-bug & the lightning." – Mark Twain
    - "A writer is a person for whom writing is more difficult than it is for other people." – Thomas Mann
    - "In my own somewhat narrow experience, the value of writing seems to be in inverse proportion to the ease of writing. Whatever flows freely and bubblingly turns out to be sorry stuff a week later." – H.L. Mencken
    - "When something can be read without effort, great effort has gone into its writing." – Enrique Jardiel Poncela
    - "Writing is hard work. Any time it comes easy, suspect it." – Chip Scanlan

- Communication
    - "The quieter you become, the more you are able to hear."
    - "Silence is the most powerful scream."
    - "Silence speaks when words can't."
- Automation and Technology
    - "If you automate a process that has errors, all you've done is automate the generation of those errors." - W.L.W. Borowiecki
    - "Automation is cost cutting by tightening the corners and not cutting them." - Haresh Sippy
- Change
    - "When you're finished changing, you're finished." - Benjamin Franklin
    - "We must become the change we want to see." - Mahatma Gandhi
    - "Never doubt that a small group of thoughtful, committed citizens can change the world; indeed, it's the only thing that ever has." - Margaret Mead
    - "Change is the only constant." - Heraclitus
    - "If you can't fly then run, if you can't run then walk, if you can't walk then crawl, but whatever you do, you have to keep moving forward." - Martin Luther King, Jr.
    - "I can be changed by what happens to me. But I refuse to be reduced by it." - Maya Angelou
- Business and Entrepreneurship
    - "We keep moving forward, opening new doors, and doing new things, because we're curious and curiosity keeps leading us down new paths." -Walt Disney.

## Portion Type and Size

Single (independent work), pairs, small groups, or whole class

Time: Variable

- As few as five minutes.
- No maximum length.
- Time will vary depending on the adopted approach to implementation.

Online and/or face to face

## Web Resources

Feedback Bank Quotation Repository. See: https://www.thefeedbackbank.com/

## I Tried This and This Is What I Learned

| DATE USED/LESSON TOPIC | REFLECTIONS/WHAT I MIGHT DO DIFFERENTLY NEXT TIME |
|---|---|
| | |
| | |
| | |

Have a "Word Soup (Quotable Text and Words Worth Savoring)" activity adaptation to share?

Submit your tweaks and experiences here:

Survey Link: https://forms.gle/G7JS4RPADQK8ykp89

# Kitchen Bingo

**Appetizers**

**Ice Breaker Title: Kitchen Bingo**

Bingo games to promote active recall

## Activity Description

Bingo games are short activities that ask players to identify shared terms on a grid-based gameboard. Using bingo activities as warm-ups provides opportunities to review past vocabulary and/or introduce new key terms.

Selected words might serve as a review of past lessons, with opportunities for active recall and retrieval practice. Alternatively, selected words might serve as a preview of a new lesson topic or content area.

Students can work collaboratively as a group or in pairs. Students can also work independently.

This activity works well as reinforcement for a prior lesson in which new terms and concepts were introduced. The activity also works well as an introductory warm-up for a substantive lesson in which a new topic, theory, or idea will be introduced.

## Recipe

Step 1: Define and explain "Kitchen Bingo" activities.

Step 2: Introduce the activity. Explain how the bingo activity will work.

Step 3: Clarify the content focus and subject area to be used for the activity. Explain whether the content will draw on previously covered material or new material.

Step 4: Create work groups (if applicable).

Step 5: Share a link, slide, Google Doc, or copy of prepared bingo gameboards. Alternatively, students might create their own board based on a presented list of terms.

Step 6: As terms are shared, students scan gameboards to identify matches. Alternatively, definitions might be shared, and students work to identify matching terms.

Step 7: Encourage students to recall term definitions at the same time they scan for gameboard matches.

Step 8: Game play might be first to five in a row. Alternatives include four corners, two rows, two columns, perimeter, and/or any other pattern.

Step 9: Facilitate a post-game discussion associated with the key terms. Share prompts that direct and promote conversation. Avoid questions that can be answered in a yes and no format.

## Prep (How to Create a Kitchen Bingo Activity)

Step 1: Prepare a list of vocabulary terms for this exercise. Select terms that are aligned with a prior lesson and/or current lesson objectives.

Step 2: Students might create grids (e.g., five by five) with a single word placed in each grid box.

Alternative Step 2: Utilize online bingo generators to create gameboards.

## The Secret Sauce (Why It Works)

This targeted activity provides a stress-free opportunity for students to increase familiarity with key terms and concepts. Students draw on and **actively recall** prior learning and knowledge. Students become more familiar with unfamiliar and/or confusing spellings and terms. Students can work collaboratively and thereby strengthen communication and problem-solving skills. This activity promotes hands-on, **active learning** that requires students to do something (interact with) with a set of vocabulary terms and concepts. Goals include increased **student comfort** with a particular set of key terms as well as increased **confidence** spelling and communicating those key terms. The activity offers opportunities for **reflection** (both individual and group). The activity also offers opportunities for **formative assessment**.

## Ingredients

- ☐ A list of key terms related to a class learning objective or lesson
- ☐ Gameboard grids (e.g., four by four, five by five) with a single word placed in each grid box
    - ☐ Online bingo generators can be used to create gameboards
- ☐ Gameboard markers (e.g., chips, seeds, paper scraps)
- ☐ Clock/Timer (as applicable)

## Activity Prep

A collection of key terms related to a prior or current lesson topic.

- Optional: Students create original lists of key terms and gameboards.

Gameboard grids (e.g., four by four, five by five) with a single word placed in each grid box.

- Online bingo generators can be used to create gameboard.

Gameboard markers (e.g., chips, seeds, paper scraps).

## Activity Adaptations/Toppings

This activity can be used and adapted in a variety of ways.

- Use key terms from an assigned reading or book.
- Use key terms from a current event or news article.
- Introduce the activity with a discussion question/reflection prompt that explores key concepts related to the terms list.
- Introduce the activity using a current event/news article related to the lesson topic and from which students will create bingo gameboards for future game play.
- Use the activity as a collaborative learning exercise where one student is responsible for defining unfamiliar vocabulary in a text-based resource, another is responsible for documenting the group's process, and another is responsible for creating bingo gameboards for future use. Depending on the desired group size, additional roles can be developed.
- Vary game play (e.g., four corners, five in a row, perimeter, diagonals, X shape).
- During game play, instructor shares definitions for key terms (those included on gameboards). Students identify the term associated with the shared definition.
- For math-based bingo, instructor shares math problems for solving. Students solve and identify a number/answer to the presented problem. Students create five by five (or four by four) number-based gameboards in advance of play.
- Show images of words, rather than stating the word or concept. Students match words with images.
- Rather than stating the word, share clues that students use to identify matches.
- Students create clues for word lists.

## Activity Extensions

Provide opportunities for students to create original term lists and bingo cards. Students might post bingo cards to a class bulletin board or gallery. A Padlet board, class Google Site, or Pinterest board are free options that work well.

Students swap generated lists and practice active recall and retrieval by writing definitions for each term from memory.

### Math Bingo Example (Addition, Subtraction, Multiplication, Division)

Students create a grid of five-by-five squares on a sheet of paper or Google Doc.

Students enter whole numbers between 1 and 50. Instructor shares randomly generated math problems for students to solve and then identify matches on gameboard grids.

Sample problems:

1. $2 \times 4$
2. $12/6$
3. $5 + 25$
4. $87 - 43$
5. $43 + 22 - 35$
6. $(2 \times 17) - (45/9)$

### Language Arts Bingo Example (Form of Speech)

Students create a box of five-by-five squares on a sheet of paper or Google Doc.

Students enter different forms of speech in each box (e.g., Noun, Verb, Adjective, Adverb).

Instructor shares randomly generated terms relating to a course topic.

Students identify the form of speech and then seek matches on gameboard grids.

## Portion Type and Size

Single (independent work), pairs, small groups, or whole class

Time: Variable

- As few as five minutes.
- No maximum length.
- Time will vary depending on the adopted approach to implementation (and the number of rounds played).
- *Note*: The activity takes significantly less time when the instructor provides pre-generated bingo game cards.

Online and/or face to face

## Web Resources

- My Free Bingo Cards
    - https://myfreebingocards.com/bingo-card-generator
- Bingo Baker
    - https://bingobaker.com/
- Canva
    - https://www.canva.com/create/bingo-cards/
- Fun Classroom Activity Bingo
    - https://www.bookwidgets.com/blog/2014/11/fun-classroom-activity-bingo
- Bingo in the Classroom: Four Ways it Can Increase Skills
    - https://autismclassroomresources.com/bingo-activities-in-the-classroom/
- Bingo Across the Curriculum
    - https://www.thoughtco.com/bingo-across-the-curriculum-2081088

## Sample Templates

Free Bingo Card Templates. See: https://www.adobe.com/express/create/bingo-card

## I Tried This and This Is What I Learned

| DATE USED/LESSON TOPIC | REFLECTIONS/WHAT I MIGHT DO DIFFERENTLY NEXT TIME |
|---|---|
| | |
| | |
| | |

Have a "Kitchen Bingo" activity adaptation to share?

Submit your tweaks and experiences here:

Survey Link: https://forms.gle/G7JS4RPADQK8ykp89

# An Extra Serving of Jam

**Appetizers**

**Ice Breaker Title: An Extra Serving of Jam**

Collaborative bulletin boards as a tool to promote collaboration and engagement

## Activity Description

Digital bulletin boards offer opportunities for students to collaborate and engage with course material in interactive and engaging ways.

Collaborative digital boards (which can be used anonymously and/or in self-identified ways) are also a way to proactively mitigate the increased cognitive load (drain on working memory) and anxiety that often emerges when a student interacts with complex concepts. This activity is designed to support and sustain increased student comfort and confidence when interacting with course concepts.

## Recipe

Step 1: Define and explain Jamboard activities.

Step 2: Introduce the activity. Demo Jamboard software application to be used in the activity (as applicable). Clarify content focus and type of resource to be used for the activity.

Step 3: Create groups (if applicable).

Step 4: Share a link or copy of a pre-designed/selected Jamboard. Alternatively, provide time for students to research and locate an original image/graphic resource for use in this activity (if applicable).

Step 5: Provide instructions for the Jamboard activity. Clarify desired interactions and actions.

Step 6: Provide active work time for students to work on Jamboard activity (recommended minimum five minutes).

- Offer support as needed.
- Share directional reminders about the activity, as applicable.

Step 7: Provide time for review and reflection.

Step 8: Open discussion and reflection on the exercise (out loud or independent journaling).

Sample prompts:

- How has this activity changed the way you feel about the shared ideas?
- How has this activity changed the way you feel about the related topic?

## The Secret Sauce (Why It Works)

This **interactive** activity breaks down complex material into manageable chunks that reduce **cognitive load** on students. Students draw on and actively **recall** prior learning and knowledge. The activity promotes **creative thinking** and hands-on, **active learning** that requires students to do something (interact with) with a course concept/topic. Goals include increased student **comfort** with a particular topic as well as increased **understanding** of the topic. The activity offers many opportunities for **reflection** (both individual and group). The activity also offers many opportunities for **formative assessment**.

## Ingredients

- ☐ A Jamboard for lesson-specific use
- ☐ Clock/Timer (as applicable)

## Activity Prep

A Jamboard for lesson-specific use.

Optional: Students create original Jamboards.

## Activity Adaptations/Toppings

This activity can be used and adapted in a variety of ways.

- Students create original Jamboards to share in a future activity.
- Students complete the activity independently on a private Jamboard and then share when ready.
- Vary time permitted to work on the Jamboard annotation.
- Vary the tools available for use on the Jamboard annotation (e.g., text, drawing, sticky notes).

## Activity Extension

Provide opportunities for students to publicly share completed Jamboards.

### Example Jamboards

Link Your Thinking. See: https://jamboard.google.com/d/11PMB1v9CQIlkJmZ-qQD8VnGu5hwuFUeanRGK5T8fdRA/edit?usp=sharing

Resource Round-Up. See: https://jamboard.google.com/d/1s3z_luvCfjyQ6ZSTTKxP7Auwi532WO7_SnbIsoFDkSY/edit?usp=sharing

60-Second Reflection/Activity Generation. See: https://jamboard.google.com/d/1x4gVU8ThKStDjZPCLVmnxfGUBlSOTt0tzhpjvE4oYfE/edit?usp=sharing

Scales of Justice Debate/Argument Construction. See: https://jamboard.google.com/d/1km9FmgDyBBNOgitKnyG5dXR6oDE2HbsgluomDbyvmSM/edit?usp=sharing

Yay or Nay. See: https://jamboard.google.com/d/1tfZPTU_wBsbbplR12QtxpigoFfsP1TQEVByUxj2TzDk/edit?usp=sharing

Pause and Reflect: What I Already Know About That. See: https://jamboard.google.com/d/1WbUpE88-4wrE5kbOtFyHMVVindy5EINURIUaSsSnqoE/edit?usp=sharing

SWOT Analysis. See: https://jamboard.google.com/d/19KeJsfuS80iBCRIe-sq1f0GiPL_UfWMDSUHlOrTYsfo/edit?usp=sharing

I Read About That In.... See: https://jamboard.google.com/d/1zUoblp1VoorlbX9m940SH4NwGCERX-HWvA90kVtRMaak/edit?usp=sharing

Puppy Tug of War. See: https://jamboard.google.com/d/1J3Wb_9UWAn3gC4JygUWAtoAi4-hGDRrtoWWEZcitaNc/edit?usp=sharing

Temperature Check. See: https://jamboard.google.com/d/1wiJ1npi645OWwdqkLX_Q7CMwUsgAU993V970JQELUU8/edit?usp=sharing

Other Ways to Use Jamboards

- Ethical Hypotheticals (Responses/Votes)
- In Support/In Opposition (For/Against Debates)
- Brainstorming, Idea Generation
- Timelines
- ADDIE Template, Problem-Solving Design Exercise. See: https://jamboard.google.com/d/1MzAjrCBbt2gsv_LAGOqamQDuNacxXMF_mnCu8sOSxS4/viewer
- What I Wish I Knew

Alternatives

- Pinterest. See: https://www.pinterest.com/
- Miro. See: https://miro.com/

## Portion Type and Size

Single (independent work), pairs, small group, or whole class

Time: Variable

- As few as five minutes.
- No maximum length.
- Time will vary depending on the adopted approach to implementation.
- *Note*: The activity takes significantly less time when the instructor prepares a lesson-specific Jamboard for class use.

Online and/or face to face

## Web Resources

- How to Use Google Jamboard tutorials
    - https://teachers.tech/how-to-use-google-jamboard/

- What's Jamboard?
    - https://support.google.com/jamboard/answer/7424836?hl=en

## I Tried This and This Is What I Learned

| DATE USED/LESSON TOPIC | REFLECTIONS/WHAT I MIGHT DO DIFFERENTLY NEXT TIME |
|---|---|
| | |
| | |
| | |

Have "An Extra Serving of Jam" activity adaptation to share?

Submit your tweaks and experiences here:

Survey Link: https://forms.gle/G7JS4RPADQK8ykp89

# I've Got Something to Say about That

**Appetizers**

**Ice Breaker Title: I've Got Something to Say About That (Class Padlets)**

Collaborative bulletin boards as a tool to promote collaboration and engagement

## Activity Description

Digital bulletin boards offer opportunities for students to collaborate and engage with course material in interactive and engaging ways.

Collaborative digital boards (which can be used anonymously and/or in self-identified ways) are also a way to proactively mitigate the increased cognitive load (drain on working memory) and anxiety that often emerges when a student interacts with complex concepts. This activity is designed to support and sustain increased student comfort and confidence when interacting with course concepts.

## Recipe

Step 1: Define and explain Padlet board activities.

Step 2: Introduce the activity. Quickly demo Padlet tools (as applicable). Clarify content focus and type of resource to be used for the activity.

Step 3: Create groups (if applicable).

Step 4: Share a link or copy of a Padlet board.

Step 5: Provide instructions for the Padlet board activity. Clarify desired interactions and actions.

Step 6: Provide active work time for students to work on the activity (recommended minimum five minutes).

- Offer support as needed.
- Share directional reminders about the activity, as applicable.

Step 7: Provide time for review and reflection.

Step 8: Open discussion and reflection on the exercise (out loud or independent journaling).

Sample prompts:

- How has this activity changed the way you feel about the shared ideas?
- How has this activity changed the way you feel about the related topic?

## The Secret Sauce (Why It Works)

This **interactive** activity breaks down complex material into manageable chunks that reduce **cognitive load** on students. Students draw on and actively **recall** prior learning and knowledge. The activity promotes **creative thinking** and hands-on, **active learning** that requires students to do something (interact) with a course concept/topic. Goals include increased student **comfort** with a particular topic as well as increased **understanding** of the topic. The activity offers many opportunities for **reflection** (both individual and group). The activity also offers many opportunities for **formative assessment**.

## Ingredients

- ☐ A Padlet board for lesson-specific use
- ☐ Clock/Timer (as applicable)

## Activity Prep

A Padlet board for lesson-specific use

Optional: Students create original Padlet boards for this activity.

## Activity Adaptations/Toppings

This activity can be used and adapted in a variety of ways.

- Students create original Padlet boards to share in a future activity.
- Students complete the activity independently on a private Padlet board.
- Vary time permitted to work on the Padlet uploads and curation.
- Vary tool features available for use on the Padlet uploads and curation.

## Activity Extensions

- Provide opportunities for students to publicly share completed Padlet boards.
- Encourage students to share resources on an ongoing basis. Curate and create classroom libraries.
- Current events assignment. Curate recent articles.

### Example Padlet Boards

Legal Technology Question Board. See: https://padlet.com/Edscripts/drzf9w0nujswe5dk

I Read About That Term In .... See: https://padlet.com/Edscripts/vr7f7bfzun6gumj5

Case-Specific Resources. See: https://padlet.com/Edscripts/7rvq25jw6ma2

Grading Feedback Resources. See: https://padlet.com/Edscripts/40zolcyulg0i

Communication Strategy Resources. See: https://padlet.com/Edscripts/19vpd6z5waz

My Learning Intention. See: https://padlet.com/Edscripts/wnlozmsdq9v2

Role Play Reflections. See: https://padlet.com/Edscripts/iosb1tzu2tb2

Reflections on Writing. See: https://padlet.com/Edscripts/732ou6sczhpr

Strengthening Writing. Sharing Makes Us Stronger. See: https://padlet.com/Edscripts/89nudgsos590

Employers and Grammar. See: https://padlet.com/Edscripts/nffunrogax2c

Resume Templates. See: https://padlet.com/Edscripts/sx68nrjrc11q

Writing: Tips, Resources, Inspiration. See: https://padlet.com/Edscripts/luhrbb9hegaj

Time Management Tips and Resources. See: https://padlet.com/Edscripts/j766zu4rnvfw

Reflection and Learning. See: https://padlet.com/Edscripts/47o7c2jm1ld3

Add to a class booklist (with optional reviews). See: https://padlet.com/Edscripts/52tih4ojamw5

Course or Discipline Special Terminology Boards. Legal Terms Example. See: https://padlet.com/Edscripts/hwn4nhlvjbsd

Real-World Applications. The Judicial System and Our Lives Example. See: https://padlet.com/Edscripts/54sec9qbn2tp

Course Resource board. Instructional Design and Theory Example. See: https://padlet.com/Edscripts/amzlcp4lh0l4

Course Resource board. Website/Webpage Design Example. See: https://padlet.com/Edscripts/y6qup7ieva2q

Inspiration: Look, Listen, Appreciate. See: https://padlet.com/Edscripts/kcdmpf20sobm

Discipline and Course Content Specific TED Talks Library. Intellectual Property Example. See: https://padlet.com/Edscripts/1bcizy6hhyqd

- *Note*: For courses using a learning management system, Padlet boards can be embedded directly into course modules and pages.

Alternatives:

- Pinterest. See: https://www.pinterest.com/
- Miro. See: https://miro.com/

## Portion Type and Size

Single (independent work), pairs, small group, or whole class

Time: Variable

- As few as five minutes.
- No maximum length.

- Time will vary depending on the adopted approach to implementation.
- *Note*: The activity takes significantly less time when the instructor prepares a lesson-specific Padlet board for the activity.

Online and/or face to face

### Web Resources

- Padlet. See: https://padlet.com/

### I Tried This and This Is What I Learned

| DATE USED/LESSON TOPIC | REFLECTIONS/WHAT I MIGHT DO DIFFERENTLY NEXT TIME |
|---|---|
| | |
| | |
| | |

Have an "I've Got Something to Say about That" activity adaptation to share?

Submit your tweaks and experiences here:

Survey Link: https://forms.gle/G7JS4RPADQK8ykp89

# Main Course/Entrée

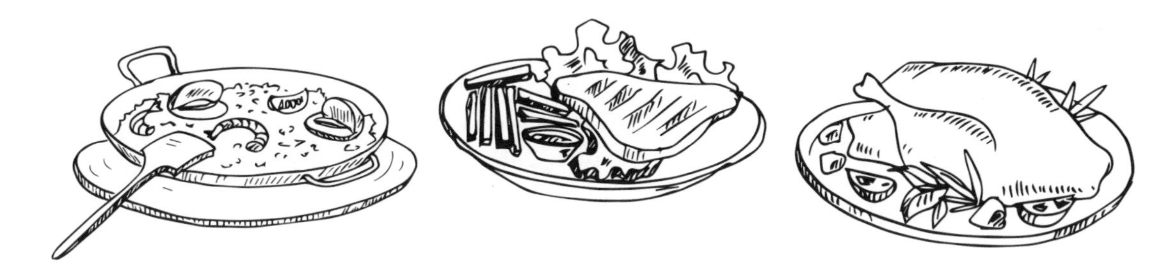

"Food is not just eating energy. It's an experience."

*Guy Fieri*

## How Similar/How Different

**Main Course/Entrée**

**Ice Breaker Title: How Similar/How Different**

Compare/contrast activities to promote active recall, reinforce long-term learning, and increase student confidence

## Activity Description

In this compare/contrast activity, students are presented two related but distinct topics or concepts. Students are prompted to generate lists of similarities and differences. Doing so supports brainstorming and elaboration as well as recall and critical thinking.

Compare/contrast activities provide opportunities for students to review key terms and concepts. Subsequent discussion and associated reflections also provide an opportunity to promote critical thinking, analysis, and related familiarity with core concepts.

In this activity, students generate similarities and differences either verbally or in writing. Digital bulletin boards (e.g., Padlet, Jamboard, Google Slides) provide opportunities for collaborative sharing. Sharing can be done anonymously, for submission, or for discussion.

Students can work collaboratively as a group or in pairs. Students can also work independently.

Students can create original compare/contrast activity topics to share with peers.

This activity works well as reinforcement for a prior lesson in which a variety of new terms and related concepts were introduced.

## Recipe

Step 1: Define and explain compare/contrast activities.

Step 2: Introduce the activity. Explain how "How Similar/How Different" activities work.

Step 3: Clarify the content focus and subject area to be used for the activity.

Step 4: Create work groups (if applicable).

Step 5: Share a link or copy of the topic(s) to be used for the activity.

Step 6: Provide time for students to conduct research (if applicable).

Step 7: Provide active work time for students to complete the assigned compare/contrast activity.

- Offer support as needed.
- Share directional reminders about the activity, as applicable.

Step 8: Provide instructions for sharing. Options include small groups or paired discussion, whole-class discussion, independent journaling and reflection, and/or instructor submission.

Step 9: Open discussion and reflection on the exercise (out loud or independent journaling)

Sample prompts:

- How has this activity changed the way you feel about the key concepts?
- How has this activity changed the way you feel about the relationship between the key concepts?

Step 10: Share reflections (either out loud or on digital bulletin board) (optional/if applicable).

## The Secret Sauce (Why It Works)

This targeted activity provides a stress-free opportunity for students to review course concepts and apply critical thinking and analysis skills. Students **compare** and **contrast** characteristics and **elaborate** in ways that increase their familiarity with key terms and concepts and deepen associated understanding. Students draw on and **actively recall** prior learning and knowledge. Students also strengthen **critical thinking** and **analysis** skills. This activity promotes hands-on, **active learning** that requires students to do something (interact) with a pair of concepts. Goals include increased **student comfort** with a particular set of course concepts as well as deeper understanding of the relationship between course concepts. The activity offers opportunities for **reflection** (both individual and group). The activity also offers opportunities for **formative assessment**.

## Ingredients

- ☐ A collection of related concepts that share similarities as well as differences.
- ☐ Clock/Timer (as applicable)

## Activity Prep

A collection of related concepts that share similarities as well as differences.

Optional: Students create paired concepts to use for this activity.

## Activity Adaptations/Toppings

This activity can be used and adapted in a variety of ways.

Conduct the activity using concepts/topics (several paragraphs, a page of text) from a current reading, assigned book, or related news article.

Introduce the activity with a discussion question/reflection prompt that explores the related topic prior to initiating the activity.

Introduce the activity with a discussion question/reflection prompt that explores the learning benefits of compare/contrast activities.

Introduce the activity with a discussion question related to each of two paired concepts and which promotes active recall.

Introduce the activity using a current event/news article related to the lesson topic and from which students identify paired concepts for this activity.

Use the activity as a collaborative learning exercise where one student is responsible for identifying and describing similarities and another student is responsible for identifying and describing differences associated with two paired concepts. After initial lists are generated, students discuss and add to both similarities and differences. Depending on the desired group size, additional roles can be developed.

Present topic characteristics. Students identify each characteristic as a shared similarity or a difference. Play with teams for points.

Students create compare/contrast infographics on a course topic of choice.

Students create compare/contrast infographics on an assigned course topic.

Provide a course topic. Students identify a related topic (one with similarities and differences to the initial topic) for use in this activity.

Vary time permitted to work on compare/contrast construction.

## Activity Extensions

Provide opportunities for students to publicly share compare/contrast infographics. Students might post to a class bulletin board or gallery. A Padlet board, class Google Site, or Pinterest board are free options that work well.

If student research leads to new resources used for compare/contrast activity generation, students can share resources in a class library (Google Docs, Google Sites, Padlet board). Source identification can be used as research reinforcement and library building.

### Law-Based Examples

Civil versus Criminal Law Characteristics

- Burden of proof
- Right to a jury trial
- Jury size
- Initiation
- Parties involved
- Possible penalties
- Average duration
- Voting threshold
- Guiding principles
- Role of precedent
- Jurisdictional issues

Sample points

- Defendants are involved.
- Court decisions may be subject to appeal.
- Lawyers/attorneys are involved.
- Juries may be involved.
- Juries are always involved.
- A judge determines outcome.
- A judge determines damages.
- Victims are involved.
- Addresses actions determined to be offenses against society.
- Parties involved are found guilty or not guilty.
- Double jeopardy applies.
- Concerned with private rights and obligations.
- Jail is/is not a possible sentence.

State and Federal Court Systems Characteristics

- Types of cases heard (examples: robbery, assault, bankruptcy, etc.)
- Rights to appeal
- Structure
- Number of courts (levels, place)
- Judge appointment—election/nomination process
- Judges—terms
- Judge removal process

Print versus Digital Research Characteristics

## Portion Type and Size

Single (independent work), Pairs, Small Group,s or Whole Class

Time: Variable

- As few as five minutes
- No maximum length
- Time will vary depending on the adopted approach to implementation.

Online and/or face to face

## Web Resources

Free Infographic Makers

- Venngage
    - https://venngage.com/
- Piktochart
    - https://piktochart.com/formats/infographics/
- Canva.
    - https://www.canva.com/create/infographics/
- Google Slides

## References

Compare and Contrast. See: https://www.phrasebank.manchester.ac.uk/compare-and-contrast/

## I Tried This and This Is What I Learned

| DATE USED/LESSON TOPIC | REFLECTIONS/WHAT I MIGHT DO DIFFERENTLY NEXT TIME |
|---|---|
| | |
| | |
| | |

Have a "How Similar/How Different" activity adaptation to share?

Submit your tweaks and experiences here:

Survey Link: https://forms.gle/G7JS4RPADQK8ykp89

# Remember When

**Main Course/Entrée**

**Ice Breaker Title: Remember When**

Reflection and chronology activities as a tool to promote active recall, reinforce vocabulary, and increase familiarity with key concepts

## Activity Description

Reflection and chronology activities prompt students to order terms, concepts, and/or events in a preferred order. Order might vary. Examples include oldest to most recent (or vice versa), by date, by time, and/or by some other marker or characteristic.

Chronology and ordering activities provide excellent opportunities for students to actively recall and review key terms and concepts. Chronology activities also provide an opportunity to increase student familiarity with vocabulary terms and meanings.

Students can work collaboratively as a group or in pairs. Students can also work independently.

This activity is designed to support student retention and recall of key terms and vocabulary words. It is often important for students to be able to group important people, events, circumstances by time (or some other characteristic) as a way to better understand and/or identify trends, influential thinking, powerful ideologies, and historical context.

Students can complete chronology activities with either a provided list of key terms or definitions only. Students can also create original chronology activities to share with peers.

This activity works well as reinforcement for a prior lesson in which a variety of new dates, events, people, or other orderable concepts were introduced.

## Recipe

Step 1: Define and explain reflection and chronology activities.

Step 2: Introduce the activity.

Step 3: Clarify content focus and subject area to be used for the activity.

Step 4: Create work groups (if applicable).

Step 5: Share a link or copy of the chronology and reflection activity resource (if applicable).

Step 6: Provide time for students to create their own list of items to be ordered (if applicable).

Step 7: Provide active work time for students to complete the assigned chronology/ordering activity.

- Offer support as needed.
- Share directional reminders about the activity, as applicable.

Step 8: Open discussion and reflection on the exercise (out loud or independent journaling)

Sample prompts:

- How has this activity changed the way you feel about the key terms?
- How has this activity changed the way you feel about the related topic?

Step 9: Share reflections (either out loud or on digital bulletin board) (optional/if applicable).

## Prep (How to Create a "Remember When" Chronology/Ordering Activity)

Step 1: Create a list of key terms and associated definitions (optional/students might also be prompted to complete definitions either by recall or with research).

Step 2: Identify the characteristic pursuant to which the terms/concepts should be ordered.

Step 3: Create as either a digital or paper-based resource for student use.

## Variations

Create using PowerPoint or Google Slides (collaborative activity).

## The Secret Sauce (Why It Works)

This targeted activity provides a stress-free opportunity for students to increase familiarity with key terms and concepts and to better understand and appreciate **context** associated with grouped/ordered events. Students draw on and **actively recall** prior learning and knowledge. Students also strengthen skills associated with context clue fluency and related communication (Gamesver, n.d.). This activity promotes hands-on, **active learning** that requires students to do something (interact) with a set of key terms or concepts and associated characteristics. Goals include increased **student comfort** with a particular set of key terms as well as increased **confidence** evaluating a set of key terms. The activity offers opportunities for **reflection** (both individual and group). The activity also offers opportunities for **formative assessment**.

## Ingredients

- ☐ A list of key terms (and definitions, optional) that is related to a class learning objective or lesson
- ☐ An associated characteristic (e.g., time, date, currency) that can be used to order shared terms
- ☐ Clock/Timer (as applicable)

## Activity Prep

A list of key terms and definitions that are related to a class learning objective or lesson

An associated characteristic (e.g., time, date, currency) that can be used to order the shared terms

- Optional: Students create original terms lists and characteristics for this activity.

## Activity Adaptations/Toppings

This activity can be used and adapted in a variety of ways.

- Introduce the activity with a discussion question/reflection prompt that explores the related course topic/concept.
- Use the activity as a collaborative learning exercise where one student is responsible for defining unfamiliar vocabulary in a text-based resource, another is responsible for identifying characteristics that can be used for ordering/chronology purposes. Depending on desired group size, additional roles can be developed.
- Students create a "Remember When" activity on a course topic of choice.
- Students create a "Remember When" activity on an assigned course topic.
- Identify characteristics (e.g., currency, birth, date of an event) and prompt students to generate a list of course terms/concepts that can be ordered. Students then swap activities.
- Students create visual timelines using free software applications. Free options include Create.ly, Google Slides, Bubbl.us.
- Once created, students swap work (in pairs or small groups). Timelines can be reviewed and annotated (either digitally or using writing instruments). If in person, tracing paper can be used to preserve students' original work.

- Create decks of cards (or sets) with events, people, topics to be ordered according to some identified characteristic or factor. Cards can be used in a variety of ways. For example, one student might deal five cards face up. A sixth card is handed to another student who must then identify where to place to sixth card. Numbers can vary. As another example, one student might deal four to six cards and then ask what is missing. Students must identify what other events/people/etc. might be placed in a presented chronology.

## Activity Extensions

- Provide opportunities for students to publicly share "Remember When" activities. Students might post timelines to a class bulletin board or gallery. A Padlet board, class Google Site, or Pinterest board are free options that work well.
- Identify characteristics (e.g., currency, birth, date of an event) and prompt students to identify associated course topics and generate a list of terms/concepts that can be ordered based on the identified characteristic. Students might create "Remember When" activities as independent, out-of-class work.

### Law-Based Examples

- Fifteen of the Most Important Supreme Court Decisions. Order by date. Landmark Supreme Court Cases. See: https://www.americanbar.org/groups/public_education/programs/constitution_day/landmark-cases/
- Famous Supreme Court Dissents. Order by date. See: https://constitutioncenter.org/blog/looking-back-famous-supreme-court-dissents
- Supreme Court Landmark Decisions. Order by date. See: https://www.uscourts.gov/about-federal-courts/educational-resources/supreme-court-landmarks
- Landmark Supreme Court Cases. See: https://www.cnn.com/2012/10/10/justice/landmark-scotus-cases/index.html
- U.S. presidents. Order by date of service

## Portion Type and Size

Single (independent work), Pairs, Small Groups, or Whole Class

Time: Variable

- As few as five minutes
- No maximum length
- Time will vary depending on the adopted approach to implementation.
- *Note*: The activity takes significantly less time when the instructor creates a list of concepts/terms and associated order/chronology prompts in advance of class.

Online and/or face to face

## Web Resources

- Chronology: Making It Stick. See: https://schoolshistory.org.uk/topics/chronology-making-it-stick/
- Creately. See: https://creately.com/
- Bubble.us. See: https://bubbl.us/
- Google Slides. See: https://docs.google.com/presentation/u/0/

## I Tried This and This Is What I Learned

| DATE USED/LESSON TOPIC | REFLECTIONS/WHAT I MIGHT DO DIFFERENTLY NEXT TIME |
|---|---|
| | |
| | |
| | |

Have a "Remember When" activity adaptation to share?

Submit your tweaks and experiences here:

Survey Link: https://forms.gle/G7JS4RPADQK8ykp89

# Let's Document How to Do That

**Main Course/Entrée**

**Ice Breaker Title: Let's Document How to Do That**

Documentation and teaching to promote long-term memory and deeper understanding

## Activity Description

Documentation and teaching are opportunities to retrieve prior learning and strengthen long-term memory of associated concepts. In this activity, students document the steps needed to complete an identified activity or process associated with course content. Alternatively, students might document (describe and explain in writing or via digital tools) the meaning of key terms and curate a library of course vocabulary for group review and sharing.

"Let's Document How to Do That" activities present opportunities for students to engage with course concepts in creative ways. Students can adopt a wide range of creative approaches and digital tools to capture the shared steps. "Let's Document How to Do That" activities also present instructional opportunities for students to strengthen long-term memory of course concepts in a stress-free environment.

The activity works well with course content that involves a series of steps or processes to complete.

This activity works well as an introductory warm-up for a substantive lesson associated with the steps/processes used for the documentation activity.

## Recipe

Step 1: Define and explain "Let's Document How to Do/Make That Again" activities.

Step 2: Explain how documentation activities work. Clarify content focus and/or type of knowledge to be used for the activity.

- Students might create graphic organizers or simple "recipes" that document the steps to complete a course-related activity.
- Documentation can be completed by hand or using a digital tool.

Step 3: Create groups (if applicable).

Step 4: Share a list of concepts/skills/processes for use in the activity (if applicable). Alternatively, provide time for students to research and locate a skill or process for this exercise.

Step 5: Explain the nature of the concepts/skills students will use for the documentation activity (if applicable).

Step 6: Provide active work time for students to generate and document the steps associated with a specific course process or procedure (recommended minimum 10 minutes).

- Offer support as needed.
- Share directional reminders about the activity, as applicable.

Step 7: Clarify the process by which students will submit and/or share their work.

Step 8: Open discussion and reflection on the exercise (out loud or independent journaling).

Sample prompts:

- How has this activity changed the way you feel about each step of the completed process?
- How has this activity changed the way you feel about the related topic?

Step 9: Share work products (either out loud or on digital bulletin board) (if applicable).

## The Secret Sauce (Why It Works)

This **scaffolded** activity breaks down complex material into manageable chunks that reduce **cognitive load** on students. Students draw on and actively **recall** prior learning and knowledge. The activity promotes hands-on, **active learning** that requires students to do something (clarify steps of a complex concept, skill, or process). Goals include increased student **comfort** with a particular process as well as increased **confidence** associated with the process. The activity offers many opportunities for **reflection** (both individual and group). The activity also offers many opportunities for **formative assessment**.

## Ingredients

- ☐ A collection of course topics or concepts that can be broken down into steps and that are related to a class learning objective or lesson
- ☐ Clock/Timer (as applicable)

## Activity Prep

Identify and curate a collection of course topics or concepts that can be broken down into steps and that are related to a class learning objective or lesson.

Optional: Students conduct research and identify skills and concepts to use for this activity.

## Activity Adaptations/Toppings

This activity can be used and adapted in a variety of ways.

- Conduct activity in small groups where students document each step as they also complete the activity.

- Conduct this activity over an extended period of time, with a class adding one new step to the "recipe" each day.
- Introduce the activity with a discussion question/reflection question that explores different ways to document steps in a process.
- Students create a "recipe" on a course-related process or procedure of choice.
- Students create a "recipe" on a specific theme (assigned by instructor).
- Students create checklists to use as self-check tools before finalizing an assignment, completing an exercise, working through a defined series of steps, etc.
- Vary time permitted to work on "recipe" construction.
- Use this activity over an extended period of time to create a "recipe book" of course-related documentation across a range of processes and procedures.
- Use this activity over an extended period of time to create a "recipe book" of course-related vocabulary and related definitions across a range of processes and procedures.
- Students create video tutorials documenting the steps to complete an activity.
- Beyond processes and procedures specifically aligned with course content, this activity can be used to document best practices and strategies for research (text or web), resource review, proofreading, etc. The activity works well as a way to create a collection of student-generated strategies and best practices for a wide range of soft and transferable skills.
    - Sample resource: Basic Steps in the Research Process example. See: https://www.nhcc.edu/student-resources/library/doinglibraryresearch/basic-steps-in-the-research-process

## Activity Extensions

- Provide opportunities for students to publicly share their documentation, checklists, and/or "recipes". Students might post work to a class bulletin board or gallery. A Padlet board, class Google Site, or Pinterest board are free options that work well.
- If student research leads to sources used for recipe generation, students might share resources in a class library (Google Docs, Google Sites, Padlet board). Source identification can be used as research reinforcement and library building.

### Law-Based Example (Case Briefs)

This activity works well for any process or procedure where a teacher wants to help students feel more comfortable with their skills and the associated steps.

Many students come to legal materials intimidated by the complex language. Activities that provide opportunities for review and student-teaching allow students to actively engage with and approach a complex skill and/or concept in a low-stakes way that is designed to help minimize the fear associated with higher-stakes settings.

- Students might document the steps required to complete a case brief of choice (e.g., by jurisdiction, topic).

## Portion Type and Size

Single (independent work), pairs, small groups, or whole class

Time: Variable

- As few as five minutes.

- No maximum length.
- Can be conducted as an extended activity with additional steps added each day.
- Time will vary depending on the adopted approach to implementation.

Online and/or face to face

## I Tried This and This Is What I Learned

| DATE USED/LESSON TOPIC | REFLECTIONS/WHAT I MIGHT DO DIFFERENTLY NEXT TIME |
|---|---|
| | |
| | |
| | |

Have a "Let's Document How to Do That" activity adaptation to share?

Submit your tweaks and experiences here:

Survey Link: https://forms.gle/G7JS4RPADQK8ykp89

# That's Up for Debate

**Main Course/Entrée**

**Ice Breaker Title: That's Up for Debate**

Debate as a tool to promote critical thinking and communication skills

## Activity Description

Debate activities offer opportunities for students to engage with complex concepts in thoughtful ways. Debate activities also present opportunities for students to practice communication skills, research, and active recall.

This activity is designed to support and sustain increased student comfort and confidence when interacting with and examining complex concepts.

This activity works well as an introductory warm-up for a substantive lesson that extends upon an earlier, related concept. The activity also works well as a review activity and as preparation for a summative assessment requiring higher-level thinking skills and analysis.

## Recipe

Step 1: Define and explain debate activities.

Step 2: Introduce the activity. Clarify content focus and type of material to be used/available for the activity.

Step 3: Create pairs and/or small groups (if applicable).

Step 4: Share applicable debate guidelines (if applicable).

Step 5: Provide time for team/groups to research and prepare for the activity (if applicable).

Step 6: Explain ground rules of the debate (expectations, process).

Step 7: Initiate debate activity.

- Offer support as needed.
- Share directional reminders, as applicable.

Step 8: Open discussion and reflection on the exercise (out loud or independent journaling).

Sample prompts:

- How has this activity changed the way you feel about public speaking?
- How has this activity changed the way you feel about group work?
- How has this activity changed the way you feel about the related topic?

## The Secret Sauce (Why It Works)

This **collaborative** activity breaks down complex concepts and questions into manageable segments that reduce cognitive load on students. Students work collaboratively, conduct research, and draw on and **actively recall** prior learning and knowledge. The activity promotes hands-on, **active learning** that requires students to do something (interact with a complex concept). Goals include increased student comfort and **confidence** with a particular concept, **public speaking, teamwork**, and **critical analysis**. The activity offers opportunities for reflection (both individual and group). The activity also offers opportunities for formative assessment.

## Ingredients

- ☐ A thought-provoking question or argumentative statement that is related to a class learning objective or lesson
- ☐ Clock/Timer (as applicable)

## Activity Prep

A collection of questions and/or argumentative statements (web-based or paper) related to a lesson topic.

Optional: Students conduct research and identify a topic to use for this activity.

## Activity Adaptations/Toppings

This activity can be used and adapted in a variety of ways.

- Students are assigned a topic and then draft original statements or questions for debate.
- Students select a course topic and draft original statements or questions for debate.
- Conduct the activity using a controversial news topic.
- Introduce the activity with a discussion question/reflection prompt that explores best practices for debates.
- Students generate guidelines for debate structure, rules, and guidelines.
- Introduce the activity with a discussion question related to the debate topic and which promotes active recall.

Examples:

- How might we locate a text that provides more on ____ (related to the topic)?
- What are some databases and/or reputable search engines to find ____ on this topic?
- What are some options and resources to locate [a particular type of text] on the topic?
- Introduce the activity using a current event/news article related to the lesson topic and from which students create debatable statements.
- Depending on desired group size, design unique roles for all group members.
- Suggest students prepare debate responses that use five (or more) course vocabulary terms. Students might submit defined vocabulary terms and/or post terms and definitions on a class wide resource.
- Students create and swap debate topics on a course topic of choice.
- Students create and swap debate topics on an assigned course topic.
- Vary time permitted to work on question construction.
- Vary time permitted to prepare for debate.
- Vary time allotted for debate.

## Activity Extensions

- Provide opportunities for students to reflect on the debate experience (either out loud or privately in writing).
- Students might post reactions to the debate anonymously on a class bulletin board or gallery. A Padlet board, class Google Site, or Pinterest board are free options that work well.

### Paralegal/Legal-Based Example

Conducting a low-stakes debate is a way for students to actively engage with and approach a complex topic in a low-stakes way that is designed to help minimize the fear associated with higher-stakes settings.

Prompt: Read an assigned fact-scenario/legal case.

Question: In whose favor should the case be decided? Plaintiff/Defendant?

Case law debates might be used as a warm-up for a deeper lesson on the legal issues involved in a particular case. (*Note*: Judicial opinions can be swapped with any piece of writing and any primary or secondary source exploring a complex topic.)

- To reinforce research skills, students might conduct research and select a judicial opinion of choice (e.g., by jurisdiction, topic) for debate.
- Instructor shares a judicial opinion, perhaps one that students will later read and brief as part of a graded activity.
- Either in pairs, in small groups, or as a whole-class exercise, students conduct a debate (e.g., for/against, in favor of plaintiff/defendant).

## Portion Type and Size

Single (independent work), pairs, small groups, or whole class

Time: Variable

- As few as five minutes.
- No maximum length.
- Time will vary depending on the adopted approach to implementation.
- *Note*: The activity takes significantly less time when the instructor selects and assigns a specific topic/question for debate.

Online and/or face to face

## Illustrative Topics (Legal Technology-Related)

- Artificial intelligence is an asset to criminal investigations.
- All law offices should use automated billing systems.
- Facial recognition software will reduce crime.
- Anyone who doesn't vote should be fined.
- All voting should be done electronically.
- All law firms should have a website.
- All law firms should be active on social media.
- Social media helps reduce crime.
- Social media improves communication in the workplace.
- All trials should be held virtually.
- Jury duty should be optional.
- All case law should be available free of charge.
- All court trials should be streamed live.
- No court trials should be streamed live.
- Voting should be required of all citizens.
- Not voting should be subject to monetary penalty.
- Not voting should be subject to jail time.
- Office dress codes are inappropriate.
- Court dress codes are appropriate.
- Recycling should be required by law.
- Not recycling should be subject to monetary fines.
- Only criminal trials should be streamed on TV.
- Only civil trials should be streamed on TV.

## Web Resources

Sample Debate Topics: https://www.thoughtco.com/debate-topics-for-high-school-8252

- Sample Debate Topics
  - https://blog.prepscholar.com/good-debate-topics
- Sample Debate Topics
  - https://owlcation.com/academia/100-Debate-Topics
- Business Law Debate Topics

    - https://www.wappingersschools.org/cms/lib01/ny01001463/centricity/moduleinstance/6049/business_law_debate_topics.doc

- Sample Debate Topics
    - https://www.5staressays.com/blog/speech-and-debate/debate-topics
- Debate Preparation Resources
    - Illustrative Debate Preparation Resources: https://www.esu.org/resources/
    - Debate Guide: https://www.wisesayings.com/debate-guide/
- Random Question Generators
    - Random Word Generator: https://randomwordgenerator.com/question.php
    - Random Question Generator: https://conversationstartersworld.com/random-question-generator/
    - Random Question Maker: https://randomquestionmaker.com/
    - Conversation Starters: https://www.conversationstarters.com/generator.php

## I Tried This and This Is What I Learned

| DATE USED/LESSON TOPIC | REFLECTIONS/WHAT I MIGHT DO DIFFERENTLY NEXT TIME |
|---|---|
| | |
| | |
| | |

Have a "That's Up for Debate" activity adaptation to share?

Submit your tweaks and experiences here:

Survey Link: https://forms.gle/G7JS4RPADQK8ykp89

# Seek and Find/Scavenger Hunt: What's in the Cabinet?

**Main Course/Entrée**

**Ice Breaker Title: Seek and Find/Scavenger Hunt: What's in the Cabinet?**

Trivia-type, randomized review of prior learning to promote active recall, reinforce long-term learning, and increase student confidence

## Activity Description

In this activity, students review a variety of randomized trivia-type questions drawn from (or based on) prior learning and course content. Questions might include key terms from a prior chapter, resource, or class reading. The activity promotes active recall and retrieval practice, along with interleaving, all of which are research-based strategies that promote long-term learning. The activity can be conducted as a closed- or open-book activity.

Seek and Find/Scavenger Hunts are useful exercises for strengthening learning, promoting connections across concepts, and developing research skills. Course resource-based scavenger hunts provide excellent opportunities for students to review key terms and course concepts. Seek and Find/Scavenger Hunts also provide an opportunity to increase student familiarity with chronology and connections related to course concepts and associated meanings.

Students are provided definitions, clues, dates, and/or trivia-type facts from prior course lessons and material. Students are tasked with locating the corresponding key term, concept, fact, or definition.

Students can work collaboratively as a group or in pairs. Students can also work independently.

Students can complete provided scavenger hunts with a provided list of key terms, facts, or definitions. Students can also create original scavenger hunts to share with peers.

Terms, facts, and events that are sometimes confusing and unfamiliar to students work well in this activity. Terms with complex and/or unusual meanings are also well suited to this activity.

This activity works well as reinforcement for a prior lesson in which a variety of new terms were introduced.

## Recipe

Step 1: Define and explain Seek and Find/Scavenger Hunt activities.

Step 2: Introduce the activity. Explain how the activity will work.

Step 3: Clarify content focus and subject area to be used for the activity.

Step 4: Create work groups (if applicable).

Step 5: Share a link or copy of the scavenger hunt resource (if applicable).

Step 6: Provide time for students to create scavenger hunt clues (if applicable).

Step 7: Provide active work time for students to complete the assigned scavenger hunt activity.

- Offer support as needed.
- Share directional reminders about the activity, as applicable.

Step 8: Open discussion and reflection on the exercise (out loud or independent journaling).

Sample prompts:

- How has this activity changed the way you feel about the shared clues?
- How has this activity changed the way you feel about the related course topic(s)?

## The Secret Sauce (Why It Works)

This targeted activity provides a stress-free opportunity for students to increase familiarity with key terms and course concepts. Students draw on and **actively recall** prior learning and knowledge. Students also strengthen **research skills** and familiarity with course resources and material. This activity promotes hands-on, **active learning** that requires students to do something (interact with a set of clues related to course terms and concepts and search for associated items). Goals include increased **student confidence** (achievable goals and successful finds) and **comfort** with a particular set of key terms and concepts as well as increased **familiarity** with course materials. This low-risk and low-stakes activity offers opportunities for **reflection** (both individual and group). The activity also offers opportunities for **formative assessment**.

## Ingredients

- ☐ A set of clues related to prior course content (readings, resources, materials)
- ☐ Clock/Timer (as applicable)

## Activity Prep

A set of clues related to prior course content.

Optional: Students create clues to use for this activity.

## Activity Adaptations/Toppings

Depending on the instructional goals and objectives, this activity can be used and adapted in a variety of ways.

- Conduct the activity using a passage (several paragraphs, a page of text) from a current reading, assigned book, or related news article.
- Introduce the activity with a discussion question/reflection prompt that prompts recall of a prior course lesson or concept.
- Students create sets of clues to share (in pairs, small groups, or in a whole-class format).
- Introduce the activity with a discussion question related to research methods and which promotes active recall.
    - Examples:
        - How might we locate an answer to a question that ___?
        - Where might we look for information on a key date?
        - Where might we locate a definition for an unfamiliar term?
        - How might we locate a judicial opinion in ___ jurisdiction?
        - What are some options and resources to locate [a particular type of text]?
- Introduce the activity using a current event/news article related to the lesson topic and from which students create scavenger hunt clues.
- Use the activity as a collaborative learning exercise where one student is responsible for defining unfamiliar vocabulary in a text-based resource, another is responsible for the creation of associated clues related to the identified vocabulary, another is responsible for ordering the created clues and finalizing the wording of the scavenger hunt, etc. Depending on desired group size, additional roles can be developed.
- Students create theme-related clues that focus on five (or more) new and/or unfamiliar terms.
- Scavenger hunts can be shared and completed in pairs, small groups, or a whole-class format.
- Vary time permitted to work on clue construction/scavenger hunt completion.
- Vary number of clues created per scavenger hunt.
- Create internet-based scavenger hunts using clues aligned with lesson objectives and course topics.
- Create library-based scavenger hunts to support research skills.

## Activity Extensions

Provide opportunities for students to publicly share scavenger hunts. Students might post scavenger hunt clues to a class bulletin board or gallery. A Padlet board, class Google Site, or Pinterest board are free options that work well.

### Law-Based Examples

Hypothetical scenarios. Clue prompts: Do the scenarios present civil or criminal cases?

Sample crimes. Clue prompts: Are they felonies or misdemeanors?

Sample civil actions. Clue prompts: Are they torts or contracts?

Legal research-based scenarios. Clue prompts: What resource/reporter might include ___?

- Judicial opinions. Clue prompts: Date of decision, deciding judge, legal issue(s), key facts, dissenting judge, etc.
- To reinforce research skills, students might conduct research and select a case of choice (e.g., by jurisdiction, topic) for purposes of creating scavenger hunt clues.

### Philadelphia-Themed Service-Based Scavenger Hunt Example

Walk around your Neighborhood. Conduct research online.

Find an example of each of the following:

1. Nonprofit
2. Small Law Firm
3. Government Agency
4. Court Building
5. Community Group

Philadelphia neighborhoods

- Center City
- Old City
- South Philly
- Graduate Area
- Washington Square
- Passyunk
- Kensington
- Fairmount
- Francisville
- Fishtown
- Northern Liberties
- More...

### Constitutional Law Scavenger Hunt Example

- A Constitutional Law Scavenger Hunt with a Serious Purpose. See: https://www.discourse.net/2005/11/a_constitutional_law_scavenger_hunt_with_a_serious_purpose/

### Technology Tool Examples

- Google Slides Scavenger Hunt. See: https://catlintucker.com/2017/08/google-slide-scavenger-hunt/
- Google Slides Scavenger Hunt. See: https://applieddigitalskills.withgoogle.com/c/middle-and-high-school/en/go-on-a-scavenger-hunt-through-italy/go-on-a-scavenger-hunt-through-italy/start-your-scavenger-hunt-in-google-slides.html

## Portion Type and Size

Single (independent work), pairs, small groups, or whole class

Time: Variable

- As few as five minutes.
- No maximum length.
- Initial development will be most time intensive.
- Time will vary depending on the adopted approach to implementation.
- *Note*: The activity takes significantly less time when the instructor creates a scavenger hunt in advance of class.

Online and/or face to face

## Web Resources

- Internet Scavenger Hunts. See: https://www.educationworld.com/a_lesson/archives/scavenger_hunt.shtml
- Finding and Using Sources and Evidence Scavenger Hunt. See: https://docs.google.com/forms/d/e/1FAIpQLSdY0nw0H7ArrVJhCCX_GwMTCPnC7KPbP4dSXoVS8WUrmiXC_A/viewform?c=0&w=1
- EBSCO-based Scavenger Hunts. See: https://connect.ebsco.com/s/article/Where-can-I-find-scavenger-hunts-to-familiarize-users-with-EBSCO-resources?language=en_US
- Research Scavenger Hunt. Sample Assignment and Instructions. See: https://courses.lumenlearning.com/englishcomp1/chapter/discussion-research-scavenger-hunt/

## I Tried This and This Is What I Learned

| DATE USED/LESSON TOPIC | REFLECTIONS/WHAT I MIGHT DO DIFFERENTLY NEXT TIME |
|---|---|
| | |
| | |
| | |

Have a "Seek and Find/Scavenger Hunt" activity adaptation to share?

Submit your tweaks and experiences here:

Survey Link: https://forms.gle/G7JS4RPADQK8ykp89

# Everything but the Kitchen Sink (Collaborative Crosswords)

**Main Course/Entrée**

**Ice Breaker Title: Everything but the Kitchen Sink (Collaborative Crosswords)**

Collaborative crosswords as a tool to promote collaboration, active recall, and familiarity with key concepts and terms

## Activity Description

A crossword is a word puzzle where players decipher numbered clues and insert corresponding answers/responses in an associated box (typically a square) (Amlen, 2019). Boxes are numbered, usually in letter and/or number format. Clues are provided for both horizontal and/or vertical placement. Many letters are used in more than one word as horizontal and vertical rows can cross.

Arthur Wynne is credited with creating the first crossword-style game in 1913 (Amlen, 2019). Wynne had designed a numbered puzzle grid. The puzzle had an empty center, the word "fun" at the top (serving as the puzzle's first "horizontal" or "across" entry) and was called "Word-Cross" (Amlen, 2019). An illustrator inadvertently swapped "Cross-Word" for "Word-Cross" and Wynne complied (Amlen, 2019). Simon & Schuster later published the first crossword puzzle book in 1924 (Amlen, 2019). The *New York Times* published its first crossword in 1942 (Amlen, 2019).

This activity is a collaborative crossword. Students work together to complete a crossword that had been created based on key terms and concepts from a course lesson. Collaborative crosswords offer opportunities for students to review concepts and reinforce understanding.

Completing a crossword collaboratively can proactively mitigate the increased cognitive load (drain on working memory) and anxiety that often emerges when a student engages independently with complex topics and terms.

The activity works well with basic terms and vocabulary.

This activity works well as an introductory warm-up and review for a prior session's substantive lesson associated with the text(s) and materials used for the collaborative crossword.

## Recipe

Step 1: Define and explain collaborative crosswords.

Step 2: Explain how collaborative crosswords work. Clarify content focus and type of resource to be used for the activity.

Step 3: Clarify whether the activity will be completed as a "closed" or "open" book exercise.

Step 4: Create groups (if applicable).

Step 5: Share a link or copy of the crossword (if applicable).

Step 6: Optional. Provide active work time for students to create and generate an original collaborative crossword using an original list of clues/responses (recommendation: chunk time, 10 minutes to create list/10 minutes to swap and solve crosswords).

Step 7: Provide active work time for students to complete the collaborative crossword.

- Offer support as needed.
- Share directional reminders about the activity, as applicable.

Step 8: Open discussion and reflection on the exercise (out loud or independent journaling)

- Sample prompt:
  - How has this activity changed the way you feel about the related topic?

## The Secret Sauce (Why It Works)

This **collaborative** activity breaks down complex material into **manageable chunks** that reduce cognitive load on students. Students draw on and actively recall prior learning and knowledge. The activity promotes hands-on, active learning that requires students to do something (interact with) with a collection of course concepts and material. Goals include increased student comfort with a particular collection of material. The activity offers opportunities for **problem-solving, critical thinking, active recall**, and application (individual and group). The activity also offers opportunities for formative assessment.

## Ingredients

- ☐ A list of clues and associated "answers" or "responses"
- ☐ Clock/Timer (as applicable)

## Activity Prep

Create a collaborative crossword using a collaborative crossword tool.

See: https://beasleydog.github.io/collaborativecrossword/

- To create a crossword, first prepare a list of clues and responses.
- Next, copy and paste desired content.
- Click Create.
- To work collaboratively, share the webpage link.
- Optional: Students prepare clues and responses to be used as content for this activity.

## Activity Adaptations/Toppings

Depending on the instructional goals and objectives, this activity can be used and adapted in a variety of ways.

- Assign students specific course topics for crossword clue generation. Students prepare lists of 5, 10, or 15 (or more) clues and responses to be used in a newly created crossword.
- Conduct the activity using student-generated crosswords (created independently or in small groups and then swapped with groups).
- Conduct the activity using characters and other craft elements from a current reading, assigned book, or related news article.
- Introduce the activity with a discussion question/reflection prompt that explores the content that is the subject of the collaborative crossword.
- Introduce the activity using a current event/news article related to the lesson topic and from which students create collaborative crosswords.
- Use the activity as a collaborative game-based learning exercise where student groups both create and solve crosswords.

- Students create crosswords that use 15 (or more) new and/or unfamiliar terms. First, scan assigned readings for unfamiliar terms. Conduct research and define 15 (or more) unfamiliar terms. Students might submit the newly defined vocabulary terms and/or post the words and definitions on a class resource.
- Students create a collaborative crossword on a topic of choice.
- Students create a collaborative crossword on an assigned topic.
- Vary time permitted to work on crossword completion.
- Provide a word length or clue limit/cap on the crossword (time and topic, too).

## Activity Extensions

- Provide opportunities for students to publicly share crosswords. Students might post crosswords to a class bulletin board or gallery. A Padlet board, class Google Site, or Pinterest board are free options that work well.
- If student research leads to sources used for crossword creation, students might share resources in a class library (Google Docs, Google Sites, Padlet board). Source identification can be used as research reinforcement and library building.

### Legal Technology/Office Software-Based Example (Excel Key Terms)

Many students come to new technologies unfamiliar with key terms and language. Creating a collaborative crossword is a way for students to actively engage with new terms in a low-stakes, fun way that is designed to help minimize the fear associated with higher-stakes settings.

This collaborative crossword activity might be used as a warm-up for a lesson introducing Excel to students.

Excel Terminology Sample Collaborative Crossword. See: https://docs.google.com/spreadsheets/d/1l5xxjP9SAsALFkhPwj9RiebG66WxOEAC_VP-Sn_OjdY/edit?usp=sharing

### High-Impact Practice Activities Example

High-Impact Practice Crossword. See: https://docs.google.com/spreadsheets/d/1KpLewAsSxNwpF7lu6ABXWCbZQ1WD1g-D4JtMdZAGaSU/edit#gid=0

Associated Digital Flashcards and Notes. See: https://remnote.com/a/high-impact-practices-and-evidence-based-learning-strategies-illustrative-examples/60ba934037bb580034cb7e46

## Portion Type and Size

Single (independent work), Pairs, Small Group, or Whole Class

Time: Variable

- As few as five minutes
- No maximum length
- Initial use/crossword clue and response creation will be most time intensive.
- Time will vary depending on the adopted approach to implementation.
- *Note*: The activity takes significantly less time when the instructor creates crosswords in advance.

Online and/or face to face

## Additional Web Resources

Collaborative Crossword Generator. See: https://beasleydog.github.io/collaborativecrossword/

Single-Use Resources:

My Crossword Maker. See: https://crosswordhobbyist.com/

Crossword Puzzle Generator. See: https://www.education.com/worksheet-generator/reading/crossword-puzzle/

## Reference

Amlen, D. (2019). *How the crossword became an American pastime.* Retrieved from https://www.smithsonianmag.com/arts-culture/crossword-became-american-pastime-180973558/

## I Tried This and This Is What I Learned

| DATE USED/LESSON TOPIC | REFLECTIONS/WHAT I MIGHT DO DIFFERENTLY NEXT TIME |
|---|---|
| | |
| | |
| | |

Have an "Everything but the Kitchen Sink (Collaborative Crosswords)" activity adaptation to share?

Submit your tweaks and experiences here:

Survey Link: https://forms.gle/G7JS4RPADQK8ykp89

## What Did We Eat Last Night? Last Week?

**Main Course/Entrée**

**Ice Breaker Title: What Did We Eat Last Night? Last Week?**

Retrieval and active recall activities to promote learning transfer from short- to long-term memory, reinforce vocabulary, and increase familiarity with key concepts

## Activity Description

This activity promotes long-term learning through active recall and spaced repetition.

Spaced repetition and retrieval practice activities prompt students to actively recall past learning.

Students practice shared terms/digital flashcards independently (on a personalized spaced repetition schedule) or in small groups and optimize their study and retention of key concepts.

This activity also promotes active reflection on notetaking and organization. Students are encouraged to consider how they might keep track of newly acquired knowledge.

Students can work collaboratively as a group or in pairs. Students can also work independently.

This activity works well as reinforcement for a prior lesson in which new terms, concepts, and topic were introduced. The activity is also helpful as ongoing review and preparation for summative assessments.

## Recipe

Step 1: Define and explain active recall and retrieval practice.

Step 2: Explain how easy it is to forget new knowledge and how repetition and practice over time can help.

Step 3: Introduce the activity. Explain how the "What Did We Eat Last Night? Last Week?" activity will work.

Step 4: Clarify content focus and subject area to be used for the activity.

Step 5: Create work groups (if applicable).

Step 6: Share a link or copy of the activity resource (if applicable).

Step 7: Provide time for students to create original documents and digital flashcards (if applicable).

Step 8: Provide active work time for students to review (applying active recall and retrieval practice) shared flashcards.

- Students might review independently, in pairs, small groups, or as a whole class.
- Students might take turns answering cards.
- Students might also write down or submit responses via polling software.
- Offer support as needed.
- Share directional reminders about the activity, as applicable

Step 9: Open discussion and reflection on the exercise (out loud or independent journaling)

Sample prompts:

- How has this activity changed the way you feel about the key terms?
- How has this activity changed the way you feel about the related topic?

## The Secret Sauce (Why It Works)

This targeted activity provides a stress-free opportunity for students to increase familiarity with key terms and concepts and to promote long-term learning and memory of such terms and concepts. Students draw on and **actively recall** prior learning and knowledge. This activity promotes hands-on, **active learning** that requires students to do something (retrieve information from memory via active recall) with a set of key terms or concepts and associated characteristics. Goals include increased **student comfort** with key terms/concepts as well as increased **confidence** associated with the terms and concepts. The activity also provides an opportunity for students to better understand how memory and learning work. The activity promotes positive study skills and habits (along with note taking) that are transferable to other learning contexts. The activity offers opportunities for **reflection** (both individual and group). The activity also offers opportunities for **formative assessment**.

## Ingredients

- ☐ Notes and flashcards that are related to a class learning objective or lesson
- ☐ Notes and Flashcard Creator.
- ☐ Clock/Timer (as applicable)

## Activity Prep

Notes and flashcards that are related to a class learning objective or lesson.

Optional: Students create their own notes/digital flashcards for use in this activity.

Step 1: Create a list of key terms and associated definitions.

Step 2: Create as either a digital or paper-based resource for student use.

## Activity Adaptations/Toppings

Depending on the instructional goals and objectives, this activity can be used and adapted in a variety of ways.

- Introduce the activity with a discussion question/reflection prompt that explores the related course topic/concept that is the focus of the flashcard activity.
- Students create notes and digital flashcards for personal and/or shared use.
- Students create a "What Did We Eat Last Night?" activity on a course topic of choice.
- Students create a "What Did We Eat Last Night?" activity on an assigned course topic.
- Vary time permitted to work on the activity and/or associated flashcard construction).
- Independent, Out-of-Class Variation:

    1. Review at least five new vocabulary terms each week.
    2. Practice with the new terms throughout the week.
    3. Submit a reflection that confirms your practice.

       Use the following questions as a guide:

       - What new terms did I learn?
       - How might I use a new term in the workplace?
       - How comfortable do I feel with the terminology and concepts?
       - How have spaced practice and active recall contributed to my learning?

## Activity Extensions

- After active flashcard practice, provide five minutes for reflective journaling. Students can write privately (or to share with the instructor) on the practice experience.
- Sample prompts/Questions:
    - What new terms did I learn?
    - How might I use a new term in the workplace?
    - How comfortable do I feel with the terminology and concepts?
    - How have spaced practice and active recall contributed to my learning?

- Provide opportunities for students to share notes/flashcards for group review. Students might post notes and flashcards to a class bulletin board or gallery. A Padlet board, class Google Site, or Pinterest board are free options that work well.
- Students might create notes/flashcards as independent, out-of-class work and then swap activities in class.

## Law-Based Examples

- Case Brief Terms. See: https://www.remnote.com/a/cj-560-case-brief-terms/W6DCnBtPw244osC9F
- United States Courts Glossary of Terms. See: https://www.remnote.com/a/qEuMmP6qR9Hyg3pkN
- Citing Case Law in APA Format. See: https://www.remnote.com/a/cj-560-how-to-cite-case-law/RM55Xmqv7DyRfbGLj
- 30 Legal Terms You'll Want to Spell Correctly. See: https://www.remnote.com/a/what-s-on-the-docket/z2oTSLdG7uP2GyckW
- Proofreading Strategies That Work. See: https://www.remnote.com/a/what-s-on-the-docket-minimizing-errors/GrZGawzocrGn5ZsjR

## Business Statistics Examples

*Introductory Business Statistics* by OpenStax

Chapter 1: Sampling and Data (Key Terms). See: https://www.remnote.com/a/openstax-cnx-article-introductory-business-statistics-chapter-1-terms/yYMM59w78bfAvxe

Chapter 2: Terms. See: https://remnote.com/a/openstax-cnxarticleintroductory-business-statistics-chapter-2-terms/Ns7XibuKR3ow5vDC2

Chapter 3: Terms. See: https://remnote.com/a/openstax-cnxarticle-chapter-3-terms/BisM4HEA3HQQdGkMG

*Introductory Business Statistics* by OpenStax is licensed under a Creative Commons Attribution License v4.0. This text is designed to meet the scope and sequence requirements of the one-semester statistics course for business, economics, and related majors.

## Political Science Examples

*American Government 2e*, by OpenStax

### Key Terms and Digital Flashcards

Folder with all chapters: https://www.remnote.com/a/american-government-2e-by-openstax/y2rZ3rQnrpQ9HbqmS

**Chapter 1:** https://www.remnote.com/a/chapter-1-key-terms/wjszmYuGtxvP2FeLw

**Chapter 2:** https://www.remnote.com/a/chapter-2-key-terms/pLP7icbyJ3PfZe7RK

**Chapter 3:** https://www.remnote.com/a/chapter-3-key-terms/ffCmWtNBiYw7cYWqy

**Chapter 4:** https://www.remnote.com/a/chapter-4-key-terms/7R24goHJLv7MEx7yN

**Chapter 5:** https://www.remnote.com/a/chapter-5-key-terms/3D5FRqDQo4YJ4sGBD

**Chapter 6:** https://www.remnote.com/a/chapter-6-key-terms/6hbGJuSQACAKbveNf

**Chapter 7:** https://www.remnote.com/a/chapter-7-key-terms/6thzjjo9LKaydnNDB

**Chapter 8:** https://www.remnote.com/a/chapter-8-key-terms/Ky2rpSccbwBPepZj5

**Chapter 9:** https://www.remnote.com/a/chapter-9-key-terms/qniR4deb7p4qxhzn6

**Chapter 10:** https://www.remnote.com/a/chapter-10-key-terms/xzF9BN8o9G2PzPCjC

**Chapter 11:** https://www.remnote.com/a/chapter-11-key-terms/PYtSzJxZkq8DzPGap

**Chapter 12:** https://www.remnote.com/a/chapter-12-key-terms/FYYasnFYqfDpRhWC4

**Chapter 13:** https://www.remnote.com/a/chapter-13-key-terms/jFRSwBk7hzhz7vWvj

**Chapter 14:** https://www.remnote.com/a/chapter-14-key-terms/GgPLQqgQ4nGTFw7Le

**Chapter 15:** https://www.remnote.com/a/chapter-15-key-terms/TgbX5zcqwfB7SGnNt

**Chapter 16:** https://www.remnote.com/a/chapter-16-key-terms/mejXpGRmejXCYM5nk

**Chapter 17:** https://www.remnote.com/a/chapter-17-key-terms/N4MfFbfYviGrg6prn

## Psychology Examples

### OpenStax Psychology, Chapter Terms

Chapter 1 Key Terms. See: https://remnote.com/a/openstax-cnxarticleintro-to-psychology-chapter-1-terms/LoYLr7EEyRSLZJa2N

Chapter 2 Key Terms. See: https://remnote.com/a/openstax-cnx-psychological-research-chapter-2-terms/yjXzSrDuB79uKy3so

Chapter 3 Key Terms. See: https://remnote.com/a/openstax-cnx-biopsychology-chapter-3-terms/gyfaJ2qmtj6QnXLA8

Chapter 4 Key Terms. See: https://remnote.com/a/openstax-cnx-states-of-consciousness-chapter-4-terms/DwPqWraPhh5EyApk6

Chapter 5 Key Terms. See: https://remnote.com/a/open-stax-cnx-chapter-5-sensation-and-perception-terms/Lm9DSXCudJrKGtapi

Chapter 6 Key Terms. See: https://remnote.com/a/openstax-cnx-chapter-6-learning-key-terms/ANuykqFud3LbQedEi

Chapter 7 Key Terms. See: https://remnote.com/a/openstax-cnx-chapter-7-thinking-and-intelligence-key-terms/sdKXmfjweqF8oMcqY

Chapter 8 Key Terms. See: https://remnote.com/a/openstax-cnx-chapter-8-memory-key-terms/Ake66J4NGn9tM6YxP

Chapter 9 Key Terms. See: https://remnote.com/a/openstax-cnx-chapter-9-lifespan-development-key-terms/my9n8hQtmqbi3LWCN

Chapter 10 Key Terms. See: https://remnote.com/a/openstax-cnx-chapter-10-emotion-and-motivation-key-terms/KaGCtidNCndEM4ier

Chapter 11 Key Terms. See: https://remnote.com/a/openstax-cnx-psychology-chapter-11-personality-key-terms-/QDKagBhbHHxSZpYQQ

Chapter 12 Key Terms. See: https://remnote.com/a/openstax-cnx-chapter-12-social-psychology-key-terms/2vbFdsrcvKfvFkoDr

The terms are derived from the following open educational resource: *Psychology*. Available at: https://cnx.org/contents/4abf04bf-93a0-45c3-9cbc-2cefd46e68cc

### Business Examples

*Introduction to Business*. Available at: https://openstax.org/details/books/introduction-business

The text includes general lists of key vocabulary terms that appear often in business law and business ethics material. The terms are derived from the above referenced open educational resource.

**Chapter 1 Key Terms** (Understanding Economic Systems and Business Terms)

See: https://www.remnote.com/a/introduction-to-business-chapter-1-understanding-economic-systems-and-business-terms/ru5aBa83tWs6QQ9ph

**Chapter 2 Key Terms** (Making Ethical Decisions and Managing a Socially Responsible Business)

See: https://www.remnote.com/a/introduction-to-business-chapter-2-making-ethical-decisions-and-managing-a-socially-responsible-business-terms/koggHvesR4bSSNh78

**Chapter 3 Key Terms** (Competing in the Global Marketplace)

See: https://www.remnote.com/a/introduction-to-business-chapter-3-competing-in-the-global-marketplace-key-terms/TDZzFCYbXzCpLJLSR

**Chapter 4 Key Terms** (Forms of Business Ownership)

See: https://www.remnote.com/a/introduction-to-business-chapter-4-forms-of-business-organization-key-terms/i9zd3LaKqtEWG3W44

**Chapter 5 Key Terms** (Entrepreneurship: Starting Your Own Business)

See: https://www.remnote.com/a/introduction-to-business-chapter-5-entrepreneurship-starting-and-managing-your-own-business-key-terms/oHNkZQAs3KkBSsMpq

**Chapter 6 Key Terms** (Management and Leadership in Today's Organizations)

See: https://www.remnote.com/a/introduction-to-business-chapter-6-management-and-leadership-in-today-s-organizations-/4nFMk3HMsZRdQWiP9

**Chapter 7 Key Terms** (Designing Organizational Structures)

See: https://www.remnote.com/a/introduction-to-business-chapter-7-designing-organizational-structures-/ZbDz8282MhbPAEEcq

**Chapter 8 Key Terms** (Performance Appraisal and Rewards)

See: https://www.remnote.com/a/organizational-behavior-chapter-8-performance-appraisal-and-rewards-/NXD2xFvWQ8aWCmzTG



*Introduction to Business*. Available at: https://openstax.org/details/books/introduction-business

## Portion Type and Size

Single (independent work), pairs, small groups, or whole class

Time: Variable

- As few as five minutes.

- No maximum length.
- Time will vary depending on the adopted approach to implementation.
- *Note*: The activity takes significantly less time when the instructor creates digital or paper-based cards in advance of class.

Online and/or face to face

## Web Resources

- RemNote. A free tool that combines note-taking and spaced repetition flashcards.
- For more on retrieval practice, see:
  - Retrieval Practice. See: https://www.retrievalpractice.org/
  - Retrieval Practice. See: http://www.learningscientists.org/retrieval-practice/
  - "Learn How to Study Using Retrieval Practice". See: http://www.learningscientists.org/blog/2016/6/23-1
  - Retrieval Practice: The Most Powerful Learning Strategy You're Not Using. See: https://www.cultofpedagogy.com/retrieval-practice/
- For more on spaced practice, see:
  - Learn How to Study... Using Spaced Practice. See: http://www.learningscientists.org/blog/2016/7/21-1
  - The Learning Scientists, Spaced Practice. See: http://www.learningscientists.org/spaced-practice/
- For more on the "Forgetting Curve," see:
  - "What is the Forgetting Curve (and How to Combat It)" See: https://elearningindustry.com/forgetting-curve-combat

## I Tried This and This Is What I Learned

| DATE USED/LESSON TOPIC | REFLECTIONS/WHAT I MIGHT DO DIFFERENTLY NEXT TIME |
|---|---|
| | |
| | |
| | |

Have a "What Did We Eat Last Night? Last Week?" activity adaptation to share?

Submit your tweaks and experiences here:

Survey Link: https://forms.gle/G7JS4RPADQK8ykp89

# Apples, Oranges, or Lemons

**Main Course/Entrée**

**Ice Breaker Title: Apples, Oranges, or Lemons**

A variation of *Apples to Apples* as a tool to promote critical thinking, analysis, and reflection associated with complex course topics

## Activity Description

In this activity, students engage in a variation of *Apples to Apples. Apples to Apples* is a game where one player is a judge for each round. The judge holds Adjective cards while the players each have hands of Noun cards.

In this variation, students take on the same roles, rotating between judge and players. The student who serves as judge plays an Adjective (Apples) card. All players hold hands of cards (three, five, or seven). Each player selects one of the Noun (Oranges) cards from their hand and plays that as a "best match" for the Adjective card. Each student makes a case for why their played card is a best match, and the judge decides each round.

This activity is designed to encourage critical thinking and support and sustain increased student comfort and confidence when interacting with complex concepts.

The activity works well with concepts for which there are a variety of examples and/or associated traits or characteristics. Concepts that are sometimes intimidating for students (because of complexity, depth, range of options, or otherwise) are especially well suited to this activity.

This activity works well as an introductory warm-up for a substantive lesson associated with the cards' concepts. The activity also works well as a review activity for concepts introduced and/or explored in a prior lesson.

## Recipe

Step 1: Define and explain the "Apples, Oranges, or Lemons" game.

Step 2: Introduce the activity. Clarify content focus and type of resource to be used for the activity.

Step 3: Create groups (if applicable).

Step 4: Share cards to be used for the activity. Index cards work well for in-person game play. Cards can be shared with students via private chat (instructor types assigned words) for virtual game play. Provide time for students to research and create collections of cards (if applicable).

Step 5: Assign roles. Students take on the role of the judge on a rotating basis.

Step 6: Demo a game-play round (if applicable).

- Judge presents an adjective card of choice.
- Players present a "best match" from their assigned noun cards.
- Players make an argument for why their presented Noun card is the best match for the associated Adjective card.
- Instructor clarifies how much time students have to prep and present.
- Instructor clarifies whether judge can ask questions and, if so, how many.
- Instructor clarifies how long judge may deliberate.

- Instructor clarifies points earned by round.
- Instructor clarifies number of rounds in the game.

Open discussion:

- Which is the "best match" for the Apple card?
- Alternative: Which is the least "best match" (becomes the Lemon card)?

Step 7: Provide active work time for students to play game rounds (recommended minimum five minutes).

- Offer support as needed.
- Share directional reminders, as applicable.

Step 8: Open discussion and reflection on the exercise (out loud or independent journaling).

Sample prompts:

- How has this activity changed the way you feel about the topic?
- How has this activity changed the way you feel about the presented examples?

## The Secret Sauce (Why It Works)

This **interactive** activity breaks down complex material into manageable chunks that reduce **cognitive load** on students. Students draw on and actively **recall** prior learning and knowledge. The activity promotes **critical thinking** and hands-on, **active learning** that requires students to do something (interact with a complex concept). Goals include increased student comfort with a particular topic as well as increased **confidence**. The activity offers opportunities for **reflection** (both individual and group). The activity also offers opportunities for **formative assessment**.

## Ingredients

- ☐ A set or deck of cards/index cards with nouns and adjectives that are related to a class learning objective or topic
- ☐ Clock/Timer (as applicable)

## Activity Prep

Select a topic for the game deck.

Create sets of Noun and Adjective cards.

Optional: Students create card decks to use for this activity.

Paper and/or index cards can be used for in-person game play.

Google Slides and/or Google Docs can be used for virtual game play.

- Create a folder with multiple documents or slides. A collection of terms (Nouns) can be populated on each document or slide. Instructor provides each student (or group) a specific URL (to a document or slide).

PowerPoint and Prezi also work well. This article, titled "Three Tools for Creating Digital, Online Card Games" provides instructions on use. See: https://www.linkedin.com/pulse/three-tools-creating-digital-online-card-games-karl-kapp

## Activity Adaptations/Toppings

Depending on the instructional goals and objectives, this activity can be used and adapted in a variety of ways.

- Vary number of rounds. Instructor and/or students determine number of rounds.
- Vary number of cards dealt to each student (three, five, or seven cards work well).
- Lemon card: A student can play a card they believe is least like the Adjective card. If persuasive, they earn double points.
- Introduce the activity with a discussion question/reflection prompt that explores the topic that will be covered in game play. Questions might promote basic recall (definitions of key terms) and/or higher-level analysis of such topic.
- Introduce the activity using a current event/news article related to the lesson topic and with respect to which students will engage in game play.
- Use the activity as a collaborative learning exercise where students collaboratively create sets of cards for use in game play.
- Students individually create Adjective and Noun cards (themed, by set) on a course topic of choice.
- Students create Adjective and Noun cards (themed, by set) on an assigned topic.
- Vary time permitted to work on the card creation.
- Vary time permitted for each round.

## Activity Extensions

- Provide opportunities for students to create a variety of card sets (decks) on a range of course topics.

Share decks as study resources. Themed decks might be shuffled and used to promote review and analysis of multiple topics at once (an opportunity for mixed practice and interleaving).

### Law-Based Example (Legal Technology)

Many students come to legal technology unfamiliar with available software applications. Creating a game environment to explore and recall key concepts is a way for students to actively engage with and approach a complex topic in a low-stakes, fun way that is designed to help minimize the fear associated with higher-stakes settings.

Apple card: Efficient.

Orange cards: Time Keeping Software, Legal Billing Software, Case Management Software.

Open discussion: Which is the best match for the Apple card?

Which is the least-best match? (Present as [or becomes] the Lemon card).

Additional sample Apple cards: Cost-Saving, Time-Saving, Protective of Confidentiality, Expensive, Risky, Research Tool.

## Portion Type and Size

Single (independent work), pairs, small groups, or whole class

Time: Variable

- As few as five minutes.
- No maximum length.
- Initial preparation will be the most time intensive.
- Time will vary depending on the adopted approach to implementation.
- *Note*: The activity takes significantly less time when the instructor creates sets of cards (decks) in advance.

Online and/or face to face

## Web Resource

Apples to Apples. See: https://en.wikipedia.org/wiki/Apples_to_Apples

## I Tried This and This Is What I Learned

| DATE USED/LESSON TOPIC | REFLECTIONS/WHAT I MIGHT DO DIFFERENTLY NEXT TIME |
|---|---|
| | |
| | |
| | |

Have an "Apples, Oranges, or Lemons" activity adaptation to share?

Submit your tweaks and experiences here:

Survey Link: https://forms.gle/G7JS4RPADQK8ykp89

# Recipe Cards Against All Legalities

**Main Course/Entrée**

**Ice Breaker Title: Recipe Cards Against All Legalities**

Interactive games based on *Cards Against Humanity* as a tool to promote critical thinking and analysis skills

## Activity Description

This activity is a variation of *Cards Against Humanity*, a card game that relies on both questions and fill-in-the-blank statements to generate conversation and debate.

One player presents a question or fill-in-the-blank card from a prepared deck. Decks can be themed or generally aligned with course content.

The presenting player reads the card out loud. All other players (whole class or small groups) write down or submit a written response to the card. The presenting player reads all submissions out loud and awards one the honor of "winning" submission along with a reason why. The player with the winning submission earns a point for the round. After each round, a new player takes on the role as card presenter/reviewer.

This activity is designed to encourage critical thinking and student confidence when interacting with complex concepts.

The activity works well with concepts for which there are a variety of examples and/or associated traits or characteristics. Concepts that are sometimes intimidating for students (because of complexity, depth, range of options, or otherwise) are especially well suited to this activity.

The activity works well as a review activity for a concept introduced and/or explored in a prior lesson.

## Recipe

Step 1: Define and explain *Cards Against Humanity* card game.

Step 2: Introduce the activity. Explain how "Recipe Cards Against All Legalities" works. Clarify content focus and type of resource to be used for the activity.

Step 3: Create groups (if applicable).

Step 4: Share a link or copy of the game cards (if applicable)/Provide time for students to research and create game cards (if applicable).

Step 5: Explain the theme of the card deck (the material to use for the game activity) (if applicable).

Step 6: Demo "Recipe Cards Against All Legalities" game (if needed).

- Presenting player shares a card of choice.
- Players submit a response (index cards, slips of paper, or online submissions).
- Presenting player selects one "winner" and explains why.
- Instructor clarifies how much time students have to prep and present.
- Instructor clarifies whether the judge can ask questions and, if so, how many.
- Instructor clarifies how long the judge may deliberate.
- Instructor clarifies points earned by round.
- Instructor clarifies number of game rounds.

Step 7: Provide active work time for students to play (recommended minimum five minutes).

- Offer support as needed.
- Share directional reminders about the activity, as applicable.

Step 8: Open discussion and reflection on the exercise (out loud or independent journaling).

- Sample prompt:
    - How has this activity changed the way you feel about the related topic?

## The Secret Sauce (Why It Works)

This **scaffolded** activity breaks down complex material into manageable chunks that reduce **cognitive load** on students. Students draw on and actively **recall** prior learning and knowledge. Students practice **active listening** and engage in associated **critical thinking** and analysis. The activity promotes hands-on, **active learning** that requires students to do something (interact with a complex concept). Goals include increased student **comfort** as well as increased confidence with complex concepts. The activity offers opportunities for **reflection** (both individual and group). The activity also offers opportunities for **formative assessment**.

## Ingredients

- ☐ A set or deck of cards/index cards with questions and fill-in-the-blank statements that are related to a class learning objective or lesson
- ☐ Clock/Timer (as applicable)

## Activity Prep

Prepare a set/deck of cards for use in this activity.

Optional: Students create card decks on an assigned topic.

## Activity Adaptations/Toppings

Depending on the instructional goals and objectives, this activity can be used and adapted in a variety of ways.

- Players make an argument for why their submission is the best match for the associated card.
- An additional deck of cards might be developed for all submitting players. Answers must be drawn from this deck.
- Open discussion:
    - Which is the best match for the presented card?
    - Which is the worst match for the presented card?
- Vary number of rounds. Instructor and/or students determine number of rounds.
- Vary number of cards used for each round (three, five, or seven cards work well).
- Introduce the activity with a discussion question/reflection prompt that explores the topic that will be covered in game play. Questions might promote basic recall (definitions of key terms) and/or higher-level analysis of such topic.
- Introduce the activity using a current event/news article related to the lesson topic and with respect to which students will engage in game play.
- Use the activity as a collaborative learning exercise where students collaboratively create sets of cards for use in game play.
- Students individually create cards (themed, by set) on a course topic of choice.
- Students create cards (themed, by set) on a specific topic (assigned by instructor).
- Vary time permitted to work on card creation.
- Vary time permitted for each round.

## Activity Extensions

- Students create a variety of card sets (decks) on a range of course topics.
- Share decks as study resources. Individual themed decks might be shuffled and used to promote review and analysis of multiple topics at once (an opportunity for mixed practice and interleaving).

### Law-Based Example (Legal Technology/Paralegal Ethics)

Presenter cards:

Which type of legal technology is most beneficial from an efficiency perspective?

Which type of legal technology is most useful as a cost-saving matter?

What type of legal technology is most helpful to ensure client confidentiality?

What is the greatest risk associated with using legal technologies?

What is the greatest risk associated with avoiding legal technologies?

What is the most significant ethical issue to consider when using legal technologies?

What ethical issue is most significantly impacted in a positive way when using legal technologies?

## Portion Type and Size

Single (independent work), pairs, small group, or whole class

Time: Variable

- As few as five minutes.
- No maximum length.
- Initial set-up will be most time intensive.
- Time will vary depending on the adopted approach to implementation.
- *Note*: The activity takes significantly less time when the instructor prepares cards in advance of use.

Online and/or face to face

## Web Resource

Cards Against Humanity. See: https://www.cardsagainsthumanity.com/

## I Tried This and This Is What I Learned

| DATE USED/LESSON TOPIC | REFLECTIONS/WHAT I MIGHT DO DIFFERENTLY NEXT TIME |
|---|---|
| | |
| | |
| | |

Have a "Recipe Cards Against All Legalities" activity adaptation to share?

Submit your tweaks and experiences here:

Survey Link: https://forms.gle/G7JS4RPADQK8ykp89

# Erasure Poems

**Main Course/Entrée**

**Ice Breaker Title: Erasure Poems**

Poetry as a tool to help mitigate student anxiety with complex and/or unfamiliar texts

## Activity Description

Erasure poems are a form of found poetry. Students draft poems that are created from existing texts. Words are "erased" (crossed out, removed, deleted) from an existing text-based resource. The remaining text emerges as a new "found" poem.

Erasure poems offer opportunities for students to engage with complex texts in creative ways. Erasure poems also present instructional opportunities for students to become familiar with complicated and/or unfamiliar texts in a stress-free environment.

Creating an erasure poem is also a way to proactively mitigate the increased cognitive load (drain on working memory) and anxiety that often emerges when a student interacts with a complex resource for the first time. This activity is designed to support and sustain increased student comfort and confidence when interacting with complex texts.

To create an erasure poem, student writers erase or cross out existing text (words and phrases), keeping only words and phrases that will eventually be a part of a newly created poem.

In this "Erasure Poems" activity, students create an erasure poem from a primary or secondary resource. The activity works well with any type of prose or expository text. Texts that are sometimes intimidating for students (because of vocabulary, writing style, familiarity, or otherwise) are especially well suited to this activity.

This activity works well as an introductory warm-up for a substantive lesson associated with the text(s) and materials used for the erasure poem.

## Recipe

Step 1: Define and explain erasure poems.

Step 2: Introduce the activity. Explain how erasure poems work. Clarify content focus and type of resource to be used for the activity.

Step 3: Create groups (if applicable).

Step 4: Share a link or copy of the resource (if applicable)/Provide time for students to research and locate a text-based resource (if applicable).

Step 5: Explain the nature of the text or resource (the material to be used for the erasure poem) (if applicable).

Step 6: Demo an online erasure poem tool (if applicable).

- See web resources for link.
- To create a poem, first click "Create Poem" at bottom of screen.
- Next, copy and paste in the text of a resource.
- Click Create.
- Begin creating an erasure poem.
- To work collaboratively, share the webpage link or copy and share the Join Code at the bottom left.
    - Direct collaborators to go to http://blackoutpoem.herokuapp.com/.
    - Collaborators input the code and then contribute to the erasure poem.
- All contributors are randomly assigned a color when they join the room.
- Explore tool bar features.

- Use pencil to cross out words.
- Use horizontal scroll bar to adjust for width.
- Use eraser to revise text.
- Click speech bubble to chat with collaborators.
- Click download arrow to save final erasure poem as a PNG.

Step 7: Upload the resource to the generator (if applicable)/walk students through the upload process.

Step 8: Provide active work time for students to create and generate an original erasure poem using the identified resource (recommended minimum five minutes).

- Offer support as needed.
- Share directional reminders about the activity, as applicable.

Step 9: Open discussion and reflection on the exercise (out loud or independent journaling).

Sample prompts:

- How has this activity changed the way you feel about the resource?
- How has this activity changed the way you feel about the related topic?

Step 10: Share erasure poems (either out loud or on digital bulletin boards) (if applicable).

## The Secret Sauce (Why It Works)

This **scaffolded** activity breaks down complex material into **manageable chunks** that reduce **cognitive load** on students. The activity promotes hands-on, **active learning** that requires students to do something (interact with a complex text). Goals include increased **student comfort** with a particular type of writing as well as increased **confidence** reading a complex text. The activity offers opportunities for **reflection** (both individual and group). The activity also offers opportunities for **formative assessment**.

## Ingredients

- ☐ A primary or secondary resource related to a class learning objective or lesson
- ☐ Clock/Timer (as applicable)

## Activity Prep

A primary or secondary resource (web-based or paper) related to a lesson topic.

Optional: Students conduct research and identify a resource for this activity.

## Activity Adaptations/Toppings

Depending on instructional goals and objectives, this activity can be used and adapted in a variety of ways.

- Conduct the activity using a passage (several paragraphs, a page of text) from a current reading, assigned book, or related news article.
- Introduce the activity with a discussion question/reflection prompt that explores the difference between primary and scholarly sources, scholarly and popular sources, etc.

- Introduce the activity with a discussion question/reflection prompt that explores different types of writing (e.g., expository versus narrative).
- Introduce the activity with a discussion question related to research methods and which promotes active recall.

Examples

- How might we locate a text that ___?
- What are some databases and/or reputable search engines to find ____?
- What are some options and resources to locate [a particular type of text]?
    - Introduce the activity using a current event/news article related to the lesson topic and from which students create erasure poems.
    - Use the activity as a collaborative learning exercise where one student is responsible for defining unfamiliar vocabulary in a text-based resource, another is responsible for documenting the group's process, another is responsible for presenting the final erasure poem, etc. Depending on desired group size, additional roles can be developed.
    - Students create erasure poems that use five (or more) new and/or unfamiliar terms. First, scan resource for unfamiliar terms. Conduct research and define [some number of] unfamiliar terms. Students might also submit newly defined vocabulary terms and/or post the words and definitions on a class resource.
    - Students create an erasure poem on a topic of choice.
    - Students create an erasure poem on an assigned topic.
    - Vary time permitted to work on poem construction.
    - Provide a word limit/cap on the poem.
    - Encourage students to read actively for meaning after creating an erasure poem.

## Activity Extensions

- Provide opportunities for students to publicly share erasure poems. Students might post poems to a class bulletin board or gallery. A Padlet board, class Google Site, or Pinterest board are free options that work well.

### Law-Based Example (Judicial Opinions)

This "Erasure Poem" activity might be used as a warm-up on a lesson for how to read and/or brief a judicial opinion. (*Note*: Judicial opinions can be swapped with any piece of writing and any primary or secondary source.)

- If an instructor wants to reinforce research skills, students might conduct research and select a judicial opinion of choice (e.g., by jurisdiction, topic).
- Alternatively, an instructor can share a pre-selected judicial opinion.
- Either individually, in pairs, in small groups, or as a whole-class exercise, students create an original erasure poem from an identified judicial opinion.

## Portion Type and Size

Single (independent work), Pairs, Small Groups, or Whole Class

Time: Variable

- As few as five minutes

- No maximum length
- Initial use will be most time intensive
- Time will vary depending on the adopted approach to implementation
- *Note*: The activity takes significantly less time when the instructor selects a resource for the poem generator

Online and/or face to face

## Web Resource

Erasure Poem Generator. See: http://blackoutpoem.herokuapp.com/

## I Tried This and This Is What I Learned

| DATE USED/LESSON TOPIC | REFLECTIONS/WHAT I MIGHT DO DIFFERENTLY NEXT TIME |
|---|---|
| | |
| | |
| | |

Have an "Erasure Poems" activity adaptation to share?

Submit your tweaks and experiences here:

Survey Link: https://forms.gle/G7JS4RPADQK8ykp89

# Ambience-Informed Insights

**Main Course/Entrée**

**Ice Breaker Title: Ambience-Informed Insights**

Podcasts as a tool to develop active listening skills and deeper understanding of course concepts and to also help mitigate student anxiety with complex and/or unfamiliar topics

## Activity Description

In this activity, students listen to brief content-related podcasts. Students take notes and then discuss the podcast after time for reflection.

Podcasts are audio programming content that can be consumed (listened to) on demand. Podcasts are often curated and produced with a focus on a particular topic. There are as many different options for podcasts as there are course topics.

Podcasts offer opportunities for students to engage with complex concepts in ways that extend beyond course readings. Podcasts also present instructional opportunities for students to become familiar with a variety of voices, perspectives, and opinions on course topics.

Listening to podcasts on specific course topics is also a way to proactively mitigate the increased cognitive load (drain on working memory) and anxiety that often emerges when a student interacts with a complex text or resource for the first time. This activity is designed to support and sustain increased student comfort and confidence when interacting with complex texts.

Podcasts can be found on virtually any topic. Topics that are controversial and/or abstract are especially well suited for this activity. Students can be introduced to a wide range of perspectives, voices, and viewpoints. Students can also gain increased awareness regarding practical applications of course concepts. Many podcasts include interviews with practitioners, and these are often especially helpful for instructional purposes.

This activity works well as a review/reflection activity and/or an introductory warm-up for a substantive lesson associated with the content of the selected podcast.

## Recipe

Step 1: Define and explain podcasts.

Step 2: Introduce the activity. Clarify content focus and type of resource to be used for the activity.

Step 3: Create groups (if applicable). Pairs or small groups can be used for either podcast selection and/or listening/reflection and discussion.

Step 4: Share a link or copy of the resource (if applicable)/Provide time for students to research and locate an applicable podcast (if applicable).

Step 5: Encourage students to take notes while listening.

- Consider providing a note-taking template.
- Consider introducing the exercise with reminders of different types of note-taking approaches.

Step 6: Provide active work time for students to listen to the selected podcast (recommended minimum three to five minutes).

- Offer support as needed.
- Share directional reminders about the activity, as applicable.

Step 7: Open discussion and reflection on the exercise (out loud or independent journaling)

Sample prompts:

- Summarize the speaker's main points.
- List three surprising insights.
- List three questions you might ask of the podcast speaker.
- How has this activity changed the way you feel about the resource?
- How has this activity changed the way you feel about the related topic?

## The Secret Sauce (Why It Works)

This **listening** activity presents complex material in a variety of creative ways (audio content that can be both "chunked" and replayed) to reduce **cognitive load** on students. The activity promotes **active listening** that requires students to do something (interact with new ideas presented in audio format). Goals include increased student **comfort** with a particular topic as well as increased **awareness** of unique perspectives related to the covered topic. The activity offers opportunities for **reflection** (both individual and group). The activity also offers opportunities for **formative assessment**.

## Ingredients

- ☐ A podcast related to a class learning objective or lesson
- ☐ A collection of follow-up discussion prompts
- ☐ Clock/Timer (as applicable)

## Activity Prep

A podcast related to a class learning objective or lesson.

A collection of follow-up discussion prompts.

Optional: Students conduct research and identify a podcast for this activity.

## Activity Adaptations/Toppings

Depending on the instructional goals and objectives, this activity can be used and adapted in a variety of ways.

- Students conduct research and identify podcasts related to course topics.
- Swap podcasts with music (songs, lyrics) related to content.
- Prepare (in advance) a collection of discussion questions for students to work on either independently, in pairs, or small groups after listening to the podcast. Provide students time to reflect and complete the questions. Questions might range across all levels of Bloom's Taxonomy.
    - 20 Question Stems Framed Around Bloom's Taxonomy. See: https://www.teachthought.com/critical-thinking/question-stems/
- Students prepare reflection-based writings in response to the podcast. Writing might first summarize the podcast's main points and then engage in critical analysis.
- Students produce their own podcasts. This might be done as a scaffolded, long-term group assignment. "Project Audio: Teaching Students How to Produce Their Own Podcasts". See: https://www.nytimes.com/2018/04/19/learning/lesson-plans/project-audio-teaching-students-how-to-produce-their-own-podcasts.html
- Introduce the activity with a discussion question/reflection prompt that explores the related course topic.

## Activity Extensions

- Students listen to assigned or self-identified podcasts as an out of class activity. Begin class with discussion and reflection.
- Provide opportunities for students to publicly share recommended podcasts. Students might post recommendations to a class bulletin board or gallery. A Padlet board, class Google Site, or Pinterest board are free options that work well.
- Students conduct research and locate podcasts on an assigned topic.

### Law-Based Example

Legal-themed podcasts:

- "20 Best Legal Podcasts". See: https://www.simplelegal.com/blog/20-best-legal-podcasts.

- "Best Legal Podcasts". See: https://www.clio.com/blog/best-legal-podcasts/

## Portion Type and Size

Single (independent work), pairs, small group, or whole class

Time: Variable

- As few as five minutes.
- No maximum length.
- Time will vary depending on the adopted approach to implementation.
- *Note*: The activity takes significantly less time when the instructor selects a podcast for use in this activity.

Online and/or face to face

## Web Resources

- Podcasts Options Examples: https://www.simplelegal.com/blog/20-best-legal-podcasts.
- "Why You Should Bring Podcasts Into Your Classroom": https://www.cultofpedagogy.com/podcasts-in-the-classroom/

## I Tried This and This Is What I Learned

| DATE USED/LESSON TOPIC | REFLECTIONS/WHAT I MIGHT DO DIFFERENTLY NEXT TIME |
|---|---|
| | |
| | |
| | |

Have an "Ambience-Informed Insights" activity adaptation to share?

Submit your tweaks and experiences here:

Survey Link: https://forms.gle/G7JS4RPADQK8ykp89

# Sides/Fruits/Vegetables

"Cooking demands attention, patience, and, above all, a respect for the gifts of the earth."
*Judith Jones*

## Recipe/Resume Review

**Sides/Fruits/Vegetables**

**Ice Breaker Title: Recipe/Resume Review**

Close reading and resume review to promote proofreading strategies, active reading, and transferable skills

## Activity Description

In this "Recipe/Resume Review" activity, students actively review and reflect on the language, tone, grammar, and overall format of a resume.

This exercise serves several purposes. Students become more familiar with the possible format and layout of a resume. Students also become more aware of the importance of proper spelling and grammar in professional contexts.

The activity promotes both active and close reading as well as reflection. Students might generate and/or identify common spelling and grammar errors in sample resumes. Students might also identify strategies that help minimize such errors.

"Recipe/Resume Review" activities provide opportunities for students to explore and analyze career-relevant topics and complex ideas in a low-stakes, safe environment.

Students can work collaboratively as a group or in pairs. Students can also work independently.

## Recipe

Step 1: Define and explain "Recipe/Resume Review" activities.

Step 2: Introduce the activity.

Step 3: Clarify the focus (resume, cover letter, job context) and content to be used for the activity.

Step 4: Create work groups (if applicable).

Step 5: Share a link, slide, or copy of a resume sample.

Step 6: Introduce an open-ended discussion question.

Sample prompts:

- Should typos on a resume matter?
- What strategies help minimize typos on a resume?
- Should all resumes look the same?
- Can you successfully proofread your own resume?
- Is it easier/harder to identify errors (grammatical, spelling, typographical) in a resume you are familiar or unfamiliar with?

Step 7: Share a brief article on resume writing.

Step 8: Students review shared sample resume(s). Review can occur independently, in pairs/small groups, or as a class. Work collaboratively or independently to identify typos.

Step 9: Students generate a list of common errors. Related discussion prompts: Where do spelling and/or grammar errors most commonly occur? What strategies help prevent such errors?

Step 10: Provide active work time for students to review a shared resume(s).

- Offer support as needed.
- Share directional reminders about the activity, as applicable.

Step 11: Facilitate a discussion associated with the shared resume. Share prompts that direct and promote conversation. Avoid questions that can be answered in a yes and no format.

Sample prompts:

- How has this activity changed the way you feel about resume writing?
- How has this activity changed the way you feel about resume review?

Step 12: Share reflections either out loud or independently.

## Prep (How to Create a "Recipe/Resume Review" Activity)

Step 1: Curate a collection of resumes (one or more) for review.

Step 2: Revise one or more resumes to include a variety of grammatical, spelling, and/or organizational errors.

## Variations

Initiate the activity with independent writing. Students spend independent time working on their own career toolbox (e.g., resumes, cover letters, email inquiries, thank-you notes). At the end of the independent work period, conduct a whole-class or small-group discussion. Provide optional opportunities for students to share their writing and/or related thoughts.

## The Secret Sauce (Why It Works)

This targeted activity provides a stress-free opportunity for students to increase familiarity with professional resume and cover letter writing. Students become more familiar with the possible format and layout of a resume. Students also become more aware of the importance of proper spelling and grammar in professional contexts. The activity promotes both **active and close reading** as well as **reflection**. "Recipe/Resume Review" activities provide opportunities for students to honestly evaluate their own **written communication skills** in a low-stakes, safe environment. This activity promotes hands-on, **active learning** that requires students to do something (interact with and identify spelling and grammatical errors in a sample resume). Goals include increased student comfort with resume writing as well as increased **confidence** associated with professional communication. The activity offers opportunities for **reflection** (both individual and group). The activity also offers opportunities for **formative assessment**.

## Ingredients

- ☐ A mock resume or cover letter, preferably with a series of typos throughout
- ☐ Clock/Timer (as applicable)

## Activity Prep

A mock resume or cover letter, preferably with a series of typos throughout.

Optional: Students prepare their own resumes and cover letters to use for this activity.

## Activity Adaptations/Toppings

Depending on the instructional goals and objectives, this activity can be used and adapted in a variety of ways. A few examples follow:

- Use an original resume created for this activity. Alternatively, conduct the activity using a resume found online.
- Introduce the activity with a discussion question/reflection prompt that explores differences between various types of professional communication (e.g., resumes, cover letters, follow-up emails, thank-you notes).
- Introduce the activity with a discussion question/reflection prompt that explores different types of professional writing.
- Introduce the activity with a discussion question related to resume writing.
- Introduce the activity with a discussion question focused on proofreading strategies. Generate and evaluate strategies that have worked well and explore why. Explore contexts in which proofreading is easier/harder (e.g., one's own work, work one is familiar with).
- Introduce the activity using a current event/news article related to resume writing.
- Use the activity as a collaborative learning exercise where one student is responsible for defining unfamiliar vocabulary in a shared resume, another is responsible for identifying spelling and grammatical errors, etc. Depending on desired group size, additional roles can be developed.
- Students create a resume for a possible career or job of choice.
- Students create a cover letter for a possible job of choice.
- Students generate a list of commonly misspelled words.
- Students generate a list of common errors that spellcheck won't catch.
    - Examples:
        - *type* versus *typo*
        - *avoid* versus *avid*
        - *statute* versus *statue*

## Activity Extensions

- Provide opportunities for students to publicly share resume annotations. Students might post to a class bulletin board or gallery. A Padlet board, class Google Site, or Pinterest board are free options that work well.
- Utilize this activity to promote digital literacy. Encourage students to conduct research and identify web-based articles on resume writing. Analyze articles for objectivity, credibility, accuracy, relevance, etc.
- Share illustrative articles. See "15 Resume Mistakes to Avoid" at https://www.indeed.com/career-advice/resumes-cover-letters/15-resume-mistakes-to-avoid/. Provide time for students to read and then, discuss. Analyze the articles for strength. Compare/contrast points shared across articles.
- If student research leads to articles and sources for resume generation, ask students to share resources in a class library (Google Docs, Google Sites, Padlet board). Source identification can be used as research reinforcement and library building.
- Either individually, in pairs, small groups, or as a whole-class exercise, students create original resumes for use in jobs of choice. Students might research on LinkedIn and other job posting sites to identify desired skills and explore how those skills might be emphasized in a resume.
- Encourage students to remain alert for typos in communications (e.g., mailings, advertisements, signs) that they come across in their personal lives. Students might take pictures and share with the class. Consider creating a class website or resource where such images are shared as a way of raising awareness and encouraging modifications to personal workflows to minimize the likelihood of such errors.

### Sample Resumes

- Resume Template 1. See: https://docs.google.com/document/d/16mIc1oVdQ40a2GWv8CY4vHvKmdRbqXMjX4p6SR9vNPk/edit?usp=sharing
- Resume Template 2. See: https://docs.google.com/document/d/1C9dMNO9_Ib4r3o3-KZTSioMretusSej92dMYW-IGpsM/edit?usp=sharing
- Resume Sample 1 (Copy and apply typos for student review). See: https://docs.google.com/document/d/1xVCl8OmiWcKpaYh0ZT2UvCdDTLcmEl3YIRRcHX6G--Q/edit?usp=sharing
- Resume Sample 2 (Copy and apply typos for student review). See: https://docs.google.com/document/d/1SFW7yTo3PF18eqSs9uTsD2WV8mtiRgjiPZ7IZ76tsXw/edit?usp=sharing

## Portion Type and Size

Single (independent work), pairs, small group, or whole class

Time: Variable

- As few as five minutes.
- No maximum length.
- Time will vary depending on the adopted approach to implementation.
- *Note*: The activity takes significantly less time when the instructor and/or students prepare sample resumes in advance.

Online and/or face to face

## Web Resources

- Can You Find the Ten Errors in this Resume? See: https://www.medixteam.com/can-you-find-errors-resume/
- 15 Common Resume Typos to Avoid. See: https://www.flexjobs.com/blog/post/resume-tip-proofread-your-resume-for-typos-and-misspellings-v2/
- Bad Resume Examples. See: https://zety.com/blog/bad-resume-examples
- Do Resume Typos Matter: Here's What 100s of LinkedIn Users Say? See: https://www.fastcompany.com/40536077/do-resume-typos-matter-heres-what-hundreds-of-linkedin-users-say
- Proofreading Strategies That Work. See: https://www.remnote.com/a/what-s-on-the-docket-minimizing-errors/GrZGawzocrGn5ZsjR
- 30 Legal Terms You'll Want to Spell Correctly. See: https://www.remnote.com/a/what-s-on-the-docket/z2oTSLdG7uP2GyckW
- Proof that Blog. See: https://proofthatblog.com/
- Functional Resume Example. See: https://www.thebalancecareers.com/functional-resume-example-2063203
- Chronological Resume Example. See: https://www.thebalancecareers.com/chronological-resume-example-for-a-retail-position-2063201
- Combination Resume Example. See: https://www.thebalancecareers.com/combination-resume-example-and-writing-tips-2061951
- Resume Profile Examples. See: https://www.thebalancecareers.com/resume-profile-examples-2062828
- How to Write a Masterpiece of a Resume. See: https://rockportinstitute.com/resources/how-to-write-a-masterpiece-of-a-resume/
- Annotation Tools (Collaborative/Individual)
    - Google Docs
    - Perusall. See: https://perusall.com/
    - Kami App. See: https://www.kamiapp.com/

## I Tried This and This Is What I Learned

| DATE USED/LESSON TOPIC | REFLECTIONS/WHAT I MIGHT DO DIFFERENTLY NEXT TIME |
|---|---|
| | |
| | |
| | |

Have a "Recipe/Resume Review" activity adaptation to share?

Submit your tweaks and experiences here:

Survey Link: https://forms.gle/G7JS4RPADQK8ykp89

# Something Smells Fishy (Language and Communication Clarity)

**Sides/Fruits/Vegetables**

**Ice Breaker Title: Something Smells Fishy (Language and Communication Clarity)**

Review and discussion of educationally focused comics to promote communication skills, proofreading strategies, active reading, and transferable skills

## Activity Description

In this "Something Smells Fishy" activity, students actively review and reflect on the messages conveyed by comics and illustrations with a focus on language, tone, grammar, and related communication skills.

This exercise serves several purposes. Students become more familiar with the multiple ways in which language might be interpreted. Students also become more aware of the importance of proper spelling and grammar in a variety of contexts.

The activity promotes both active and close reading as well as reflection.

Students can work collaboratively as a group or in pairs. Students can also work independently.

## Recipe

Step 1: Define and explain "Something Smells Fishy" activities.

Step 2: Introduce the activity.

Step 3: Clarify the focus (e.g., communication, grammar, spelling) and content to be used for the activity.

Step 4: Create work groups (if applicable).

Step 5: Share a link, slide, or copy of a pre-selected comic/graphic.

Step 6: Open with an open-ended discussion question.

Sample prompts:

- Why does communication matter?
- What is professional communication?
- What causes miscommunication?
- What are some strategies that help minimize ambiguity in writing?

Step 7: Students review shared graphics. Review can occur independently, in pairs/small groups, or as a class. Work collaboratively or independently to discuss.

Optional: Share a series of questions to which students respond.

Step 8: Ask students to generate takeaways relating to preferred communication strategies.

Step 9: Facilitate a discussion associated with the shared graphic. Share prompts that direct and promote conversation. Avoid questions that can be answered in a yes and no format.

Sample prompts:

- How has this activity changed the way you feel about communication?

- How has this activity changed the way you approach communication?

Step 10: Share reflections (either out loud or independently) (optional/if applicable).

## Variations

Initiate the activity with independent writing. Students spend independent time reflecting on their relative strengths and weaknesses when communicating. Students might distinguish between verbal and written communication. Students might respond to specific prompts and/or experiment with specific and identified strategies. At the end of the independent writing period, conduct a whole-class or small-group discussion. Provide optional opportunities for students to share their writing and/or related thoughts.

## The Secret Sauce (Why It Works)

This targeted activity provides a stress-free opportunity for students to strengthen a variety of transferable and soft skills. The activity promotes both **active and close reading** as well as **reflection**. This activity promotes hands-on, **active learning** that requires students to do something (interact with a provided graphic/comic). Goals include increased **student comfort** with professional writing as well as increased confidence associated with professional communication. The activity offers opportunities for **reflection** (both individual and group). The activity also offers opportunities for **formative assessment**.

## Ingredients

- ☐ A curated collection of graphics/comics for review and discussion
- ☐ Clock/Timer (as applicable)

## Activity Prep

A curated collection of graphics/comics for review and discussion.

Optional: Students conduct research and identify comics to share.

Optional: Students create original comics for use in this activity.

## Activity Adaptations/Toppings

Depending on the instructional goals and objectives, this activity can be used and adapted in a variety of ways.

- Students conduct research and identify comics to share.
- Students create original comics for use in this activity.
- Introduce the activity with a discussion question/reflection prompt that explores different types of writing.
- Introduce the activity with a discussion prompt focused on clarity in communication and associated strategies.
- Introduce the activity using a current event/news article related to communication.
- Find comics that explore course-related concepts and share with students for reflection and discussion. Pose substantive prompts to facilitate conversation.

- Criminal law example
    - Inkygirl.com Comic, See: https://twitter.com/UDPLibrary/status/1435377574625087491/photo/1

Discuss: What crime might this individual be charged with?

## Activity Extensions

- Open class with a discussion of a grammar or punctuation rule or convention. Students create a related comic to illustrate the perils of its misuse.
- Provide opportunities for students to publicly share original graphics/comics created for this activity. Students might post graphics to a class bulletin board or gallery. A Padlet board, class Google Site, or Pinterest board are free options that work well.

### Samples

- "I thought it was fine to park here." See: https://ifunny.co/picture/i-thought-it-was-fine-to-park-here-RsF7hnSK8
- 3 Punctuation Mistakes That Can Make You Look Like a Cannibal. See: https://www.grammarly.com/blog/3-punctuation-mistakes-that-can-make-you-look-like-a-cannibal/
- Punctuation Headlines. See: https://wronghands1.tumblr.com/post/182823489460
- "I know I am an inverted comma, but I still hate being quoted." See: https://www.cartoonstock.com/directory/i/inverted_comma.asp
- 23 Witty Grammar Jokes and Puns. See: https://blog.hubspot.com/marketing/grammar-jokes

## Portion Type and Size

Single (independent work), pairs, small groups, or whole class

Time: Variable

- As few as five minutes
- No maximum length
- Time will vary depending on the adopted approach to implementation.
- *Note*: The activity takes significantly less time when the instructor curates a collection of comics for review.

Online and/or face to face

## Web Resources

Comic Creation Tools. See: https://www.canva.com/create/comic-strips/

- Annotation Tools (Collaborative/Individual)
    - Google Docs
    - Perusall. See: https://perusall.com/
    - Kami App. See: https://www.kamiapp.com/

## I Tried This and This Is What I Learned

| DATE USED/LESSON TOPIC | REFLECTIONS/WHAT I MIGHT DO DIFFERENTLY NEXT TIME |
|---|---|
| | |
| | |
| | |

Have a "Something Smells Fishy" activity adaptation to share?

Submit your tweaks and experiences here:

Survey Link: https://forms.gle/G7JS4RPADQK8ykp89

# Let's Check That Recipe

**Sides/Fruits/Vegetables**

**Ice Breaker Title: Let's Check That Recipe**

Syllabus or assignment expectation quick checks to promote student understanding, time management, and communication

## Activity Description

In "Let's Check That Recipe" activities, students re-engage with fundamental course documents (aka "recipes for success") including syllabi and assignment guidelines to support student success. Students practice active recall and solidify understanding of course expectations and requirements.

In this activity, students are presented "quick checks" in the form of brief questions regarding course syllabi, assessment guidelines, and assignment rubrics. Questions can vary and might be presented in multiple formats, including true/false and multiple choice.

Quick-check questions provide opportunities for students to reinforce prior understanding and awareness of course and assignment expectations. Quick-check questions also present instructional opportunities that can increase the likelihood of student success.

This activity is designed to support and sustain increased student comfort and confidence when completing course assignments. The activity works well at any point in a term or semester.

## Recipe

Step 1: Define and explain "Let's Check That Recipe" activities.

Step 2: Introduce the activity. Explain how course materials including syllabi, assignment guidelines, and assessment rubrics can be thought of as both critical ingredients and spices for a rich and meaningful course experience. Clarify content focus and type of resource to be used for the activity.

Step 3: Create groups (if applicable).

Step 4: Share a link or copy of the associated resource (if applicable).

Step 5: Present quick-check questions.

Step 6: Provide time for students to respond and then discuss.

- Offer support as needed.
- Share directional reminders about the activity, as applicable.

Step 7: Open discussion and reflection on the exercise (out loud or independent journaling)

Sample prompts:

- How has this activity changed the way you feel about your understanding of course expectations?
- How has this activity impacted how confident you feel about your ability to complete a course assignment?

## The Secret Sauce (Why It Works)

This **retrieval** and **reinforcement** activity breaks down complex material into manageable chunks that reduce **cognitive load** on students. Students draw on and actively **recall** prior learning and knowledge. The activity promotes hands-on, **active learning** that requires students to do something (interact with a fundamental course resource such as a syllabus, rubric, and/or assessment guidelines). Goals include increased student **comfort** with a particular course component as well as increased **confidence** regarding course and assignment expectations. The activity offers opportunities for **reflection** (both individual and group). The activity also offers opportunities for **formative assessment**.

## Ingredients

- ☐ Course documents that are related to a current or prior class learning objective or lesson
- ☐ Clock/Timer (as applicable)

## Activity Prep

Course documents that are related to a current or prior class learning objective or lesson

## Activity Adaptations/Toppings

Depending on the instructional goals and objectives, this activity can be used and adapted in a variety of ways.

- Students create original questions based on a review of course syllabi, assignment guidelines, and/or rubrics and present those to peers in pairs, small groups, or as a whole class.

## Activity Extensions

- Provide opportunities for students to review course assessment materials and share suggestions, highlight points of confusion, and/or ask clarifying questions.
- Open discussion on how course syllabi might be improved for the benefit of all students.
- Resources on inclusive syllabi:
    - Creating Inclusive Syllabi: https://cte.ku.edu/creating-inclusive-syllabus

- The Syllabus as a Tool for Setting Class Climate: https://provost.tufts.edu/celt/the-syllabus-as-a-tool-for-setting-the-climate/
- Syllabus Design: https://ceils.ucla.edu/resources/teaching-guides/syllabus-design/
- Syllabus Design Checklist: Syllabus Design_Check-list.pdf
- Designing Inclusive Syllabi: https://ctl.columbia.edu/resources-and-technology/resources/designing-inclusive-syllabus/

**Sample Syllabus Quiz Questions:**

- What day are initial discussion posts due?
- What time are assignments due?
- How many weeks does our course run?
- How many times a week am I expected to log into our online classroom?
- What is our course late policy?
- When are office hours?
- What is the best way to reach your instructor?
- If I receive an email from an instructor or classmate, what are response-time expectations?
- Are assignment revisions and resubmissions accepted?
- What is academic honesty and how do we ensure it in our class?
- What are the elements of a substantive discussion post?

**Sample Assignment Expectations Questions:**

- What formats are acceptable for assignment submission?
- What formatting style should be used for references and citations?
- What time are assignments due?
- What is the course late policy?

**Sample Rubric Expectations Questions:**

- How many resources must be included in written work?
- Are there font and margin expectations?

## Portion Type and Size

Single (independent work), pairs, small group, or whole class

Time: Variable

- As few as two minutes.
- No maximum length.
- Time will vary depending on the adopted approach to implementation.

Online and/or face to face

## I Tried This and This Is What I Learned

| DATE USED/LESSON TOPIC | REFLECTIONS/WHAT I MIGHT DO DIFFERENTLY NEXT TIME |
|---|---|
| | |
| | |
| | |

Have a "Let's Check That Recipe" activity adaptation to share?

Submit your tweaks and experiences here:

Survey Link: https://forms.gle/G7JS4RPADQK8ykp89

## Chef, There's a Fly in the Soup: What Do We Do?

**Sides/Fruits/Vegetables**

**Ice Breaker Title: Chef, There's a Fly in the Soup: What Do We Do?**

Ethical puzzles and moral dilemmas as a tool to promote reflection, critical analysis, and discussion

## Activity Description

"Chef, there's a fly in the soup" activities offer opportunities for students to explore a topic from a variety of ethical perspectives. The activity is well-suited for promoting debate and reflection, as well as a focused analysis on ethical issues associated with core course topics. The activity presents instructional opportunities for students to review prior concepts and reinforce key aspects and ethical components of core course topics.

This activity works well with a range of course topics and concepts. One of the goals (or possibilities) of this exercise is the ability to highlight variations in perception and experience.

This activity is designed to support and sustain increased student comfort and confidence when reviewing challenging course topics, processes, and/or problems that pose ethical dilemmas. This activity works well as an introductory warm-up for a substantive lesson that involves core concepts and previously explored concepts. The activity also serves as a form of formative assessment.

## Recipe

Step 1: Define and explain "Chef, There's a Fly in the Soup" activities.

Step 2: Introduce the activity. Clarify content focus and type of resource to be used for the activity.

Step 3: Share a link or copy of the concept, topic, activity, and/or procedure to be used for purposes of the activity.

Step 4: Share student response options.

- Students might share responses privately in writing, anonymously (polling software such as Poll Everywhere, Padlet, and Google Jamboard work well), or out loud.

Step 5: Present an ethical or moral dilemma associated with course content.

Prompt students to reflect and then free-write an initial response.

Sample questions follow:

- How would you describe the ethical dilemma presented in the scenario?
- What would you do?
- What are the possible actions?
- To whom might you go with questions and/or to discuss?
- How likely is such a scenario?

Step 6: Provide active work time for students to reflect and document responses (one to five minutes).

- Offer support as needed.
- Share directional reminders about the activity, as applicable.
- Vary time based on the complexity and number of ethical dilemmas and/or shared prompts.

Step 7: Responses can be shared anonymously or as a whole class. Alternatively, students can keep responses private.

Step 8: Once responses are collected and/or shared, discuss.

## The Secret Sauce (Why It Works)

This content-aligned and **focused** activity breaks down complex material into **discrete chunks and concepts** that reduce **cognitive load** on students. Students draw on and **actively recall** prior learning and knowledge related to a specific concept. The activity promotes hands-on, **active learning** that requires students to do something (reflect on a posed ethical dilemma and document reactions) in connection with a shared scenario. Goals include increased **student comfort** with a particular concept as well as increased **confidence** analyzing and responding to ethical dilemmas and conflicts of interest (as well as articulating associated reasoning).

The activity promotes **critical thinking**, problem solving, and application of course concepts. Students practice **transferable skills** such as argument construction, communication, ethical analysis, public speaking (as applicable), and conflict resolution. This activity works well for any concept where a teacher wants to help students explore multiple sides, perspectives, and use cases.

The activity offers opportunities for **reflection** (both individual and group). The activity also offers opportunities for **formative assessment**.

## Ingredients

- ☐ An ethical or moral dilemma and hypothetical scenario aligned with a prior course lesson or learning objective
- ☐ Clock/Timer (as applicable)

## Activity Prep

An ethical or moral dilemma and hypothetical scenario aligned with a prior course lesson or learning objective.

Optional: Students generate ethical dilemmas and hypothetical scenarios for this activity.

## Activity Adaptations/Toppings

Depending on the instructional goals and objectives, this activity can be used and adapted in a variety of ways.

- Whole-class discussion.
- Whole-class activity where hypothetical scenarios involving possible ethical dilemmas associated with course concepts are generated and documented.
- Introduce and/or extend the activity with discussion questions related to the lesson topic and which promote active recall of associated concepts.
- Introduce the activity using a current event/news article related to the lesson topic and which presents an ethical dilemma.

## Activity Extensions

- Provide opportunities for students to publicly share original ethical dilemmas and associated hypothetical scenarios for future review. Students might post dilemmas and scenarios to a class bulletin board or gallery. A Padlet board, class Google Site, or Pinterest board are free options that work well.
- Student hypotheticals might be consolidated into an open educational resource and published online.

### Business-Based Example (Workplace Dilemmas)

- "What Would You Do?" See: https://www.corporatecomplianceinsights.com/what-would-you-do/
- "Common Ethical Workplace Dilemmas". See: https://smallbusiness.chron.com/common-ethical-workplace-dilemmas-748.html

## Portion Type and Size

Single (independent work), pairs, small group, or whole class

Time: Variable

- As few as five minutes.
- No maximum length.
- Time will vary depending on the adopted approach to implementation.

Online and/or face to face

## Web Resources

- Moral Dilemma Questions. See: https://icebreakerideas.com/moral-dilemma-questions/
- The Daily Dilemma. See: https://www.goodcharacter.com/the-daily-dilemma/
- Benefits of Teaching Ethical Dilemmas. See: https://www.edutopia.org/article/benefits-teaching-ethical-dilemmas
- Ethical Dilemmas to Pose to Students. See: https://classroom.synonym.com/ethical-dilemmas-pose-students-8066466.html
- How to Talk About Ethical Dilemmas in the Classroom. See: https://greatergood.berkeley.edu/article/item/how_to_talk_about_ethical_issues_in_the_classroom

## I Tried This and This Is What I Learned

| DATE USED/LESSON TOPIC | REFLECTIONS/WHAT I MIGHT DO DIFFERENTLY NEXT TIME |
|---|---|
| | |
| | |
| | |

Have a "Chef, There's a Fly in the Soup" activity adaptation to share?

Submit your tweaks and experiences here:

Survey Link: https://forms.gle/G7JS4RPADQK8ykp89

# Let's Dissect That Rubric

**Sides/Fruits/Vegetables**

**Ice Breaker Title: Let's Dissect That Rubric**

Focused rubric analysis to promote student success and shared understanding of assignment expectations

## Activity Description

"Let's Dissect that Rubric" exercises offer opportunities for students to think carefully, and in a focused way, about assignment requirements and expectations. Students review and discuss individual rubric elements and components so as to ensure a shared understanding on the part of all learners and the course instructor.

The activity is well suited for promoting critical analysis of assignment rubric phrases. The activity also presents instructional opportunities for students to review course concepts as described in rubric elements and simultaneously reinforce assignment expectations.

This activity works well with a range of course assignments. Any assignment typically scored using a pre-developed and shared rubric works well for this activity.

This activity is designed to support and sustain increased student comfort and confidence when completing course assignments. This activity works well as a review activity before an assignment is due for submission.

## Recipe

Step 1: Define and explain "Let's Dissect that Rubric" activities.

Step 2: Introduce the activity. Clarify assignment focus and type of rubric to be used for the activity.

Step 3: Create pairs and/or small groups (if applicable).

Step 4: Share a link or copy of the rubric to be used for purposes of the activity.

Step 5: Identify specific phrases in the rubric to raise for discussion. Pose questions related to individual rubric phrases. Share student response options.

- Students might share responses privately in writing, anonymously (polling software such as Poll Everywhere, Padlet, and Google Jamboard work well), or out loud.
- Students might also journal and/or discuss in small groups.

Step 6: Provide independent time for students to reflect on presented questions. Questions might be shared as a group or one by one.

Step 7: Provide active work time for students to deconstruct identified rubric phrase and reflect on the meaning of component parts.

- Vary time (based on phrase length, complexity of the language, student familiarity with topic, etc.).
- Offer support as needed.
- Share directional reminders about the activity, as applicable.

Step 8: Facilitate a follow-up discussion (either independently, in pairs, small groups, or whole class).

Step 9: Open discussion and reflection on the exercise (out loud or independent journaling)

Sample prompts:

- How has this activity changed the way you feel about the assignment?
- How has this activity changed the way you feel about your understanding of assignment expectations?
- How has this activity impacted your confidence regarding your ability to successfully complete the assignment?

## The Secret Sauce (Why It Works)

This content-aligned and **focused** activity breaks down complex material (assignment rubrics) into **discrete chunks and concepts** that reduce **cognitive load** on students. The activity promotes hands-on, **active learning** that requires students to do something (identify and describe components of a shared rubric criteria). Goals include increased **student comfort** with a particular concept as well as increased **confidence** analyzing course-related concepts and topics.

The activity offers opportunities for **reflection** (both individual and group). The activity also offers opportunities for **formative assessment**.

## Ingredients

- ☐ An assignment rubric (the activity works best when a shared rubric is associated with an upcoming assignment or one almost due for submission)
- ☐ Clock/Timer (as applicable)

## Activity Prep

An assignment rubric (the activity works best when a shared rubric is associated with an upcoming assignment or one almost due for submission).

Optional: Students select assignment rubrics to be used for this activity.

## Activity Adaptations/Toppings

Depending on the instructional goals and objectives, this activity can be used and adapted in a variety of ways. A few examples follow:

- Introduce the activity with an open-ended discussion question/reflection prompt that revisits the larger course topic most closely aligned with the rubric.
- Introduce and/or extend the activity with recall-based discussion questions related to the assignment topic.
- Students draft original questions relating to rubric language.
- Students create scavenger hunt clues based on rubric language to be swapped and then solved.

## Activity Extensions

- Provide opportunities for students to publicly share definitions for commonly used rubric phrases that might be beneficial when completing assignments. Students might post definitions associated with a specific rubric or rubric element to a class bulletin board or gallery. A Padlet board, class Google Site, or Pinterest board are free options that work well.
- Provide opportunities for students to curate a list of resources that might be beneficial when completing assignments aligned with a shared rubric. Students might post resources associated with a specific rubric (element or entire rubric) to a class bulletin board or gallery. A Padlet board, class Google Site, or Pinterest board are free options that work well.

### Sample Rubric, General Example

A criteria element on a linked rubric distinguishes between "Weak," "Satisfactory," and "Strong."

- "Grading Rubric: Sample Scales". See: https://www.brown.edu/sheridan/teaching-learning-resources/teaching-resources/course-design/classroom-assessment/grading-criteria/rubrics-scales
- Discussion Prompt: What is the difference between each criteria level? Can anyone share examples of a response that might fall in ___ category?

A criteria element on a linked rubric distinguishes between "Poor," "Minimal," "Sufficient," "Above Average," and "Excellent."

- "Grading Rubric: Sample Scales". See: https://www.brown.edu/sheridan/teaching-learning-resources/teaching-resources/course-design/classroom-assessment/grading-criteria/rubrics-scales
- Prompt for discussion: What is the difference between each criteria level? Can anyone share examples of a response that might fall in ___ category?

## Portion Type and Size

Single (independent work), pairs, small group, or whole class

Time: Variable

- As few as five minutes.
- No maximum length.
- Time will vary depending on the adopted approach to implementation.

Online and/or face to face

## Web Resources

- Types of Rubrics. See: https://resources.depaul.edu/teaching-commons/teaching-guides/feedback-grading/rubrics/Pages/types-of-rubrics.aspx
- "Know Your Terms: Holistic, Analytic, and Single-Point Rubrics). See: https://www.cultofpedagogy.com/holistic-analytic-single-point-rubrics/
- Deciding Which Type of Rubric to Use. See: https://www.southwestern.edu/offices/writing/faculty-resources-for-writing-instruction/designing-rubrics/deciding-which-type-of-rubric-to-use/

Sample Rubrics

- Rubric Template: https://www.thoughtco.com/rubric-template-2081369
- Simple Rubric Examples: https://examples.yourdictionary.com/simple-rubric-examples-for-teachers.html
- Rubric Scales: https://www.brown.edu/sheridan/teaching-learning-resources/teaching-resources/course-design/classroom-assessment/grading-criteria/rubrics-scales
- Rubric Examples: https://uwf.edu/academic-affairs/departments/cutla/supporting-pages/examples-of-rubrics/

## I Tried This and This Is What I Learned

| DATE USED/LESSON TOPIC | REFLECTIONS/WHAT I MIGHT DO DIFFERENTLY NEXT TIME |
|---|---|
| | |
| | |
| | |

Have a "Let's Dissect That Rubric" activity adaptation to share?

Submit your tweaks and experiences here:

Survey Link: https://forms.gle/G7JS4RPADQK8ykp89

# Observing the Chef and the Guests

**Sides/Fruits/Vegetables**

**Ice Breaker Title: Observing the Chef and the Guests**

Reflection on shared experiences as a tool to improve communication and understanding

## Activity Description

"Observing the Chef and the Guests" activities are designed to promote heightened awareness of varying perspectives with a goal of deeper shared understanding and improved communication. In this activity, students reflect on presented questions and share responses based on personal experiences. Responses are then shared collectively, and a related discussion explores varying perspectives and responses to the same question.

Reflection activities offer opportunities for students to deepen self-awareness of individual growth and progress.

This activity works well as an introductory warm-up for a substantive lesson that involves group work and/or whole-class discussions.

## Recipe

Step 1: Define and explain the "Observing the Chef and the Guests" exercise.

Step 2: Introduce the activity. Clarify how question prompts and responses will be shared for the activity.

Step 3: Present questions either one-by-one or in digital quiz/paper format.

*Note*: Prompts might focus on a particular topic, a classroom exercise or session, an assignment, etc.

Step 4: Open discussion and reflection on the similarities and differences across shared responses.

Step 5: Reflection (out loud or independent journaling).

Sample prompts:

- How has this activity changed the way you feel about the reflection process?
- How has this activity changed the way you feel about communicating understanding/misunderstanding?

## The Secret Sauce (Why It Works)

This **reflection-based** activity promotes deeper understanding of varying perspectives and associated communication challenges and potential barriers. The activity promotes hands-on, **active learning** that requires students to do something (reflect and respond to questions involving a specific, course-related experience). Goals include increased student comfort with peers as well as increased **awareness** of varying interpretation and communication challenges (associated with both written and verbal communication). The activity offers many opportunities for **reflection** (both individual and group).

## Ingredients

- ☐ A collection of observational and/or experience-based questions. Questions should be answered with a quantitative response.
- ☐ Clock/Timer (as applicable)

## Activity Prep

A collection of observational and/or experience-based questions. All should be answerable with a numerical, quantitative response.

Optional: Students draft original questions.

## Activity Adaptations/Toppings

Depending on instructional goals and objectives, this activity can be used and adapted in a variety of ways. A few examples follow:

- Vary response collection procedures. Questions might be assigned in advance of class with answers collected via a Google Form.
- Students generate lists of questions to be used for this activity.
- Introduce the activity with a discussion question/reflection prompt that explores the value of observation in connection with a course topic.

## Activity Extensions

- Students share actionable suggestions and strategies to ensure shared understanding when communicating with others.
- Students brainstorm and generate a list of course-related terms and concepts that are subject to multiple meanings.

### Sample Questions

This exercise promotes reflection and a deeper understanding of how individuals often approach and evaluate similar experiences from very different perspectives. Perception can influence how we interact with others, how we communicate with others, and how we understand the needs and experiences of others. The exercise also provides opportunities to use analytical observation to identify needs.

The exercise also demonstrates how individuals can, and often do, use the same words in very different ways. Finally, the exercise highlights the importance of fact-finding and questioning to fully understand an issue, situation and/or experience.

Answer the following questions in writing.

1. "Traffic was awful yesterday. It took me so much longer than usual to get into town." How much extra time were you traveling?

   ____ minutes
2. "Because of the traffic, I was very late for my appointment." How late were you?

   ____ minutes
3. "When I finally arrived at the building, I realized it had only recently been constructed. I had to climb many steps to reach the proper floor." How many steps did you have to climb?

   ____ steps
4. "After reaching the proper office, I got in a long line to wait my turn at the counter." How many people were already in line?

   ____ people
5. "While I was waiting, I listened to an old podcast on my phone." In what year was the podcast likely recorded?

   ____ (year)
6. The speaker had just returned to the area after spending a long time overseas. How much time did the speaker spend overseas?

   _____ months/years
7. "I also replied to a few emails." How many is a few?

   ____
8. "The lady in front of me was older." How old was she?

   ____ years old

9. "She had several young children with her." How many children were with her?

   _____ number of children

10. "I wondered if I had anything in my bag that I could share with the children." What types of items might you look for in your bag?

    _____

11. "Finally, my turn arrived. I was forced to wait a very long time." How long did you have to wait?

    ______ minutes

12. "I submitted my payment. It was much more than I expected. The amount was very large. I had never paid so much for a textbook before." How much did you pay?

    ______

Students should provide a single number, word and/or short phrase in response to each of the 12 questions. Write down the first response that comes to mind. There are no right or wrong questions. Can submit responses via Google Forms.

A related discussion can follow.

Compile and anonymously present results from question responses.

Remind students that the exercise is intended as an opportunity to reflect and better understand how individuals often approach similar experiences from very different perspectives.

Compare/contrast how students interpreted the setting and the described situations.

Discuss how to improve observational skills and how individuals can use the power of observation to help them succeed.

## Portion Type and Size

Combination of single (independent work and reflection) and whole class (discussion).

Time: Variable

- As few as five minutes.
- No maximum length.
- Time will vary depending on the adopted approach to implementation.

Online and/or face to face

## Web Resources

- Chapter 5, Perceiving Others. https://opentextbc.ca/socialpsychology/part/perceiving-others/
- Entrepreneurship and Innovation Toolkit, Chapter 2 ("Opportunity Recognition and Design Thinking," pages 18–24). https://open.umn.edu/opentextbooks/textbooks/entrepreneurship-and-innovation-toolkit

## I Tried This and This Is What I Learned

| DATE USED/LESSON TOPIC | REFLECTIONS/WHAT I MIGHT DO DIFFERENTLY NEXT TIME |
|---|---|
| | |
| | |
| | |

Have an "Observing the Chef and the Guests" activity adaptation to share?

Submit your tweaks and experiences here:

Survey Link: https://forms.gle/G7JS4RPADQK8ykp89

# Let's Update That Recipe with a New Spice

**Sides/Fruits/Vegetables**

**Ice Breaker Title: Let's Update That Recipe with a New Spice**

Review of currency-related tools and resources to strengthen transferable skills

## Activity Description

In "Let's Update That Recipe with a New Spice" activities, students explore resources that support extended learning on a course topic in real-world contexts. In this activity, students are either introduced to or identify a new resource to which they might follow and/or subscribe in order to remain informed on trends and developments in the associated discipline or learning context.

In this activity, students are encouraged to think of course concepts as knowledge with real-world applications and relevance. Identifying and reviewing resources that offer opportunities to remain informed of new developments in the field present opportunities to both deepen concept mastery and extend knowledge. This activity is designed to support and sustain increased student comfort and confidence when interacting with course concepts in real-world contexts.

## Recipe

Step 1: Define and explain "Let's Update That Recipe with a New Spice" activities.

Step 2: Introduce the activity. Explain how course concepts can be thought of as ingredients for continued developments in a field(s) aligned with the course and course topics. Clarify content focus and type of resource to be used for the activity.

Step 3: Create groups (if applicable).

Step 4: Share a link or copy of a resource students might subscribe to and/or bookmark for future reference.

Step 5: Provide time for students to review the resource. Students might identify one or more aspects for review and discussion.

- Offer support as needed.

- Share directional reminders about the activity, as applicable.

Step 6: Open discussion and reflection on the exercise (out loud or independent journaling)

Sample prompts:

- How has this activity changed the way you feel about your understanding of the associated course concepts?
- How has this activity changed the way you feel about your ability to remain informed on developments in the content area?

## The Secret Sauce (Why It Works)

This **forward-focused** activity presents course material as dynamic and relevant. Students identify and explore opportunities to apply and solidify existing knowledge in real-world applications. The activity promotes hands-on, **active learning** that requires students to interact with a timely resource or collection of resources. Goals include increased student **comfort** with a particular course concept as well as increased **confidence** applying existing knowledge in real-world situations and changing contexts. The activity offers opportunities for **reflection** (both individual and group).

## Ingredients

- ☐ A resource or collection of resources that illustrate ways to remain informed about new developments and new learning in a particular discipline or area of study
- ☐ Clock/Timer (as applicable)

## Activity Prep

A resource or collection of resources that illustrate ways to remain informed about new developments and new learning in a particular discipline or area of study.

Optional: Students conduct original research and identify resources for ongoing updates in a particular context.

## Activity Adaptations/Toppings

Depending on the instructional goals and objectives, this activity can be used and adapted in a variety of ways.

- Conduct the activity using a passage (several paragraphs, a page of text) from a current reading, assigned book, or related news article. Prompt students to reflect and consider how they might learn more about the related topic going forward.
- Introduce the activity with a discussion question/reflection prompt that explores a variety of ways to explore trends and new research on a topic of interest. Discussions might explore blogs, list-serves, podcasts, YouTube channel subscriptions, research databases, etc.

## Activity Extensions

- Provide opportunities for students to review extension resources and discuss advantages and disadvantages of various options. Students might be prompted to consider issues of credibility, currency, objectivity, authority, etc. The discussion can be used as an instructional opportunity to support digital literacy, resource review, and critical analysis.

- If student research leads to sources for ongoing updates and topic news, encourage students to share resources in a class library (Google Docs, Google Sites, Padlet board). Source identification can be used as research reinforcement and as library building.

### Science Examples

Subscribe for alerts for new studies

- Google Scholar. See: https://scholar.google.com/
- Stork. See: https://www.storkapp.me/

### Entrepreneurship/Business Examples

- Small Business Blogs. See: https://www.zoomshift.com/blog/small-business-blogs/

### Political Science/Legal/Business-Based Examples (Case Law Updates)

- For students interested in receiving updates on case law, consider subscribing to Justia opinion summaries. See: https://law.justia.com/subscribe.
- Students might listen to oral arguments for cases argued before the Supreme Court. Summaries of the Supreme Court's most recent decisions. See: https://www.law.cornell.edu/supremecourt/text/home.

## Portion Type and Size

Single (independent work), pairs, small groups, or whole class

Time: Variable

- As few as two minutes.
- No maximum length.
- Initial use will be most time intensive.
- Time will vary depending on the adopted approach to implementation.

## Web Resource

- The Best Research Alert Services: How to Stay on Top of Your Field. See: https://ideas.newsrx.com/blog/the-best-research-alert-services-how-to-stay-on-top-of-your-field

## I Tried This and This Is What I Learned

| DATE USED/LESSON TOPIC | REFLECTIONS/WHAT I MIGHT DO DIFFERENTLY NEXT TIME |
|---|---|
| | |
| | |
| | |

Have a "Let's Update That Recipe with a New Spice" activity adaptation to share?

Submit your tweaks and experiences here:

Survey Link: https://forms.gle/G7JS4RPADQK8ykp89

## In the Kitchen: I Am, I Need, I Wish, I Offer

**Sides/Fruits/Vegetables**

**Ice Breaker Title: In the Kitchen: I Am, I Need, I Wish, I Offer**

Reflection as a means of building community and confidence

## Activity Description

In "In the Kitchen: I Am, I Need, I Wish, I Offer" activities, students reflect and post (anonymously) words or phrases that capture their current feelings from a variety of perspectives. This activity is designed to promote trust in a learning community and a deeper appreciation of the value of each member of such learning community.

The activity involves both generation and reflection as strategies to strengthen student comfort and connection.

## Recipe

Step 1: Define and explain "I Am, I Need, I Wish, I Offer" activities.

Step 2: Introduce the activity. Explain how the "I Am, I Need, I Wish, I Offer" activity works.

Step 3: Present questions that will be used for purposes of the activity.

Students might select three to respond to.

Students can respond in one word, phrases, etc.

Question variations:

I am ___

I need ___

I offer ____

I bring ___

I give ____

I wish ___

I can be ___

I know ___

Students answer anonymously (either on index cards or via anonymous digital bulletin boards).

Collect responses at start of class or course and again at the end. Review for reflection on growth and transformation.

Step 4: Provide active work time for students to respond (recommended minimum one minute).

- Offer support as needed.
- Share directional reminders about the activity, as applicable.

Step 5: Open discussion and reflection on the exercise (out loud or independent journaling). Optional sharing.

## The Secret Sauce (Why It Works)

This **reflection-based** activity promotes self-reflection. The activity promotes hands-on, **active learning** that requires students to do something (complete a phrase or sentence associated with reflection-based question stems). Goals include increased **trust** on the part of a learning community. The activity also offers opportunities for **formative assessment**.

## Ingredients

- ☐ A collection of question stems/prompts
- ☐ Clock/Timer (as applicable)

## Activity Prep

A collection of question stems/prompts.

Optional: Students generate original question stems.

## Activity Adaptations/Toppings

This activity can be used and adapted in a variety of ways.

- Vary number of words to be used when completing the prompt.
- Vary number of prompts for response.
- Vary time permitted to work on prompt completion.
- Post shared responses on a class Padlet, Instagram, etc. (anonymously, with student approval).

### English Example (Literature)

Students might complete prompts based on a character in a recently read/studied novel or short story.

### History Example (World Leaders)

Students might complete prompts based on a specified world leader (e.g., U.S. president, leader of a studied country).

## Portion Type and Size

Single (independent work), pairs, small group, or whole class

Time: Variable

- As few as one minute.
- No maximum length.
- Time will vary depending on the adopted approach to implementation.

Online and/or face to face

## I Tried This and This Is What I Learned

| DATE USED/LESSON TOPIC | REFLECTIONS/WHAT I MIGHT DO DIFFERENTLY NEXT TIME |
|---|---|
| | |
| | |
| | |

Have an "I Am, I Need, I Wish, I Offer" activity adaptation to share?

Submit your tweaks and experiences here:

Survey Link: https://forms.gle/G7JS4RPADQK8ykp89

## Recipe Formatting Checks

**Sides/Fruits/Vegetables**

**Ice Breaker Title: Recipe Formatting Checks**

Formatting quick-checks and quiz activities to reinforce existing knowledge and strengthen confidence associated with formatting conventions

## Activity Description

In "Recipe Formatting Checks" activities, students work through a collection of citation and formatting quizzes (APA, MLA, or another applicable citation convention). Students practice active recall and deepen understanding of formatting conventions and expectations through a related question-and-answer process.

In this activity, students are encouraged to think of formatting expectations as fundamental ingredients in a larger course recipe. Students are also reminded of the importance of a strong foundation (recipe and ingredients) for a final product or outcome. By reviewing statements associated with formatting guidelines and expectations, students can solidify existing knowledge and strengthen long-term memory.

Formatting activities provide opportunities for students to reinforce prior learning. The activity also creates opportunities to discuss and explore real-world applications and contexts for formatting conventions.

This activity is designed to support and sustain increased student comfort and confidence when applying formatting conventions.

This activity works well as an introductory warm-up for a substantive lesson or assignment overview that requires students to incorporate and apply formatting conventions.

## Recipe

Step 1: Define and explain "Recipe Formatting Checks" activities.

Step 2: Introduce the activity. Explain how formatting conventions and related concepts can be thought of as ingredients for clear and impactful written communications. Reinforce the importance of proper formatting in written work. Clarify formatting conventions to be used for the activity.

Step 3: Create groups (if applicable).

Step 4: Share a link or copy of a collection of formatting quick checks (if applicable)/Provide time for students to research and create original lists and collections of formatting quick check activities and questions (if applicable).

Step 5: Provide instructions (these will vary based on the selected resource). See sample resources for instructions.

Step 6: Provide active work time for students to work through exercises. Answers can be shared anonymously, in pairs, small groups, or whole-class scenarios. Questions might be reviewed and addressed one by one, or as a collection.

- Offer support as needed.
- Share directional reminders about the activity, as applicable.

Step 7: Open discussion and reflection on the exercise (out loud or independent journaling).

Sample prompts:

- How has this activity changed the way you feel about formatting conventions?

## The Secret Sauce (Why It Works)

This **targeted** activity breaks down complex material into manageable chunks that reduce **cognitive load** on students. Students draw on and actively **recall** prior learning and knowledge associated with formatting conventions. The activity promotes hands-on, **active learning** that requires students to do something (interact with a collection of formatting questions and quick checks). Goals include increased student **comfort** with formatting conventions as well as increased **confidence** applying formatting conventions. The activity offers opportunities for **reflection** (both individual and group). The activity also offers opportunities for **formative assessment**.

## Ingredients

- ☐ A collection or list of formatting questions and quick checks related to course and/or discipline specific formatting conventions
- ☐ Clock/Timer (as applicable)

## Activity Prep

A collection or list of formatting questions and quick checks related to course and/or discipline specific formatting conventions

Optional: Students draft original formatting quick-check questions and activities for this activity.

## Activity Adaptations/Toppings

Depending on the instructional goals and objectives, this activity can be used and adapted in a variety of ways. A few examples follow:

- Introduce the activity with a discussion question/reflection prompt that explores reasons for adopting formatting conventions and formatting standards.
- Vary time permitted to work on formatting quick-check activities.
- Students create a collection of formatting quick-check questions by topic. Swap collections across small groups. Complete and discuss.

## Activity Extensions

- Provide opportunities for students to share original formatting quick-check questions for ongoing review and study by peers. A Padlet board, class Google Site, or Pinterest board are free options that work well.

- Create formatting quick-check digital flashcards using spaced repetition note-taking software. See RemNote: https://www.remnote.com/

### Formatting Checks (APA Style Examples)

- Citing Case Law in APA Format. Sample Resource. See: https://www.remnote.com/a/citing-case-law-in-apa-format/pfgLkWsARG7z3hZoG

APA Style Quizzes

- APA Quizzes. See: https://www.niu.edu/writingtutorial/style/quizzes/APA.htm
- APA Quick Guide. See: https://guides.libraries.psu.edu/apaquickguide/quiz
- APA Style Quizzes. See: https://www.proprofs.com/quiz-school/topic/apa-style
- Citation Games. See: https://depts.washington.edu/trio/quest/citation/apa_mla_citation_game/
- General APA Exercises. See: https://libguides.royalroads.ca/apa7/generalexercises
- Citations Practice. See: https://libguides.royalroads.ca/apa7/citationspracticeexercise
- Reference Practice. See: https://libguides.royalroads.ca/apa7/referencespracticeexercises
- General Paper Formatting Practice. See: https://libguides.royalroads.ca/apa7/formattingexercises
- APA Knowledge Check Activities. See: http://owl.excelsior.edu/research-and-citations/documenting/apa-style/apa-activity/

### Citation Games (APA and MLA)

- Citation Game. See: http://www.citationgame.org/
- Citation Game. See: https://depts.washington.edu/trio/quest/citation/apa_mla_citation_game/
- Citation Game. See: http://depts.washington.edu/trio/quest/citation/apa_mla_citation_game/mla_book.htm
- Grammar Quizzes. See: https://www.grammar-quizzes.com/wrcite1_book.html
- "The Cite is Right Quiz". See: https://library.camden.rutgers.edu/EducationalModule/Plagiarism/citeisright.html

### Plagiarism Resources

- Plagiarism Game. See: https://www.lycoming.edu/library/plagiarism-game/
- How Well Do You Know Plagiarism Quiz. See: https://libguides.mssu.edu/c.php?g=185283&p=1223312
- Paraphrasing Exercise. See: https://gsi.berkeley.edu/gsi-guide-contents/academic-misconduct-intro/plagiarism/paraphrase-exercise/

## Portion Type and Size

Single (independent work), pairs, small group, or whole class

Time: Variable

- As few as one minute.
- No maximum length.
- Time will vary depending on the adopted approach to implementation.

Online and/or face to face

## Web Resources

- The Efficacy of a Classroom Game for Teaching APA Style Citation
  Daniel A. Clark, Walter Murphy. See:
  https://journals.sagepub.com/doi/abs/10.1177/0098628320977263?journalCode=topa
- An Evaluation of Production Versus Error-Recognition Techniques for Teaching APA-Style Citations and References
  Guy A. Boysen (2019). See: https://journals.sagepub.com/doi/10.1177/0098628319872609?icid=int.sj-abstract.similar-articles.2
- Van Note Chism, N., & Weerakoon, S. (2012). APA, Meet Google: Graduate students' approaches to learning citation style. *Journal of the Scholarship of Teaching and Learning, 12*(2), 27–38. See: https://scholarworks.iu.edu/journals/index.php/josotl/article/view/2020
- The Plagiarism Spectrum. See: https://www.turnitin.com/static/plagiarism-spectrum/

## I Tried This and This Is What I Learned

| DATE USED/LESSON TOPIC | REFLECTIONS/WHAT I MIGHT DO DIFFERENTLY NEXT TIME |
|---|---|
| | |
| | |
| | |

Have a "Recipe Formatting Checks" activity adaptation to share?

Submit your tweaks and experiences here:

Survey Link: https://forms.gle/G7JS4RPADQK8ykp89

# Recipe Reviews: 5 Stars! True for You?

**Sides/Fruits/Vegetables**

**Ice Breaker Title: Recipe Reviews: Five Stars! True for You?**

Quotations to promote reflection and application of course concepts

## Activity Description

"Recipe Reviews: Five Stars! True for You?" is a content-related quotation review and reflection activity designed to promote critical thinking and analysis.

Quotations describe words or phrases that are taken directly from another source and shared in either written or oral form. Using quotations as prompts for classroom discussions (small or whole group) provides opportunities for deep learning, critical thinking, connected thought, and reflection. Shared quotes can be closely or loosely aligned with a specific course topic or content area. Quotes might highlight the work and thinking of an influential researcher or scholar. Quotes might also highlight controversial ideas, opposing perspectives, or novel ways of thinking about and/or describing a topic.

Quotations offer opportunities for students to reimagine the application of course concepts in real-world applications. In this activity, students reflect on presented quotations and then either journal independently or discuss in small groups or whole-class settings.

This activity is designed to support and sustain student development of critical thinking skills and awareness of varying perspectives. The activity is also designed to promote both comfort and confidence in connection with course content and career-relevant transferable skills, including communication and awareness of varying perspectives.

## Recipe

Step 1: Define and explain "Recipe Reviews: Five Stars! True for You?" activities.

Step 2: Introduce the activity. Clarify content focus and type of quotation to be used.

Step 3: Create groups (if applicable).

Step 4: Share a link or copy of a selected quotation.

Step 5: Students review quotation(s) independently, in small groups, or as a whole class.

Sample prompts:

- Do you agree with the quotation? Why? Explain.
- Rate your degree of alignment with the quotation. Scale 1–5 stars.
- Propose a counter-position to the perspective in the quotation.
- How might the perspective reflected in the quotation relate to [an identified course-related career]?

Step 6: Provide active work time for students to reflect on shared quotation(s).

Step 7: Provide reflection-based prompts for students to complete in independent journaling or discussion (e.g., small group, whole class) (optional, as desired).

- Offer support as needed.
- Share directional reminders about the activity, as applicable.

Step 8: Open discussion and reflection on the exercise (out loud or independent journaling).

Sample prompts:

- How has the shared quotation changed your perspective on the related topic?
- How has our discussion impacted the way you feel about the related topic?

## The Secret Sauce (Why It Works)

This **reflection-based** activity promotes critical thinking and reflection. Students practice **active listening** and communication skills as a part of class discussions. The activity promotes hands-on, **active learning** that requires students to do something (listen, reflect, discuss) with a variety of perspectives. The activity offers opportunities for **reflection** (both individual and group). The activity also offers opportunities for **formative assessment**.

## Ingredients

- ☐ A quotation (or series of quotations) related to lesson objectives and course concepts
- ☐ Clock/Timer (as applicable)

## Activity Prep

A quotation (or series of quotations) related to lesson objectives and course concepts.

Optional: Students conduct research and identify a quotation to use for this activity.

## Activity Adaptations/Toppings

Depending on the instructional goals and objectives, this activity can be used and adapted in a variety of ways. A few examples follow:

- This activity can be adapted from quotes that focus on substantive course-related content to quotes that focus on soft skills that are transferable to a wide range of career applications.
- Introduce the activity with a reflection prompt that asks students to draft an original statement that captures their own feelings on a course topic. Then, present a quotation that shares a perspective on the same topic. Compare, contrast, and discuss.
- Introduce the activity with a discussion question/reflection prompt that explores a topic, theme, term, or concept that is the focus of the selected quotation.

## Activity Extensions

- Provide opportunities for students to research and locate quotations that explore a specific course topic or career-relevant soft skill. Students might post quotations and/or reactions to a class bulletin board or gallery. A Padlet board, class Google Site, or Pinterest board are options that work well.
- Students conduct research and locate quotations on an assigned course topic or soft skill.

### Sample Quotations/Collections

Quotations to Encourage Questions. See: https://www.remnote.com/a/quotations-to-encourage-questions/kuz7SKXPes6MA3692

Quotations that Inspire a Growth Mindset. See: https://www.remnote.com/a/quotations-that-inspire-a-growth-mindset/Hn44x9AxAumM5qPdX

Quotations to Inspire. See: https://www.remnote.com/a/quotations-to-inspire/6TeocZ7wEkBSbPYWW

Quotations on Feedback. See: https://www.remnote.com/a/quotations-on-feedback/fNQzAkPRu7ahwbrHK

Content Agnostic Quotation Collection. See: https://www.remnote.com/a/quotations/61342fe8fcf00800355edf65

Entrepreneurship Quotes. See: https://www.remnote.com/a/entrepreneurship-quotes/613430d0fcf00800355edfed

Quotations on Writing. See: https://www.remnote.com/a/writing-quotes/61343178fcf00800355ee012

Quotations on Small Business Operations. See: https://www.remnote.com/a/small-business-operation-quotes/613432c7fcf00800355ee01f

Quotations on Professional Selling and Sales. See: https://www.remnote.com/a/professional-selling-and-sales-quotations/6134334dfcf00800355ee036

## Portion Type and Size

Single (independent work), pairs, small group, or whole class

Time: Variable

- As few as two to three minutes.
- No maximum length.
- Time will vary depending on the adopted approach to implementation.

Online and/or face to face

## Web Resource

The Feedback Bank. See: https://www.thefeedbackbank.com/ (Click on Feedback Quotations)

## I Tried This and This Is What I Learned

| DATE USED/LESSON TOPIC | REFLECTIONS/WHAT I MIGHT DO DIFFERENTLY NEXT TIME |
|---|---|
| | |
| | |
| | |

Have a "Recipe Reviews: Five Stars! True for You?" activity adaptation to share?

Submit your tweaks and experiences here:

Survey Link: https://forms.gle/G7JS4RPADQK8ykp89

# So Many Ingredients/Spices, So Many Terms

**Sides/Fruits/Vegetables**

**Ice Breaker Title: So Many Ingredients/Spices, So Many Terms (Vocabulary Reflection and Application)**

Vocabulary review and scenario construction as a tool to practice recall, promote long-term learning, and make connections to real-world applications

## Activity Description

In "So Many Ingredients/Spices, So Many Terms" activities, students use course vocabulary to write original scenarios. Students practice active recall and deepen understanding of course terms through the process of drafting original hypothetical scenarios.

Students are encouraged to think of course vocabulary as core ingredients and complementary spices that can make discipline-specific language richer, more meaningful, and more persuasive. Vocabulary review and active drafting activities provide opportunities for students to reinforce prior learning of key terms. Drafting original scenarios also presents the opportunity to apply creative thinking skills and imagine (or re-imagine) the applications of key terms to real-world scenarios and situations.

Vocabulary review and drafting exercises present opportunities for students to review complicated and/or ambiguous terms in a stress-free environment. This activity is designed to support and sustain increased student comfort and confidence when interacting with core vocabulary terms.

The activity works well with any collection of course vocabulary terms. Terms that are fundamental to a discipline and/or course unit and/or sometimes intimidating for students are especially well-suited to this activity.

This activity works well as an introductory warm-up for a substantive lesson that relies on and/or is aligned with prior vocabulary terms and concepts.

## Recipe

Step 1: Define and explain "So Many Ingredients/Spices, So Many Terms" activities.

Step 2: Introduce the activity. Explain how course vocabulary can be thought of as both ingredients and spices for a rich and meaningful course-related writing or communication. Clarify content focus and type of resource to be used for the activity.

Step 3: Create groups (if applicable).

Step 4: Share a link or copy of key terms (if applicable)/Provide time for students to research and create original lists of course-related terms (if applicable).

- Recommended: Share a minimum of five to 10 terms.

Step 5: Provide instructions. Sample prompt follows:

- Review the provided list of vocabulary terms. Draft a hypothetical scenario using a minimum of (enter some number) terms. Terms should be drawn from the provided terms lists.
- Your scenario should provide a hypothetical interaction you might experience in your work as a (enter a career related to course content here). Be creative. There is no one right or wrong approach to this exercise. Use the scenario as an opportunity to practice using your newly expanded vocabulary and to demonstrate your understanding of the selected terms.
- Identify (bold, underline, or highlight) your selected terms.
- Then, reflect on the process of reviewing and then applying the noted vocabulary.
- How might weekly review terms and flashcards impact your long-term learning?

Step 6: Provide active work time for students to draft original scenarios/hypotheticals using identified course terms (recommended minimum five to ten minutes).

- Offer support as needed.
- Share directional reminders about the activity, as applicable.

Step 7: Open discussion and reflection on the exercise (out loud or independent journaling).

Sample prompts:

- How has this activity changed your understanding of the key terms?

- How has this activity changed your understanding of the related topic?

Step 8: Share original writing (either out loud or on digital bulletin boards) (if applicable). Provide time for students to read and reflect on peer work. Provide opportunities for discussion, workshopping, and peer feedback (as applicable).

## The Secret Sauce (Why It Works)

This **application-based** activity breaks down complex material into manageable chunks that reduce **cognitive load** on students. Students apply prior knowledge and make connections between course content and real-world applications. The activity promotes hands-on, **active learning** that requires students to interact with a collection of key terms and concepts. Goals include increased student **comfort** with a collection of course concepts as well as increased **confidence** with both writing and course material. The activity offers opportunities for **reflection** for both individuals and groups. The activity also offers opportunities for **formative assessment**.

## Ingredients

- ☐ A collection or list of vocabulary terms that are related to a current or prior class learning objective or lesson
- ☐ Clock/Timer (as applicable)

## Activity Prep

A collection or list of vocabulary terms that are related to a current or prior class learning objective or lesson.

Optional: Students prepare lists of key terms for this activity.

## Activity Adaptations/Toppings

Depending on the instructional goals and objectives, this activity can be used and adapted in a variety of ways.

- Introduce the activity with a discussion question/reflection prompt that explores course concepts and objectives that are aligned with the key terms.
- Introduce the activity with a discussion question/reflection prompt that explores different types of writing (e.g., expository versus narrative). Provide options for students as they plan their associated written work.
- Introduce the activity with a discussion question related to the meaning of collected terms in ways that promote active recall.
- Vary time permitted to work on scenario construction.

## Activity Extensions

- Provide opportunities for students to publicly share their writing. Students might post scenarios to a class bulletin board or gallery. A Padlet board, class Google Site, or Pinterest board are free options that work well.
- Students might swap scenarios and conduct peer reviews with feedback. Scenarios can be used as a base for a class blog or journal with writings designed to teach and illustrate applications of a course topic.

### OpenStax Introduction to Psychology Text, Sample Terms

Chapter One Key Terms. See: https://remnote.com/a/openstax-cnxarticleintro-to-psychology-chapter-1-terms/LoYLr7EEyRSLZJa2N

Chapter Two Key Terms. See: https://remnote.com/a/openstax-cnx-psychological-research-chapter-2-terms/yjXzSrDuB79uKy3so

Chapter Three Key Terms. See: https://remnote.com/a/openstax-cnx-biopsychology-chapter-3-terms/gyfaJ2qmtj6QnXLA8

Chapter Four Key Terms. See: https://remnote.com/a/openstax-cnx-states-of-consciousness-chapter-4-terms/DwPqWraPhh5EyApk6

Chapter Five Key Terms. See: https://remnote.com/a/open-stax-cnx-chapter-5-sensation-and-perception-terms/Lm9DSXCudJrKGtapi

Chapter Six Key Terms. See: https://remnote.com/a/openstax-cnx-chapter-6-learning-key-terms/ANuykqFud3LbQedEi

Chapter Seven Key Terms. See: https://remnote.com/a/openstax-cnx-chapter-7-thinking-and-intelligence-key-terms/sdKXmfjweqF8oMcqY

Chapter Eight Key Terms. See: https://remnote.com/a/openstax-cnx-chapter-8-memory-key-terms/Ake66J4NGn9tM6YxP

Chapter Nine Key Terms. See: https://remnote.com/a/openstax-cnx-chapter-9-lifespan-development-key-terms/my9n8hQtmqbi3LWCN

Chapter Ten Key Terms. See: https://remnote.com/a/openstax-cnx-chapter-10-emotion-and-motivation-key-terms/KaGCtidNCndEM4ier

Chapter Eleven Key Terms. See: https://remnote.com/a/openstax-cnx-psychology-chapter-11-personality-key-terms-/QDKagBhbHHxSZpYQQ

Chapter Twelve Key Terms. See: https://remnote.com/a/openstax-cnx-chapter-12-social-psychology-key-terms/2vbFdsrcvKfvFkoDr

See: https://cnx.org/contents/Sr8Ev5Og@10.24:sbd9BH2f@10.24/Key-Terms



## Portion Type and Size

Single (independent work), pairs, small group, or whole class

Time: Variable

- As few as five minutes
- No maximum length
- Time will vary depending on the adopted approach to implementation.
- *Note*: The activity takes significantly less time when the instructor provides terms for use in drafting.

Online and/or face to face

## I Tried This and This Is What I Learned

| DATE USED/LESSON TOPIC | REFLECTIONS/WHAT I MIGHT DO DIFFERENTLY NEXT TIME |
|---|---|
| | |
| | |
| | |

Have a "So Many Ingredients/Spices, So Many Terms" activity adaptation to share?

Submit your tweaks and experiences here:

Survey Link: https://forms.gle/G7JS4RPADQK8ykp89

## Take Note! My Recipe Book

**Sides/Fruits/Vegetables**

**Ice Breaker Title: Take Note! My Recipe Book**

Note-taking review and reflection to promote evidenced-based study and note-taking strategies

## Activity Description

Effective note-taking is a critical component of every learner's personal study process. It is important for students to be aware of a wide range of note-taking tools, resources, and strategies so that each learner can identify and develop a process best suited for their own needs and situations.

In this activity, the instructor might facilitate a discussion on the value of note-taking. The instructor might also share resources that demonstrate a variety of note-taking tools, resources, and approaches. Students might reflect and share their own strategies and workflows, with emphasis on continuous improvement and refinement.

The activity works well at any time during a semester and with any type of lesson. Discussion of note-taking strategies and tools at the start of a term or unit is especially beneficial.

## Recipe

Step 1: Define and explain the goal of a "Take Note! My Recipe Book" activity and note-taking in general.

Step 2: Introduce a discussion prompt related to note-taking. Ask for student volunteers to share their note-taking process.

Step 3: Share an illustrative tool, resource, or strategy for note-taking.

Step 4: Provide time for students to review and reflect.

Step 5: Discuss.

Sample prompts:

- What are your thoughts on paper versus digital/computer note-taking?
- Have you used paper notes in the past?

- Have you used digital notes in the past?
- What are some advantages and disadvantages of each method?
- What are some strategies for personalizing and optimizing your own approach to note-taking?
- Do you think your preferred approach to note-taking might differ by context?
- Do you have any favorite note-taking apps to recommend? What do you most appreciate about the note-taking apps you use?
- What are some gaps in your current note-taking approach?
- What are some specific steps you might take to improve your current note-taking approach?
- Describe and define outlining.
- Describe and define mind maps.
- Describe and define Cornell note-taking.
- Compare and contrast outlining, mind maps, SQ3R, and Cornell note-taking.

Step 6: Provide active work time for students to test a new resource, tool, or strategy.

- Offer support as needed.
- Share directional reminders about the activity, as applicable.

Step 7: Open discussion and reflection on the exercise (out loud or independent journaling)

Sample prompts:

- How has this activity changed the way you feel about note-taking?
- What, if anything, might you change in connection with your current process (and why)?

## The Secret Sauce (Why It Works)

This **targeted** activity focuses specifically on a core skill that all learners rely on in some form or fashion. Note-taking is both a skill and a practice which benefits from review and refinement. The activity promotes **reflection** while simultaneously encouraging **critical analysis** of current practice and processes. Goals include increased student **comfort** with a particular type of note-taking (or related tool/strategy) as well as increased **confidence** associated with an adopted practice or process. The activity offers opportunities for **reflection** (both individual and group). The activity also offers opportunities for **formative assessment**.

## Ingredients

- ☐ A note-taking resource, strategy, or tool
- ☐ Clock/Timer (as applicable)

## Activity Prep

A note-taking resource, strategy, or tool.

Optional: Students conduct research and identify a note-taking resource, strategy, or tool for this activity.

## Activity Adaptations/Toppings

Depending on the instructional goals and objectives, this activity can be used and adapted in a variety of ways.

- Conduct a hands-on, note-taking activity using a passage (several paragraphs, a page of text) from a current reading, assigned book, or related news article.
- Introduce the activity with a discussion question/reflection prompt that explores the benefits of note-taking.
- Introduce the activity with a discussion question/reflection prompt that explores a variety of note-taking processes.
- Student volunteers share current note-taking processes for review and improvement.
- Conduct a group note-taking activity involving a current reading.
- Analyze a collection of notes for opportunities to improve the related process or product.

## Activity Extensions

- Provide opportunities for students to share their note-taking experiences (both positive and less than positive).
- In the online classroom, the instructor might first encourage students to take notes. As a nongraded assessment, the instructor might ask students to submit individual notes via email and/or classroom gradebooks. Alternatively, students might post their notes in an online forum for peer review, discussion, and analysis.

### Example Resources

- Note-Taking Templates. See: https://freeology.com/graphicorgs/note-taking-organizer/
- Business Course Example:
    - The linked document provides an example of how this formative assessment activity can be used in a module introducing the "value proposition" concept to students. See: https://docs.google.com/document/d/1NnCTozAqrK5RWSZU6dw2zOvKTtvdV0QbgH67olrOVUg/edit?usp=sharing

### Articles/Strategies

Improving Your Note Taking. See: https://www.educationcorner.com/note-taking.html

The Best Resources on Effective Note-Taking Strategies. See: https://larryferlazzo.edublogs.org/2015/06/23/the-best-resources-on-effective-note-taking-strategies-help-me-find-more/

Notetaking. See: https://students.dartmouth.edu/academic-skills/learning-resources/learning-strategies/notetaking

Note-taking: A Research Roundup. See: https://www.cultofpedagogy.com/note-taking/

Crash Course Study Skills #1, Taking Notes. See: https://youtu.be/E7CwqNHn_Ns

The Science of Note-Taking. See: https://nesslabs.com/note-taking

### Note-Taking Tools

RemNote. See: https://www.remnote.com/

"The Best Note-Taking Apps for College Students". See: https://www.digitaltrends.com/computing/best-note-taking-apps-for-college-students/

### Sample Note-Taking Strategies

Learning the SQ3R Method. See: https://library.sewanee.edu/note/document

SQ3R Guide. A step-by-step guide to using SQ3R from St. Louis University. See: https://www.slu.edu/Documents/student_development/student_success_center/retention_student_success/SQ3R.pdf

SQ3R Strategy Sheet. A one-page reference sheet from Oregon State librarians. See: http://success.oregonstate.edu/sites/success.oregonstate.edu/files/LearningCorner/Tools/sq3r.pdf

SQ3R Reference. A one-page summary of the SQ3R method. See: http://studywell.library.qut.edu.au/pdf_files/READINGNOTETAKING_TheSQ3RReadingMethod.pdf

Cornell Method. See: https://library.sewanee.edu/note/lecture

Cornell Notes. See: https://www.youtube.com/watch?v=4vOsVKWeyAA

## Portion Type and Size

Single (independent work), pairs, small group, or whole class

Time: Variable

- As few as one minute.
- No maximum length.
- Time will vary depending on the adopted approach to implementation.

Online and/or face to face

## I Tried This and This Is What I Learned

| DATE USED/LESSON TOPIC | REFLECTIONS/WHAT I MIGHT DO DIFFERENTLY NEXT TIME |
|---|---|
| | |
| | |
| | |

Have a "Take Note! My Recipe Book" activity adaptation to share?

Submit your tweaks and experiences here:

Survey Link: https://forms.gle/G7JS4RPADQK8ykp89

# That Recipe Worked Out Well

**Sides/Fruits/Vegetables**

**Ice Breaker Title: That Recipe Worked Out Well**

Reflection and focus on positive experiences as a tool to inspire and develop confidence

## Activity Description

This activity is based on the "Three Good Things" exercise. In this activity, students reflect on an experience and/or a period of time (e.g., course work, a course project, content-related experiences) and identify things that went well.

Reflection activities offer opportunities for students to deepen self-awareness of individual growth and progress. Reflection-based activities that focus on positive experiences also offer opportunities for students to more deeply appreciate their growth and overall progress.

This activity is designed to support and sustain increased student comfort and confidence in connection with learning and course progress.

This activity works well as a warm-up for a substantive lesson that comes at the end of a week or course unit.

## Recipe

Step 1: Define and explain the "Three Good Things" exercise.

Step 2: Introduce the activity. Explain how "That Recipe Worked Out Well" works. Clarify content focus, assignment, and/or lesson to be used for the activity.

Step 3: Students read the following article on "Three Good Things." See: Three Good Things Happiness Exercise: Shortest Guide. https://happyproject.in/three-good-things/

Step 4: Explain the prompt and the expectation that students reflect and free-write.

Prompt: Describe and explain three good things that happened to you in connection with your coursework this week.

*Note*: Prompts can be modified as desired. Focus might be on study of a particular topic, a classroom exercise or session, an assignment, etc.

Step 5: Provide active work time for students to reflect and write (recommended minimum five minutes).

- Offer support as needed.
- Share directional reminders about the activity, as applicable.

Step 6: Create groups (if applicable).

Step 7: Students share. Either in pairs, small groups, or as a whole class.

If virtual, an online discussion forum might be used for this activity. Students can comment on peer posts and experiences.

Step 8: Open discussion and reflection on the exercise (out loud or independent journaling)

## The Secret Sauce (Why It Works)

This **reflection-based** activity promotes **positive thinking**, appreciation, and deeper understanding of personal growth. Students draw on and actively **recall** prior learning and knowledge. The activity promotes hands-on, **active learning** that requires students to reflect and write about a specific course experience from a positive lens. Goals include increased student **comfort** with a particular course topic as well as increased **confidence** regarding personal growth. The activity offers opportunities for **reflection** for both individuals and groups. The activity also offers opportunities for **formative assessment**.

## Ingredients

- ☐ A course topic, exercise, or activity for purposes of reflection
- ☐ Clock/Timer (as applicable)

## Activity Prep

A course topic, exercise, or activity for purposes of reflection.

Optional: Students suggest a topic, exercise, or course experience.

## Activity Adaptations/Toppings

Depending on the instructional goals and objectives, this activity can be used and adapted in a variety of ways.

- Vary time allotted for reflection and free-writing.
- Suggest students share three good things on a course-related experience of choice.
- Provide a word limit/cap on the three good things.

## Activity Extensions

Provide opportunities for students to share their three good things (optional participation).

### Law-Based Example (Judicial Opinions and Case Briefs)

A few sessions after students work on a case brief, prompt reflection on the activity and its utility.

Sample prompts:

- Identify three good things that are associated with knowing how to read a judicial opinion.
- Identify three good things that are associated with being able to prepare a case brief.
- Identify three good things that are associated with our lesson(s) on case briefs.

## Portion Type and Size

Single (independent work), pairs, small group, or whole class

Time: Variable

- As few as five minutes.
- No maximum length.
- Time will vary depending on the adopted approach to implementation.

Online and/or face to face

## Web Resources

"Three Good Things: The Shortest Guide to What Went Well". See: https://happyproject.in/three-good-things/

"Three Good Things". See: https://ggia.berkeley.edu/practice/three-good-things

"Find Three Good Things Each Day". See: https://www.actionforhappiness.org/take-action/find-three-good-things-each-day

## I Tried This and This Is What I Learned

| DATE USED/LESSON TOPIC | REFLECTIONS/WHAT I MIGHT DO DIFFERENTLY NEXT TIME |
|---|---|
| | |
| | |
| | |

Have a "This Recipe Worked Out Well" activity adaptation to share?

Submit your tweaks and experiences here:

Survey Link: https://forms.gle/G7JS4RPADQK8ykp89

# Get Cooking: I Can Do This!

**Sides/Fruits/Vegetables**

**Ice Breaker Title: Get Cooking: I Can Do This!**

TED Talks as a tool to promote confidence, reflection, and development of transferable skills

## Activity Description

TED Talks offer opportunities for students to reimagine their skills and their potential to contribute to a team, workplace, or project of interest. TED Talks also offer opportunities for students to engage with challenging concepts (both course and career specific) in creative ways.

This activity is designed to support and sustain increased student comfort and confidence in connection with both course content and career-relevant transferable skills. Students view and discuss TED Talks selected specifically to instill confidence and empower students to continue to grow and develop their transferable skills.

This activity works well as an introductory warm-up for a substantive lesson that might require students to exercise presentation, public speaking, and/or other skills that can often be intimidating for students.

## Recipe

Step 1: Define and explain "Get Cooking: I Can Do This!" activities.

Step 2: Introduce the activity. Explain what TED Talks are and how the activity will work. Clarify content focus and type of resource to be used for the activity.

Step 3: Create groups (if applicable).

Step 4: Share a link or copy of a selected TED Talk.

Step 5: Explain the nature of the TED Talk to be used for purposes of this activity.

Step 6: Play the TED Talk. Students can view independently, in small groups, or as a whole class.

Step 7: Provide active work time for students to watch the recording (and re-watch as needed/desired).

Step 8: Provide reflection-based prompts for students to complete (optional, as desired).

- Offer support as needed.
- Share directional reminders about the activity, as applicable.

Step 9: Open discussion and reflection on the exercise (out loud or independent journaling).

Sample prompts:

- How has this activity changed the way you feel about your potential?
- How has this activity changed the way you feel about the related topic?
- How has this activity impacted your confidence?
- How has this activity impacted your intended strategies to continue to improve your related skills?

## The Secret Sauce (Why It Works)

This **multimedia** activity presents positive and motivating material in audio and visual ways. Students practice **active listening** and engage with content selected to support personal growth and reflection. The activity promotes hands-on, **active learning** that requires students to listen, reflect, and/or discuss a compelling presentation. Goals include increased student **comfort** with a particular career-relevant skill as well as increased **confidence** in their abilities. The activity offers opportunities for **reflection** for both individuals and groups. The activity also offers opportunities for **formative assessment**.

## Ingredients

- ☐ A TED Talk that explores career-relevant soft and/or transferable skills
- ☐ Clock/Timer (as applicable)

## Activity Prep

A TED Talk that explores career-relevant soft and/or transferable skills.

Optional: Students conduct research and identify a TED Talk to use for this activity.

## Activity Adaptations/Toppings

Depending on the instructional goals and objectives, this activity can be used and adapted in a variety of ways. A few examples follow:

- Although this activity is specifically focused on soft skills that are transferable to a wide range of career applications, the activity can also be conducted using TED Talks focused on substantive, course-related content.
- Introduce the activity with a reflection prompt that asks students to journal or reflect on their relative strengths and weaknesses associated with the soft skill that is the subject of the TED Talk.
- Introduce the activity with a discussion question/reflection prompt that explores the soft skill that is the focus on the selected TED Talk.
- For classes with online learning management systems, utilize discussion forums for ongoing and extended discussions on the TED Talk.

## Activity Extensions

- Provide opportunities for students to research and locate TED Talks or videos that explore a specific soft skill. Students might post TED Talks to a class bulletin board or gallery. A Padlet board, class Google Site, or Pinterest board are free options that work well.
- Students conduct research and locate TED Talks on an assigned soft skill.
- While this activity is shared as a way to inspire and nurture student confidence, TED Talks cover all topics. Students might conduct research and locate an informative TED Talk on a course-related topic.
- Students as creators: Students might write a script and then record an original TED Talk on a course-related or soft skills topic.

### Examples

Confidence-Building and Transferable Skills Examples:

- "How to Overcome our Biases? Walk Boldly Toward Them". See: https://www.ted.com/talks/verna_myers_how_to_overcome_our_biases_walk_boldly_toward_them?utm_campaign=tedspread&utm_medium=referral&utm_source=tedcomshare
- "What Makes Us Feel Good About Our Work?" See: https://www.ted.com/talks/dan_ariely_what_makes_us_feel_good_about_our_work?utm_campaign=tedspread&utm_medium=referral&utm_source=tedcomshare
- "Positive Self Talk". See: https://positivepsychology.com/positive-self-talk/
- "Elizabeth Gilbert: Your Elusive Creative Genius". See: https://www.ted.com/talks/elizabeth_gilbert_your_elusive_creative_genius?utm_campaign=tedspread&utm_medium=referral&utm_source=tedcomshare
- "The Puzzle of Motivation". See: https://www.ted.com/talks/dan_pink_the_puzzle_of_motivation?utm_campaign=tedspread&utm_medium=referral&utm_source=tedcomshare
- Celeste Headlee—10 ways to have a better conversation. See: https://www.youtube.com/watch?v=R1vskiVDwl4
- "Dare to Disagree". See: https://www.ted.com/talks/margaret_heffernan_dare_to_disagree?utm_campaign=tedspread&utm_medium=referral&utm_source=tedcomshare
- "The Power of Introverts". See: https://www.ted.com/talks/susan_cain_the_power_of_introverts?utm_campaign=tedspread&utm_medium=referral&utm_source=tedcomshare
- "The Danger of a Single Story". See: https://www.ted.com/talks/chimamanda_ngozi_adichie_the_danger_of_a_single_story?utm_campaign=tedspread&utm_medium=referral&utm_source=tedcomshare
- "Everyday Leadership". See: https://www.ted.com/talks/drew_dudley_everyday_leadership?utm_campaign=tedspread&utm_medium=referral&utm_source=tedcomshare
- "The Happy Secret to Better Work". See: https://www.ted.com/talks/shawn_achor_the_happy_secret_to_better_work?utm_campaign=tedspread&utm_medium=referral&utm_source=tedcomshare
- "Simon Sinke on How Reflection Informs Personal Growth". See: https://www.youtube.com/watch?v=_Ky-mKuhKgU
- "Lex Gillette, Wings are Just a Detail". See: https://www.tedxsandiego.com/wings-are-just-a-detail-lex-gillette-at-tedxsandiego-2016/
- "How to Disagree with Someone More Powerful than You". See: https://hbr.org/2016/03/how-to-disagree-with-someone-more-powerful-than-you

Self-Reflection

- "Why You Should Make Time for Self-Reflection". See: https://hbr.org/2017/03/why-you-should-make-time-for-self-reflection-even-if-you-hate-doing-it
- "The Value of Self-Reflection". See: https://www.youtube.com/watch?v=G1bgdwC_m-Y

Presentations

- "10 TED Talks that Used Visual Graphics to Win the Audience". See: https://www.inc.com/anna-guerrero/10-ted-talks-that-used-visual-graphics-to-win-the-audience.html

Resilience and Problem Solving

- "Gaming Can Make a Better World". See: https://www.ted.com/talks/jane_mcgonigal_gaming_can_make_a_better_world?language=en

## Building Creative Thinking

- Sample Prompts:
    - For anyone who began our course questioning your creativity, I hope you are already developing a stronger sense of your creative self and associated confidence in your creative thinking abilities.
    - We need creative, critical thinking in the workplace. Please don't "opt out" of recognizing, cultivating, and nurturing your creative confidence.
    - Creativity involves thinking differently about challenges and the way we approach them. Any of the many issues we encounter in our own professional work (present and future) will require creative approaches to problem solving.
    - Today, we'll view a related TED Talk. It's one of my favorites. "How to Build Your Creative Confidence". See: https://www.ted.com/talks/david_kelley_how_to_build_your_creative_confidence (11:46)
    - "How to Build Your Creative Confidence" Transcript. See: https://www.ted.com/talks/david_kelley_how_to_build_your_creative_confidence/transcript

## Creative and Reflection-Based Thinking, Additional Options

- Sample Law-Based Prompt: As you reflect on what we've learned through our studies of important cases in our criminal system history, I encourage you to consider what all key parties emphasized. What did the defense focus on? The prosecution? The media?

The following TED Talk offers some important reminders of the impact of what we emphasize, talk about, and present.

"Titus Kaphar, Can Art Amend History?" See: https://www.ted.com/talks/titus_kaphar_can_art_amend_history
Share your related thoughts.

- TED Talk to Inspire Questions

TED Talk by Karen Maeyens: The Value of Asking Questions. See: https://www.youtube.com/watch?v=aZIuAQw8RA4

- Reflection Prompts:
    - How can we as students, professionals, peers, etc. (insert any role present or future here), ask more questions?

- How can asking the right questions help us learn more about your peers, colleagues, work, (insert any present or future category of work or person here), etc.?

**Article-Based Prompt (Reflection, Real-World Applications, Legal Example)**

How might what we have studied over the past several weeks (including our review of the many different roles, responsibilities, and influences within our courts) influence our interactions in the workplace?

Consider, as well, how mentoring (and related decisions) might be influenced as a result of our work.

Farnell, R. (2017). *Mentor people who aren't like you.* See: https://hbr.org/2017/04/mentor-people-who-arent-like-you?utm_campaign=hbr&utm_source=facebook&utm_medium=social

## Portion Type and Size

Single (independent work), pairs, small group, or whole class

Time: Variable

- As few as five minutes.
- No maximum length.
- Time will vary depending on the adopted approach to implementation.
- *Note*: The activity takes significantly less time when the instructor selects TED Talk videos to share in advance.

Online and/or face to face

## Web Resources

- "Talks to Give You a Confidence Boost". See: https://www.ted.com/playlists/259/talks_to_give_you_a_confidence
- "10 Inspiring TED Talks That'll Boost Your Self-Confidence". See: https://blog.hubspot.com/marketing/ted-talks-confidence-boost

## I Tried This and This Is What I Learned

| DATE USED/LESSON TOPIC | REFLECTIONS/WHAT I MIGHT DO DIFFERENTLY NEXT TIME |
|---|---|
| | |
| | |
| | |

Have a "Get Cooking: I Can Do This!" activity adaptation to share?

Submit your tweaks and experiences here:

Survey Link: https://forms.gle/G7JS4RPADQK8ykp89

# What Did You Think of That Recipe?

**Sides/Fruits/Vegetables**

**Ice Breaker Title: What Did You Think of That Recipe?**

Reflection and feedback as tools to promote dialogue, engagement, feedback loops, and active learning

## Activity Description

This activity provides an opportunity for students to reflect on prior lessons and associated learning. The activity also provides an opportunity for students to provide instructor feedback.

Students compete an anonymous survey (Google Forms works well). Doing so supports recall, reflection, and insights regarding lesson efficacy for the benefit of both students and instructors.

The activity works well at any point during a semester/school year. The activity is especially beneficial after a new instructional activity or strategy is implemented.

## Recipe

Step 1: Introduce the activity. Explain how "What Did You Think of That Recipe?" activities work.

Step 2: Clarify survey purpose and explain the form of the survey to be used for the activity.

Step 3: Share link to survey. Sample Survey: https://forms.gle/ZQnHUMyiyqt8SDeM7

Copy and edit as needed. For in-person settings, students can respond to questions anonymously on paper if preferred.

Step 4: Provide time for students to complete survey (recommended minimum five minutes).

- Offer support as needed.
- Share directional reminders about the activity, as applicable.

Step 5: Open discussion and reflection on the exercise (out loud or independent journaling)

Sample prompts:

- How has this activity changed the way you feel about the lesson?
- How has this activity changed the way you feel about the related topic?

## The Secret Sauce (Why It Works)

This **reflective** activity prompts students to **recall** prior learning and actively reflect on the value of a particular instructional strategy on their learning experience. Students draw on and **actively recall** prior learning and knowledge. Students simultaneously provide instructors valuable **feedback** on the learning experience. The activity promotes hands-on, **active learning** that requires students to do something (complete a reflection-based survey). Goals include increased **student awareness** of individual learning preferences as well as increased **dialogue** and **communication** to instructors regarding the student experience.

## Ingredients

- ☐ A reflection-based survey (general or aligned with a class session, learning objective, or lesson) that can be completed anonymously and in five minutes or less
- ☐ Clock/Timer (as applicable)

## Activity Prep

A reflection-based survey (general or aligned with a class session, learning objective, or lesson) that can be completed anonymously and in five minutes or less

- Optional: Students create their own feedback surveys for completion.
- Sample Survey: https://forms.gle/9csYoWEiRXuSSyan9

## Activity Adaptations/Toppings

Depending on the instructional goals and objectives, this activity can be used and adapted in a variety of ways. A few examples follow:

- Open discussion regarding a prior session or instructional exercise.
- Open journaling, independent student writing to reflect on a prior session or instructional exercise.
- Students work in pairs or small groups to create feedback survey questions.

## Activity Extensions

- Provide opportunities for students to draft feedback independently.
- Provide opportunities to discuss feedback in small groups or as a whole class.
- Provide opportunities for students to create questions for future feedback surveys.

## Portion Type and Size

Single (independent work), pairs, small group, or whole class

Time: Variable

- As few as five minutes.
- No maximum length.
- *Note*: The activity takes significantly less time when the instructor prepares a survey in advance of use.

Online and/or face to face

## Web Resource

- Sample survey. See: https://forms.gle/9csYoWEiRXuSSyan9

## I Tried This and This Is What I Learned

| DATE USED/LESSON TOPIC | REFLECTIONS/WHAT I MIGHT DO DIFFERENTLY NEXT TIME |
|---|---|
| | |
| | |
| | |

Have a "What Did You Think of That Recipe?" activity adaptation to share?

Submit your tweaks and experiences here:

Survey Link: https://forms.gle/G7JS4RPADQK8ykp89

# After-Meal Listening Entertainment

**Sides/Fruits/Vegetables**

**Ice Breaker Title: After-Meal Listening Entertainment**

Song list generation, lyric review, and discussion as a tool to promote application, reflection, and deeper understanding of course concepts

> "Music is the universal language of mankind."
>
> *Henry Wadsworth Longfellow*

## Activity Description

Creating lists offer opportunities to generate a collection of resources for ongoing review and access. In this activity, students reflect on songs (past and current) and/or song lyrics and identify examples that are related to a particular course concept or topic.

This activity is designed to support application of course concepts and add to a library of resources.

This activity works well as an introductory warm-up and/or review activity for a substantive lesson associated with the topic shared for song generation.

## Recipe

Step 1: Define and explain "After-Meal Listening Entertainment" activities.

Step 2: Introduce the activity. Explain how the "After-Meal Listening Entertainment" activity will work. Clarify content focus and type of resource to be used for the activity.

Step 3: Create groups (if applicable).

Step 4: Identify the topic of focus.

Step 5: Prompt students to generate and share songs (or lyrics) related to the topic.

- Recommended songs can relate either directly or indirectly to themes associated with the presented topic.

Step 6: Alternatively, provide time for students to research and locate a song/lyric-based resource (if applicable).

- Provide active work time for students to create and generate lists (recommended minimum five minutes).
  - Offer support as needed.
  - Share directional reminders about the activity, as applicable.

Step 7: Upload recommended songs to a class Padlet, Google Doc, Pinterest board, etc., for ongoing access. Digital bulletin boards work well for both onsite and online classrooms.

Step 8: Open discussion and reflection on the exercise (out loud or independent journaling).

Sample prompts:

- How has this activity changed the way you feel about the recommended songs?
- How has this activity changed the way you feel about the related topic?

## The Secret Sauce (Why It Works)

This **open-ended** activity promotes learning transfer and application of course concepts to new contexts and prior experiences. Students draw on and actively **recall** prior learning, prior knowledge, and prior learning experiences. The activity promotes hands-on, **active learning** that requires students to actively identify a related resource or song. Goals include increased student **comfort** with a particular topic as well as increased **engagement** and **application/transfer** associated with the topic. The activity offers opportunities for **reflection** for both individuals and groups.

| Ingredients |
| --- |
| ☐ A course topic that is related to a class learning objective or lesson |
| ☐ Clock/Timer (as applicable) |

## Activity Prep

A course topic that is related to a class learning objective or lesson.

Optional: Students select a course topic for this activity.

## Activity Adaptations/Toppings

Depending on the instructional goals and objectives, this activity can be used and adapted in a variety of ways. A few examples follow:

- Introduce the activity with a discussion question/reflection prompt that explores the topic used for the activity.
- Introduce the activity using a current event/news article related to the lesson topic and from which students generate song/lyric options.
- Instructor creates a pre-selected collection of lyrics that relate to course content and lesson objectives then uses lyrics to initiate discussion of the related topic.
- "Tuning Into Students' Interests: Using Song Lyrics to Teach Literary and Writing Concepts" See: https://www.nwmissouri.edu/library/researchpapers/2013/graves,%20marissa.pdf

- "Advice for Teaching Poetry Through Song Lyrics". See: https://resilienteducator.com/classroom-resources/advice-for-teaching-poetry-through-song-lyrics/
- Students create a library or list of song options for a course-related topic of choice.

## Activity Extensions

- Provide opportunities for students to listen to recommended songs. Students review lyrics from a recommended list and submit a reflection or complete a related activity as part of a course assignment.
- Students post their favorite course- or topic-themed songs to a class bulletin board or gallery. A Padlet board, class Google Site, or Pinterest board are free options that work well.
- Students write reviews of a selected song. Reviews can range in length from 50 to 500 (or more) words.

### Law-Based Example (Legal-Related Songs)

- "Songs About the Law" See: http://www.thecavanproject.com/songs-about-the-law/
- "The Law in Music: 20 Cool Songs About Courtrooms, Lawyers, and the Law". See: https://onward.justia.com/the-law-in-music-20-cool-songs-about-courtrooms-lawyers-and-the-law/

### Science Example

- "Fifteen Songa About Science". See: https://www.pastemagazine.com/science/music/15-songs-about-science/

### Poetry Based Lessons

- Five Poetry Lesson Plans Inspired by Music and Sound. See: https://poetry.arizona.edu/blog/five-poetry-lesson-plans-inspired-music-sound

## Portion Type and Size

Single (independent work), pairs, small groups, or whole class

Time: Variable

- As few as five minutes.
- No maximum length.
- Time will vary depending on the adopted approach to implementation.

Online and/or face to face

## Web Resources

- "Five Poetry Lesson Plans Inspired by Music & Sound". See: https://poetry.arizona.edu/blog/five-poetry-lesson-plans-inspired-music-sound
- Nine Teaching Ideas for Using Music to Inspire Student Writing. See: https://www.nytimes.com/2018/05/10/learning/lesson-plans/nine-teaching-ideas-for-using-music-to-inspire-student-writing.html
- How to Teach Your Students English Through Popular Songs. See: https://owlcation.com/academia/How-to-Use-Popular-Songs-to-Help-English-Language-Students-Learn-English

## References

Stygles, J. (2014). *Building schema: Exploring content with song lyrics and strategic reading*. Retrieved from https://files.eric.ed.gov/fulltext/EJ1034915.pdf

Zagerman, J. M. (2018). *Using song lyrics in teaching an undergraduate statistics course*. All Theses and Dissertations. 157. https://dune.une.edu/theses/157

## I Tried This and This Is What I Learned

| DATE USED/LESSON TOPIC | REFLECTIONS/WHAT I MIGHT DO DIFFERENTLY NEXT TIME |
|---|---|
| | |
| | |
| | |

Have an "After-Meal Listening Entertainment" activity adaptation to share?

Submit your tweaks and experiences here:

Survey Link: https://forms.gle/G7JS4RPADQK8ykp89

# After-Meal Reading Entertainment

**Sides/Fruits/Vegetables**

**Ice Breaker Title: After-Meal Reading Entertainment**

Book generation and discussion to promote application, reflection, and deeper understanding of course concepts

## Activity Description

In this activity, students reflect on books (past and current) and identify examples that are related to a particular course concept or topic.

This activity supports the application of course concepts and adds to a library of resources.

This activity works well as an introductory warm-up and/or review activity for a substantive lesson associated with the topic shared for book recommendation generation.

## Recipe

Step 1: Define and explain "After-Meal Reading Entertainment" activities.

Step 2: Introduce the activity. Explain how the "After-Meal Reading Entertainment" activity will work.

Step 3: Create groups (if applicable).

Step 4: Identify the topic of focus.

Step 5: Students generate and share books related to the topic.

- Recommended books can relate either directly or indirectly to themes associated with the presented topic.
- Provide active work time for students to create and generate lists (recommended minimum five minutes).
    - Offer support as needed.
    - Share directional reminders about the activity, as applicable.

Step 6: Upload recommended books to a class Padlet, Google Doc, Pinterest board, etc.. Digital bulletin boards work well for both onsite and online classrooms.

Step 7: Open discussion and reflection on the exercise (out loud or independent journaling)

Sample prompts:

- How has this activity changed the way you feel about the related topic?

## The Secret Sauce (Why It Works)

This **open-ended** activity promotes learning transfer and application of course concepts to new contexts and prior experiences. The activity promotes hands-on, **active learning** that requires students to do something (actively identify a related resource/book). Goals include increased student **comfort** with a particular topic as well as increased **engagement** and **application/transfer** associated with the topic. The activity offers many opportunities for **reflection** (both individual and group).

## Ingredients

- ☐ A course topic related to a class learning objective or lesson
- ☐ Clock/Timer (as applicable)

## Activity Prep

A course topic related to a class learning objective or lesson.

Optional: Students identify a course topic for this activity.

## Activity Adaptations/Toppings

Depending on the instructional goals and objectives, this activity can be used and adapted in a variety of ways. A few examples follow:

- Introduce the activity with a discussion question/reflection prompt that explores the activity topic.
- Introduce the activity using a current event/news article related to the lesson topic and from which students will generate book options.

## Activity Extensions

- Provide opportunities for students to read recommended books. Students might be encouraged to read one book from a recommended list and submit a reflection or complete a related activity as part of a course assignment.
- Students post their favorite course- or topic-themed books to a class bulletin board or gallery. A Padlet board, class Google Site, or Pinterest board are free options that work well.

- Students write reviews of a selected book. Reviews can range in length from 50 to 500 (or more) words.

### Law-Based Examples

- *Troubled Memory* (Lawrence N. Powell)
- *You Have the Right to Remain Innocent* (James Duane)
- *A Civil Action* (Jonathan Harr)
- *Gideon's Trumpet* (Anthony Lewis)
- *The Buffalo Creek Disaster* (Gerald M. Stern)
- *The Nine* (Jeffrey Toobin)
- *Solitary* (Albert Woodfox)
- *We Do This Till We Free Us* (Mariame Kaba)
- *Are Prisons Obsolete?* (Angela Y. Davis)
- *Prison By Any Other Name* (Maya Schenwar and Victoria Law)
- *Beyond Survival* (Ejeris Dixon and Leah Lakshmi Piepzna-Samarasinha)
- *The End of Policing* (Alex S. Vitale)
- *"Prisons Make Us Safer" and 20 Other Myths about Mass Incarceration* (Victoria Law)
- *Change Everything* (Ruth Wilson Gilmore and Naomi Murakawa)
- *Just Mercy* (Bryan Stevenson)

### Teamwork Examples

- Teamwork Books. See: https://teambuilding.com/blog/teamwork-books

## Portion Type and Size

Single (independent work), pairs, small group, or whole class

Time: Variable

- As few as five minutes.
- No maximum length.
- Time will vary depending on the adopted approach to implementation.

Online and/or face to face

## Web Resources

Law Books. See: https://www.lawstudies.com/article/seven-must-read-books-for-law-students/

## I Tried This and This Is What I Learned

| DATE USED/LESSON TOPIC | REFLECTIONS/WHAT I MIGHT DO DIFFERENTLY NEXT TIME |
|---|---|
| | |
| | |
| | |

Have an "After-Meal Reading Entertainment" activity adaptation to share?

Submit your tweaks and experiences here:

Survey Link: https://forms.gle/G7JS4RPADQK8ykp89

# After-Meal Viewing Entertainment

**Sides/Fruits/Vegetables**

**Ice Breaker Title: After-Meal Viewing Entertainment**

Movie recommendations and discussion to promote application, reflection, and deeper understanding of course concepts

## Activity Description

Creating lists offers opportunities to generate a collection of resources for ongoing review and access. In this activity, students reflect on movies (past and current) and identify examples that are related to a course concept or topic.

This activity supports the application of course concepts and adds to a library of resources.

This activity works well as an introductory warm-up and/or review activity.

## Recipe

Step 1: Define and explain "After-Meal Viewing Entertainment" activities.

Step 2: Introduce the activity. Explain how the "After-Meal Viewing Entertainment" activity will work. Clarify content focus and type of resource to be used for the activity.

Step 3: Create groups (if applicable).

Step 4: Identify the topic of focus.

Step 5: Students generate and share movies related to the topic.

- Recommended movies can relate either directly or indirectly to themes associated with the presented topic.
- Provide active work time for students to create and generate original lists (recommended minimum five minutes).
    - Offer support as needed.
    - Share directional reminders about the activity, as applicable.

Step 6: Post recommended movies to a class Padlet, Google Doc, Pinterest board, etc., for ongoing access. Digital bulletin boards work well for both onsite and online classrooms.

Step 7: Open discussion and reflection on the exercise (out loud or independent journaling).

Sample prompts:

- How has this activity changed the way you feel about the recommended movies?
- How has this activity changed the way you feel about the related topic?

## The Secret Sauce (Why It Works)

This **open-ended** activity promotes learning transfer and application of course concepts to new contexts and prior experiences. Students draw on and actively **recall** prior learning, prior knowledge, and prior learning experiences. The activity promotes hands-on, **active learning** that requires students to actively identify a related resource or movie. Goals include increased student **comfort** with a particular topic as well as increased **engagement** and **application/transfer** associated with the topic. The activity offers many opportunities for reflection for both individuals and groups.

## Ingredients

- ☐ A course topic related to a class learning objective or lesson
- ☐ Clock/Timer (as applicable)

## Activity Prep

A course topic related to a class learning objective or lesson.

Optional: Students identify a course topic for this activity.

## Activity Adaptations/Toppings

Depending on the instructional goals and objectives, this activity can be used and adapted in a variety of ways.

- Introduce the activity with a discussion question/reflection prompt that explores the activity topic.
- Introduce the activity using a current event/news article related to the lesson topic and from which students generate movie options.
- Students create a library or list of movie options on a course-related topic of choice.

## Activity Extensions

- Provide opportunities for students to view recommended movies. Students might view one movie from the recommended list and submit a reflection or complete a related activity.
- Students post their favorite course- or topic-themed movies to a class bulletin board or gallery. A Padlet board, Google Site, or Pinterest board are free options that work well.
- Students write reviews of a selected movie. Review can range in length from 50 to 500 (or more) words.

### Legal-Related Movies

- *A Civil Action*
- *Erin Brockovich*
- *Twelve Angry Men*
- *Inherit the Wind*
- *To Kill a Mockingbird*
- *The Insider*
- *The Trial of the Chicago 7*
- *My Cousin Vinnie*
- *Just Mercy*
- ABA Journal, "Top 25 Movies". See: https://www.abajournal.com/gallery/top25movies/

### Teamwork Examples

- "10 More Films that Highlight the Best in Humanity". See: https://greatergood.berkeley.edu/article/item/ten_more_films_that_highlight_the_best_in_humanity

### Films for Aspiring Medics/Med Students

- "Films Aspiring Medics Should Watch". See: https://www.themedicportal.com/blog/films-aspiring-medics-should-watch/
- "5 movies Every Medical Student Should See". See: https://raindance.org/5-movies-every-medical-student-see/
- "Movies for Medical Students". See: https://www.imdb.com/list/ls070273228/

### Films for Writers

- "Best Movies for Writers to Watch". See: https://www.ranker.com/list/best-movies-for-writers-to-watch/ranker-film
- "Best Movies About Aspiring Writers". See: https://screenrant.com/best-movies-about-aspiring-writers/

## Portion Type and Size

Single (independent work), pairs, small group, or whole class

Time: Variable

- As few as five minutes.
- No maximum length.
- Time will vary depending on the adopted approach to implementation.

Online and/or face to face

## Web Resources

Law Movies. See: https://www.abajournal.com/gallery/top25movies/

Using Films as a Tool for Active Learning in Teaching Sociology. See: https://files.eric.ed.gov/fulltext/EJ1092141.pdf

Ideal Ways Movies Can Serve as Educational Tools. See: https://www.filmink.com.au/ideal-ways-movies-can-serve-educational-tools/

## I Tried This and This Is What I Learned

| DATE USED/LESSON TOPIC | REFLECTIONS/WHAT I MIGHT DO DIFFERENTLY NEXT TIME |
|---|---|
| | |
| | |
| | |

Have an "After-Meal Viewing Entertainment" activity adaptation to share?

Submit your tweaks and experiences here:

Survey Link: https://forms.gle/G7JS4RPADQK8ykp89

# Sweet Treats/Desserts

"Life is uncertain. Eat dessert first."

*Ernestine Ulmer*

## Finding My Perfect Recipe (Career Fits)

**Sweet Treats/Desserts**

**Ice Breaker Title: Finding My Perfect Recipe (Career Fits)**

Career fit and aptitude test activities to promote real-world applications of course concepts

### Activity Description

"Finding My Perfect Recipe" and related career fit activities support the application of course concepts to real-world applications and future career paths.

In this activity, students complete free career-related self-assessments and reflect on results to better understand career opportunities.

"Finding My Perfect Recipe" activities offer opportunities for students to develop a deeper understanding of themselves and connect course concepts to real-world contexts and associated career opportunities.

The activity promotes forward-focused (career-related) thinking as well as reflective thinking and recall of past learning. This activity is designed to support creative thinking and student confidence associated with possible career paths. Students gain additional insights into their relative strengths and values, information which can help focus and optimize job search processes.

This activity works well at the conclusion of a unit or at the mid- or endpoint of a semester.

### Recipe

Step 1: Define and explain "Finding My Perfect Recipe" (Career Fit) activities.

Step 2: Introduce the activity. Clarify content focus and type of resource (e.g., paper-based assessment, digital assessment) to be used for the activity.

Step 3: Provide tips and reminders for how to complete the self-assessment.

- Answer truthfully.

- Reflect carefully before selecting a response.
- Carefully read all options.

Step 4: Share a link to suggested assessment (if applicable).

Step 5: Provide active work time for students to complete the self-assessment.

Step 6: Students reflect on results. Options include paired, small group, and/or whole-class discussions. Students might also reflect independently through written reflections.

- Offer support as needed.
- Share directional reminders about the activity, as applicable.

Step 7: Open discussion and reflection on the exercise (out loud or independent journaling).

Sample prompts:

- How has this activity changed the way you feel about your preferred/desired career path?

Step 8: Facilitate an open discussion that critically analyzes the shared self-assessment.

  - Encourage students to reflect on possible biases, flaws, and inaccuracies associated with the test design and/or results.

## The Secret Sauce (Why It Works)

This **interactive** activity breaks down course concepts into forward-focused activities that increase **relevance** for students. Students engage in **self-reflection** and develop greater **self-awareness** of personal strengths. The activity promotes hands-on, **active learning** that requires students to do something (complete personal self-assessments) with course and related career concepts. Goals include increased **student comfort** with a particular area of course content as well as increased **confidence** and **awareness** of associated career opportunities. The activity offers opportunities for **reflection** (both individual and group), **career-related awareness**, and **application**.

## Ingredients

- ☐ A career-related self-assessment
- ☐ Clock/Timer (as applicable)

## Activity Prep

A career-related self-assessment.

## Activity Adaptations/Toppings

Depending on the instructional goals and objectives, this activity can be used and adapted in a variety of ways. A few examples follow:

- Introduce the activity with a discussion question/reflection prompt that explores the value of breaking down jobs into specific skills.
- Introduce the activity with a discussion question/reflection prompt that explores the benefits of applying course concepts to career applications.
- Introduce the activity using a current event/news article related to the lesson topic and from which students generate job profiles.

- Introduce the activity with a discussion question that explores the value of self-assessments to identify personal strengths.
- Use the activity as a collaborative learning exercise where one student is responsible for posing a course-related scenario and another is tasked with identifying a variety of job options that are related to such a scenario.
- Students create hypothetical job postings that might require knowledge and skills learned in a prior course unit or session.

## Activity Extensions

- Students conduct independent research and share career-related articles and resources. Students post resources to a class bulletin board or gallery. A Padlet board, class Google Site, or Pinterest board are free options that work well.
- Students review job postings (and noted skills) in fields of interest.
- Discuss how to interpret and apply self-assessment test results.

### Example Self-Assessments

- Free Career Aptitude Tests. See: https://www.thebalancecareers.com/free-career-aptitude-tests-2059813
- 123 Career Aptitude Test. See: https://www.123test.com/career-test/
- Career One Stop. See: https://www.careeronestop.org/toolkit/careers/interest-assessment.aspx
- Career One Stop. Work Values Matcher. See: https://www.careeronestop.org/Toolkit/Careers/work-values-matcher.aspx
- Jung Typology Test. See: http://www.humanmetrics.com/cgi-win/jtypes2.asp#questionnaire
- Keirsey Temperament Sorter. See: https://profile.keirsey.com/#/b2c/assessment/start
- O*NET Interest Profiler. See: https://www.mynextmove.org/explore/ip
- Myers-Brigg Test (describes preferred ways of interesting with others). See: http://www.humanmetrics.com/cgi-win/jtypes2.asp. See also: https://www.16personalities.com/
- The Strong Interest Inventory. See: https://www.themyersbriggs.com/en-US/Products-and-Services/Strong
- Values Assessments. See: https://www.myplan.com/assess/values.php

## Portion Type and Size

Single (independent work), pairs, small group, or whole class

Time: Variable

- As few as five minutes.
- No maximum length.
- Time will vary depending on the adopted approach to implementation.

Online and/or face to face

## Web Resources

- Job-Related Resources

- Bureau of Labor Statistics. See: https://www.bls.gov/
- Occupational Outlook Handbook. See: https://www.bls.gov/ooh/
- Free Career Aptitude Tests. See: https://www.thebalancecareers.com/free-career-aptitude-tests-2059813
- Career Assessment Matrix. See: https://career-intelligence.com/career-assessment-matrix/

## I Tried This and This Is What I Learned

| DATE USED/LESSON TOPIC | REFLECTIONS/WHAT I MIGHT DO DIFFERENTLY NEXT TIME |
|---|---|
| | |
| | |
| | |

Have a "Finding My Perfect Recipe" activity adaptation to share?

Submit your tweaks and experiences here:

Survey Link: https://forms.gle/G7JS4RPADQK8ykp89

# That's a Creative Recipe

**Sweet Treats/Desserts**

**Ice Breaker Title: That's a Creative Recipe**

Idea generation to promote creative thinking and problem-solving

## Activity Description

Idea generation activities provide opportunities to explore creative ideas related to a specific topic. In this activity, students generate ideas for possible use cases associated with a presented object or item related to a course lesson or learning objective.

This activity works well as an introductory warm-up and/or review activity for a substantive lesson associated with an assigned topic, object, or item.

## Recipe

Step 1: Define and explain "That's a Creative Recipe" activities.

Step 2: Introduce the activity. Explain how the idea generation activity works. Clarify content focus and topic to be used for the activity.

Step 3: Create groups (if applicable).

Step 4: Identify an object or item related to course material and/or lesson objectives. Share a link or copy of a resource related to the topic (if applicable).

Step 5: Explain the nature of the topic, text, or resource (the material to be used for the activity).

Step 6: Prompt students to generate a list of possible uses for the object. Students might identify key characteristics of the object or item. Students might also reflect on past uses of the object and then identify how those uses might inform and influence future uses of the object (in similar and dissimilar situations).

Step 7: Provide active work time for students to create and generate ideas.

- Offer support as needed.
- Share directional reminders about the activity, as applicable.

Step 8: Open discussion and reflection on the exercise.

Sample prompts:

- How has this activity changed the way you feel about the related course topic?

## The Secret Sauce (Why It Works)

This **idea generation** activity breaks down complex material into manageable chunks that reduce **cognitive load** on students. Students exercise **creative thinking**, practice **divergent thinking** skills, and draw on and actively **recall** and then **apply** prior learning and knowledge. The activity promotes hands-on, **active learning** that requires students to generate a list of new uses for an object or concept. Goals include increased student **comfort** with idea generation as well as increased **confidence** generating ideas. The activity offers opportunities for **reflection** (both individual and group). The activity also offers opportunities for **formative assessment**.

## Ingredients

- ☐ A concept or topic related to a class learning objective or lesson
- ☐ Clock/Timer (as applicable)

## Activity Prep

A concept or topic related to a lesson topic.

Optional: Students identify a concept or topic to use for this activity.

## Activity Adaptations/Toppings

Depending on the instructional goals and objectives, this activity can be used and adapted in a variety of ways.

- Introduce the activity with a discussion question/reflection prompt that explores past uses of the concept or topic.

## Activity Extensions

Provide opportunities for students to publicly share lists of generated ideas. Students might discuss and/or debate strengths and weaknesses of shared ideas.

### Science Example (Laboratory Equipment)

Prompt students to reflect on a specific piece of laboratory equipment. Students generate a list of all possible uses for the noted equipment. Use cases might be both lab- and non-lab based.

- Sample List, "School Science Laboratory Equipment List and Uses": https://www.labkafe.com/blog/20-common-school-science-laboratory-equipment-and-their-uses

### Culinary Example (Kitchen Utensils/Equipment)

Prompt students to reflect on a specific kitchen utensil. Students generate a list of all possible uses for the noted utensil. Use cases might be both kitchen and non-kitchen based.

- Sample Kitchen Utensil List: https://listonic.com/kitchen-utensils-list/

## Portion Type and Size

Single (independent work), pairs, small groups, or whole class

Time: Variable

- As few as one minute.
- No maximum length.
- Time will vary depending on the adopted approach to implementation.

Online and/or face to face

## Web Resources

- Fuel Creativity through Divergent Thinking in the Classroom. See: https://www.edutopia.org/blog/fueling-creativity-through-divergent-thinking-classroom-stacey-goodman
- Convergent versus Divergent Thinking. See: https://www.psychestudy.com/cognitive/thinking/convergent-vs-divergent#

## Additional Resources/Readings

- Improving Student Idea Generation in the Classroom. See: https://www.teachingentrepreneurship.org/improve-idea-generation/
- Divergent Thinking. See: https://www.sciencedirect.com/topics/psychology/divergent-thinking
- How to Teach Divergent Thinking Skills in the Classroom. See: https://www.waterford.org/education/divergent-thinking-skills-classroom/

## I Tried This and This Is What I Learned

| DATE USED/LESSON TOPIC | REFLECTIONS/WHAT I MIGHT DO DIFFERENTLY NEXT TIME |
|---|---|
| | |
| | |
| | |

Have a "That's a Creative Recipe" activity adaptation to share?

Submit your tweaks and experiences here:

Survey Link: https://forms.gle/G7JS4RPADQK8ykp89

# I Have a Caption/Label for That

**Sweet Treats/Desserts**

**Ice Breaker Title: I Have a Caption/Label for That**

Labels and captioning to promote reflection and critical thinking

## Activity Description

Captioning activities offer opportunities for students to reflect on course concepts in creative ways. Captioning activities present opportunities for students to review complicated concepts in a stress-free environment. Captioning activities are a way to proactively mitigate the increased cognitive load (drain on working memory) and anxiety that often emerges when a student interacts with complex concepts. In this activity, students review and reflect on a presented image and draft an original caption for the graphic. Concepts that are sometimes intimidating for students (because of vocabulary, writing style, familiarity, or otherwise) are especially well-suited to this activity.

This activity is inspired by games such as What Do You Meme? and Caption This.

This activity works well as an introductory warm-up and/or reflection activity for a substantive lesson associated with the topic used for the captioning exercise.

## Recipe

Step 1: Define and explain captioning activities.

Step 2: Explain how captioning activities work. Clarify content focus and type of resource to be used for the activity.

Step 3: Create groups (if applicable).

Step 4: Share a link or copy of the resource/Provide time for students to research and locate an original image/graphic resource for use in this activity (if applicable).

Step 5: Explain the source and/or context of the image or resource to students (if applicable).

Step 6: Provide instructions for the captioning activity. Clarify desired length of caption (number of words/number of sentences) and method of sharing or submission.

- Students create original captions for a course-related image.
- Captions might define an assigned term and/or explain an assigned topic.
- Instructor shares a content-related image. Students then caption the image (using some pre-defined number of words or characters) to define or explain. Annotation is also an option.
- Instructor provides a term and ask students to locate and/or create an image to use for captioning.
- Captions can be submitted via polling software (anonymously), via classroom chat, on a Google Doc, via a Padlet board, on index cards (if in person), or via any other desired methods.

Step 7: Provide active work time for students to create and generate an original caption for the identified resource (recommended minimum five minutes).

- Offer support as needed.
- Share directional reminders about the activity, as applicable

Step 8: Share student submissions. Provide time for review and reflection.

- Student volunteers share and explain.
- Post to an online gallery (Padlet, Google Slides).
- When captions are aligned to course vocabulary, students might review all captions and try to guess the associated term.

Step 9: Points might be provided for the funniest, most unexpected, most original, etc., caption. Rounds played can vary.

Step 10: Open discussion and reflection on the exercise (out loud or independent journaling).

Sample prompts:

- How has this activity changed the way you feel about the resource?
- How has this activity changed the way you feel about the related topic?

Step 11: Share student captions (either out loud or on digital bulletin boards) (if applicable).

## The Secret Sauce (Why It Works)

This **interactive** activity breaks down complex material into manageable chunks that reduce **cognitive load** on students. Students draw on and actively **recall** prior learning and knowledge. The activity promotes **creative thinking** and hands-on, **active learning** that requires students to interact with a course concept/topic. Goals include increased student **comfort** with a particular topic as well as increased **understanding** of the topic. The activity offers opportunities for **reflection** for both individuals and groups. The activity also offers opportunities for **formative assessment**.

## Ingredients

- ☐ An image or graphic related to a class learning objective or lesson
- ☐ Clock/Timer (as applicable)

## Activity Prep

An image or graphic related to a class learning objective or lesson.

- Optional: Post an image to a Google Slide. Force copy. Students then complete annotation activity.
- Optional: Students identify a resource to use for this activity.

## Activity Adaptations/Toppings

Depending on the instructional goals and objectives, this activity can be used and adapted in a variety of ways. A few examples follow:

- Conduct the activity using an image from a current reading, assigned book, or related news article.
- Introduce the activity with a discussion question/reflection prompt that explores the course topic most closely aligned with selected images.
- Introduce the activity using an image associated with a current event/news article related to the lesson topic and from which students will create captions.

- Students create a caption for an image of choice (aligned with an identified course concept or topic).
- Students create an image and an associated caption on an assigned topic.
- Vary time permitted to work on caption drafting.
- Vary length allowed for captions (word limits, number of sentences).
- Students choose topic and then search for related images to caption.
- Whole class captioning of a single image.
- Students caption images in pairs or small groups and then present to whole class.
- Add quote bubbles for students to complete.
- Students might caption for a predetermined number of rounds, with points awarded for different categories (e.g., most unique, funniest, best instructional caption).

## Activity Extensions

- Provide opportunities for students to publicly share their captions and associated image. Students might post captions to a class bulletin board or gallery. A Padlet board, class Google Site, or Pinterest board are examples of free options that work well.
- Offer instruction and/or review for appropriate citation and attribution format for shared images.
- If student research leads to a collection of images associated with a course topic, ask students to share resources in a class library (Google Docs, Google Sites, Padlet board). Source identification can be used as research reinforcement and library building. Students might use the images (along with associated citations) for future projects.
- Students conduct research to locate images that best represent or capture an assigned topic. Captioning can be assigned as independent work.

### Law-Based Examples

Case Law/Judicial Opinions. Creating a caption for a case opinion is a way for students to actively engage with and approach a complex text in a low-stakes, fun way that is designed to help minimize the fear associated with higher-stakes settings.

- To reinforce research skills, students might conduct research and select an image of choice on an identified legal topic.
- An instructor might share a judicial opinion, perhaps one that students have previously read and briefed as part of a graded activity.
- Either individually, in pairs, in small groups, or as a whole-class exercise, students create an original caption for an identified judicial opinion.

Signing of the U.S. Constitution (Sample Image)

- https://pixabay.com/illustrations/usa-america-constitution-signing-1779925/
    - Caption: What is happening in the image?
- Courtroom (Sample Image)
    - Caption: What does the space represent?
    - Annotate: Participants in a trial

- https://pixabay.com/photos/courtroom-benches-seats-law-898931/
- Scales of Justice Example
    - Caption: What do they mean to you?

- https://pixabay.com/illustrations/scale-gavel-court-equality-balance-5665991/

### Literature/Media Examples

- Image from a content-related text or movie
  - Law Movies: https://www.abajournal.com/magazine/article/the_25_greatest_legal_movies
  - Students select an image from an assigned text or movie and create a related caption (either open-ended or in response to a prompt).

### Math Example

- Image of a house. Students caption dimensions with math-themed content.

## Portion Type and Size

Single (independent work), pairs, small group, or whole class

Time: Variable

- As few as five minutes.
- No maximum length.
- Time will vary depending on the adopted approach to implementation.
- *Note*: The activity takes significantly less time when the instructor selects a resource for captioning.

Online and/or face to face

## Web Resources

- *What Do You Meme?* See: https://whatdoyoumeme.com/
- "Games Like Cards Against Humanity." See: https://www.bustle.com/life/games-like-cards-against-humanity
- *Caption This* Game. See: https://www.baamboozle.com/game/376431
- *Caption It!* Board Game. See: http://www.boardgamecity.com/games/CaptionItBoardGame.php
- Caption This! With Google Drawings. See: https://ditchthattextbook.com/caption-this-a-fun-deep-thinking-google-drawings-activity/

### Tools

Free Online Meme Makers and Photo Captioning Tools

- Canva. See: https://www.canva.com/create/memes/
- Kapwing Meme Generator. See: https://www.kapwing.com/meme-maker
- Adobe Meme Maker. See: https://www.adobe.com/express/create/meme
- Imgflip Meme Generator. See: https://imgflip.com/memegenerator
- Google Slides (pre-load an image, create enough slides for each student or instruct students to make a copy of a slide)
- Google Draw. See: https://docs.google.com/drawings/d/16O6j00gWoHSUR80peZ9ZNxrrlPLoqQWJkppXuPtro8s/edit
- Google Jamboard (pre-load an image), group captioning/annotating. See: https://jamboard.google.com/

Free Photo Sites

- Unsplash. See: https://unsplash.com/
- Pixabay. See: https://pixabay.com/
- Pexels. See: https://www.pexels.com/

Articles

- The Best Tools for Making Internet Memes. See: https://larryferlazzo.edublogs.org/2013/06/27/the-best-tools-for-making-internet-memes/

## I Tried This and This Is What I Learned

| DATE USED/LESSON TOPIC | REFLECTIONS/WHAT I MIGHT DO DIFFERENTLY NEXT TIME |
|---|---|
| | |
| | |
| | |

Have a "I Have a Caption/Label for That" activity adaptation to share?

Submit your tweaks and experiences here:

Survey Link: https://forms.gle/G7JS4RPADQK8ykp89

## Snack Break: Time for a Laugh

**Sweet Treats/Desserts**

**Ice Breaker Title: Snack Break: Time for a Laugh**

Comics to promote deeper understanding, reflection, and critical thinking

## Activity Description

Comic review and discussion activities offer opportunities for students to reflect on course concepts in creative ways. Comic review and discussion activities also present opportunities for students to review complicated concepts in a stress-free environment.

Comic review and discussion activities can help proactively mitigate the increased cognitive load (drain on working memory) and anxiety that often emerges when a student interacts with complex concepts. This activity is designed to support and sustain increased student comfort and confidence when interacting with course concepts. In this activity, students review and reflect on a presented comic and engage in related critical analysis and discussion.

This activity works well as an introductory warm-up and/or reflection activity for a substantive lesson associated with the topic used for the comic review and discussion exercise.

## Recipe

Step 1: Define and explain the comic review and discussion activity.

Step 2: Introduce the activity. Clarify content focus and type of resource to be used for the activity.

Step 3: Create groups (if applicable).

Step 4: Share a link or copy of the selected comic/Provide time for students to research and locate a comic for use in this activity (if applicable).

Step 5: Provide active work time for students to reflect and write on the meaning of the comic. Time can vary (30 seconds/60 seconds/two minutes).

- Offer support as needed.
- Share directional reminders about the activity, as applicable.

Step 6: Discuss, either in small groups or as a whole class.

## The Secret Sauce (Why It Works)

This **interactive** activity breaks down complex material into manageable chunks that reduce **cognitive load** on students. Students draw on and actively **recall** prior learning and knowledge. The activity promotes **creative thinking** and hands-on, **active learning** that requires students to interact with a course concept/topic. Goals include increased student **comfort** with a particular topic as well as increased **understanding** of the topic. The activity offers opportunities for **reflection** for both individuals and groups. The activity also offers opportunities for **formative assessment**.

## Ingredients

- ☐ A comic related to a class learning objective or lesson
- ☐ Clock/Timer (as applicable)

## Activity Prep

A comic related to a class learning objective or lesson.

Optional: Post an image to a Google Slide. Force copy. Students then complete annotation activity.

Optional: Students conduct research and identify a comic for this activity.

## Activity Adaptations/Toppings

Depending on the instructional goals and objectives, this activity can be used and adapted in a variety of ways.

- Conduct the activity using a comic associated with a current reading, assigned book, or related news article.
- Introduce the activity with a discussion question/reflection prompt that explores the course topic most closely aligned with a selected image.
- Students create an original caption for a selected comic (aligned with an identified course concept or topic).
- Vary time permitted to work on comic summary.
- Vary recommended length for comic summary (word limits, number of sentences).
- Whole class captions a single comic.
- Students caption comics in pairs or small groups and then present to class.
- Add quote bubbles for students to complete.

## Activity Extensions

- Provide opportunities for students to publicly share comic summaries. Students might post summaries to a class bulletin board or gallery. A Padlet board, class Google Site, or Pinterest board are free options that work well.
- Offer instruction and/or review for appropriate citation and attribution format for shared comics.
- If student research leads to a collection of comics associated with a course topic, ask students to share resources in a class library (Google Docs, Google Sites, Padlet board). Students might use shared comics (along with associated citations) for future projects.
- Students conduct research and locate comics that best represent or capture an assigned topic. Summarizing can be assigned as independent work.
- Students create original content-related comics either in class or independently.

### Law-Based Examples

Alamy. (2015). *Stock photo—3d illustration of prosecution title on legal document*. Alamy. https://www.alamy.com/stock-photo-3d-illustration-of-prosecution-title-on-legal-document-175836582.html

Editor. (2010). *Jury cartoons images*. Shutterstock. https://www.shutterstock.com/search/jury+cartoons.

Editor. (2020). *Judge and jury*. Judge & Jury. https://www.facebook.com/judgejur/

Jury. Illustration by Eric Molinsky. Flickr. https://www.flickr.com/photos/caliorg/6882839119/

Grammar-Based Examples

- Parking fine example. "I thought it was fine to park here." See: https://ifunny.co/picture/i-thought-it-was-fine-to-park-here-RsF7hnSK8

## Portion Type and Size

Single (independent work), pairs, small group, or whole class

Time: Variable

- As few as five minutes.
- No maximum length.
- Time will vary depending on the adopted approach to implementation.
- *Note*: The activity takes significantly less time when the instructor pre-selects comics.

Online and/or face to face

## Web Resources

### Law-Themed Comics

- LawComic. See: https://lawcomic.net/guide/
- Lawyer Cartoons. See: https://www.pinterest.com/huntsvillelaw/lawyer-cartoons/
- Legal Cartoons. See: https://www.pinterest.com/tadpole4449/legal-cartoons/
- Lawyer Cartoons. See: https://andertoons.com/cartoons/lawyer

### Create Your Own Comics Resources

Canva. See: https://www.canva.com/create/comic-strips/

## I Tried This and This Is What I Learned

| DATE USED/LESSON TOPIC | REFLECTIONS/WHAT I MIGHT DO DIFFERENTLY NEXT TIME |
|---|---|
| | |
| | |
| | |

Have a "Snack Break: Time for a Laugh" activity adaptation to share?

Submit your tweaks and experiences here:

Survey Link: https://forms.gle/G7JS4RPADQK8ykp89

# I Know That! Rebus Puzzle

**Sweet Treats/Desserts**

**Ice Breaker Title: I Know That! Rebus Puzzle**

Rebus puzzles to promote creative thinking and active recall

## Activity Description

"I Know That! Rebus Puzzle" activities offer opportunities for students to engage with course terms and concepts in creative ways. Students solve picture puzzles where course terms are represented in a puzzle format with the use of emojis and other graphics.

Rebus puzzles present instructional opportunities for students to review and recall key terms in a fun and stress-free environment.

This activity is designed to support and sustain increased student comfort and confidence in connection with course content. This activity works well as an introductory warm-up for a substantive lesson that might require students to actively recall and apply prior course terminology and concepts.

## Recipe

Step 1: Define and explain "I Know That! Rebus Puzzle" activities.

Step 2: Introduce the activity. Describe and explain rebus puzzles. Clarify content focus and type of resource to be used for the activity.

Step 3: Create groups (if applicable).

Step 4: Share a link or copy of the rebus puzzles for use in this activity.

Step 5: Provide active work time for students to solve rebus puzzles. Puzzles might be presented in batches or individually. Teams can be formed for a gamified approach.

- Offer support as needed.
- Share directional reminders about the activity, as applicable.

Step 6: Provide reflection-based prompts for students to complete (optional, as desired). Open discussion and reflection on the exercise (out loud or independent journaling).

## The Secret Sauce (Why It Works)

This **puzzle-based** activity presents course concepts in **creative** and **visual** ways. The activity promotes hands-on, **active learning** that requires students to do something (solve a rebus puzzle) and practice **active recall** of key course terms. Goals include increased student **comfort** with course terms as well as stronger retention and long-term learning. The activity offers opportunities for **reflection** (both individual and group). The activity also offers opportunities for **formative assessment**.

## Ingredients

- ☐ A collection of rebus puzzles related to a course or lesson objective
- ☐ Clock/Timer (as applicable)

## Activity Prep

A collection of rebus puzzles related to a course or lesson objective.

Optional: Students create original rebus puzzles for use in this activity.

## Activity Adaptations/Toppings

Depending on the instructional goals and objectives, this activity can be used and adapted in a variety of ways.

- Students create original rebus puzzles for use in future activities.
- Create teams or small groups and present rebus puzzles one by one. Points are earned for solving rebus puzzles.
- Introduce the activity with a discussion question/reflection prompt that explores the course concepts that are the focus of the related rebus puzzles.

## Activity Extensions

- Provide opportunities for students to research and create original rebus puzzles that align with specific collections of chapter or module terms. Students might post puzzles to a class bulletin board or gallery. A Padlet board, class Google Site, or Pinterest board are free options that work well.
- Students as creators: Students design and sketch original graphics for use in rebus puzzle creation.
    - For a related reading on the benefits of sketching, see: Using Drawings for Formative Assessment. https://www.edutopia.org/article/using-drawings-formative-assessmentf
- Students create rebus stories on a course-related topic or theme.
- Rebus puzzles can be created using hand-drawn sketches as well as text.

### Law-Themed Examples

1. Right On
2. Nobody
   ---------
   Law

### Health Care Examples

- Heartbeat: Heart + Beat
- Brainwave: Brain + Ocean Wave
- Bandage: Musical Band + Numbers
- Cardiac Arrest: Heart + Police Officer
- Stroke: Golf Swing
- Airway: Airplane + Street
- Supine: Soup + Pine Tree - P
- Sprain: Spring (season or bouncy) - Ring + Rain
- Band Aid: Band + Extended Hand
- High Blood Pressure: Wave Hi + Blood + Pressure

### Anatomy Examples

- Sternum: Mad Face + Bum - B
- Humerus: Funny Face Emoji + Group of People

### Legal (General)

- Briefcase: Briefs + Case
- Court: Fort - F + C
- Scales of Justice: Scale + of + Just + Ice Cubes
- Defendant: D + Car Fender - er + Ant
- Litigator: Light + Eye + Alligator - Alli
- Reporter: Sheets of Paper/Memos + er
- Judgment: Judge + Men + T
- On the Right Side of the Law: Law On
- Appellant: Apple + Ant
- Applicant: Apple – e + I + Ant

### Intellectual Property

Intellectual Property: Brain + Buildings

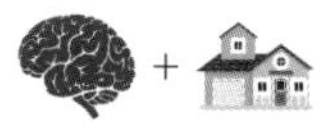

Patent: Pat a Dog + Tent

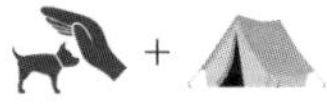

Copyright: Copier Machine + Pen and Pencil

Form: 4 + m

Trademark: Stock Market Ticker Tape + Check Mark

Trade Secret: Barter + Sshhh Sign

Contract: Prisoner + Train Tracks

Idea: Eye + D + A

Invention: A House or Inn + Air Vent + Shin - I + U

Filing: Nail File + -ing

Protect: Professional Golfer + -tect

### Contracts

Bargained for Exchange: For Sale Sign + 4 + Coins/Pennies

Contract: Railroad Track + T

Offer: Light Switch in Off Mode + -er

For more Rebus Puzzle examples, see: https://docs.google.com/document/d/19oyulesvrJNMh3PWDGiP5mcikhgeP0i7sjWWZOwcnSQ/edit?usp=sharing

## Portion Type and Size

Single (independent work), pairs, small group, or whole class

Time: Variable

- As few as five minutes.
- No maximum length.
- Time will vary depending on the adopted approach to implementation.
- *Note*: The activity takes significantly less time when the instructor creates puzzles in advance.

Online and/or face to face

## Web Resources

Just for Fun

- "Twenty Rebus Puzzles that are Almost Impossible to Solve". See: https://www.rd.com/list/rebus-puzzles/
- "25 Rebus Puzzles". See: https://parade.com/1175283/marynliles/rebus-puzzles/
- Rebus Puzzles Brainteasers". See: https://kids.niehs.nih.gov/games/brainteasers/rebus-puzzles/index.htm

### Emoji Libraries

- Emojipedia. See: https://emojipedia.org/
- Emoji Library. See: https://getemoji.com/

## Web Resources

Classroom Rebuses. See: https://education.yourdictionary.com/for-teachers/classroom-rebuses.html

Rebus Puzzles. See: http://www.fun-with-words.com/rebus_puzzles_01.html

## I Tried This and This Is What I Learned

| DATE USED/LESSON TOPIC | REFLECTIONS/WHAT I MIGHT DO DIFFERENTLY NEXT TIME |
|---|---|
| | |
| | |
| | |

Have an "I Know That! Rebus Puzzle" activity adaptation to share?

Submit your tweaks and experiences here:

Survey Link: https://forms.gle/G7JS4RPADQK8ykp89

# Picture Perfect

**Sweet Treats/Desserts**

**Ice Breaker Title: Picture Perfect**

Image and graphic (meme) identification and retrieval to promote creativity, reflection, and critical thinking

## Activity Description

Identifying representative graphics and images offer opportunities for students to reflect on course concepts in creative ways. Active research and identification of memes related to a specific course concept also present instructional opportunities for students to review complicated concepts in a stress-free environment. This activity is designed to support and sustain increased student comfort and confidence when interacting with course concepts.

In this meme-retrieval activity, students review and reflect on a presented course concept. Students then conduct research and identify a graphic or meme that best captures the meaning of the concept (or the students' feelings and thoughts related to the concept). Concepts that are sometimes intimidating for students (because of vocabulary, writing style, familiarity, or otherwise) are especially well suited to this activity.

This activity is inspired by games such as *What Do You Meme?* and *Caption This*.

## Recipe

Step 1: Define and explain memes.

Step 2: Introduce the activity. Explain how "Picture Perfect" activities work. Clarify content focus and type of resource to be used for the activity.

Step 3: Create groups (if applicable).

Step 4: Present a course concept (or collection of course concepts).

Step 5: Provide time for students to reflect on the meaning of the concept. Alternatively, encourage students to reflect on how they feel when asked to explain or apply the concept.

Step 6: Provide time for students to research and locate a meme, image, or graphic that best captures the concept or their feelings associated with the concept (as applicable).

- Offer support as needed.
- Share directional reminders about the activity, as applicable.

Step 7: Open discussion.

- Student volunteers share.
- Post to an online gallery (Padlet, Google Slides).

## The Secret Sauce (Why It Works)

This **interactive** activity provides a visual-oriented approach to engagement with a presented concept. The activity promotes **creative thinking** and hands-on, **active learning** that require students to interact with a course concept or topic. Goals include increased student **comfort** with a particular topic as well as increased **understanding** of the topic. The activity offers opportunities for **reflection** for both individuals and groups. The activity also offers opportunities for **formative assessment**.

## Ingredients

- ☐ A specific course concept (or collection/list of concepts)
- ☐ Clock/Timer (as applicable)

## Activity Prep

Identify a course concept related to a lesson's theme or learning objective(s).

## Activity Adaptations/Toppings

Depending on the instructional goals and objectives, this activity can be used and adapted in a variety of ways.

- Conduct the activity using a current reading, assigned book, or related news article.
- Introduce the activity with a discussion question/reflection prompt that explores the related course topic.
- Students create original memes in response to a presented course concept.
- Vary time permitted to work on meme-related research.
- Students identify a course topic and then swap with peers before searching for related memes.

## Activity Extensions

- Provide opportunities for students to publicly share found memes. A Padlet board, class Google Site, or Pinterest board are free options that work well.
- Offer instruction and/or review for appropriate citation and attribution format for shared memes.
- If student research leads to a collection of memes associated with a course topic, ask students to share resources in a class library (Google Docs, Google Sites, Padlet board). Source identification can be used as research reinforcement and library building.

### Science Examples

Biology Memes. See: https://www.pinterest.com.au/lisaparsons33/biology-memes/

Chemistry Memes. See: https://www.thoughtco.com/best-chemistry-memes-604332

## Portion Type and Size

Single (independent work), pairs, small groups, or whole class

Time: Variable

- As few as five minutes.
- No maximum length.
- Time will vary depending on the adopted approach to implementation.

Online and/or face to face

## Web Resources

Where to Find Memes

- Imgur: https://imgur.com/
- GIPHY: https://giphy.com
- Tenor: https://tenor.com
    - Search Engine Journal: https://www.searchenginejournal.com/find-gifs-memes/351988/

Related Games

- What Do You Meme?: https://whatdoyoumeme.com/
- Bustle: https://www.bustle.com/life/games-like-cards-against-humanity
- Baamboozle: https://www.baamboozle.com/game/376431
- Board Game City: http://www.boardgamecity.com/games/CaptionItBoardGame.php

Additional educational activity resource. "Caption This! A fun, deep-thinking Google Drawings activity". See: https://ditchthattextbook.com/caption-this-a-fun-deep-thinking-google-drawings-activity/

### Tools

Free Online Meme Makers and Photo Captioning Tools

- Canva: https://www.canva.com/create/memes/
- Meme Maker: https://www.kapwing.com/meme-maker
- Adobe: https://www.adobe.com/express/create/meme
- Imgflip, Meme Generator: https://imgflip.com/memegenerator
- Google Slides (can pre-load an image, students then make a copy of the slide or create multiple slides, enough for each student)
- Google Jamboard (can pre-load an image), group captioning/annotating
- Google Draw

Free Photo Sites

- Unsplash: https://unsplash.com/
- Pixabay: https://pixabay.com/
- Pexels: https://www.pexels.com/

### Articles

- The Best Tools for Making Internet Memes. See: https://larryferlazzo.edublogs.org/2013/06/27/the-best-tools-for-making-internet-memes/

## I Tried This and This Is What I Learned

| DATE USED/LESSON TOPIC | REFLECTIONS/WHAT I MIGHT DO DIFFERENTLY NEXT TIME |
|---|---|
| | |
| | |
| | |

Have a "Picture Perfect" activity adaptation to share?

Submit your tweaks and experiences here:

Survey Link: https://forms.gle/G7JS4RPADQK8ykp89

## House Kitchen and Table Rules

**Sweet Treats/Desserts**

**Ice Breaker Title: House, Kitchen, and Table Rules**

Creation of a class or small group "learning contract" to promote collaboration and communication

### Activity Description

This activity provides an opportunity for students to collaborate and create an original "learning contract" that will govern the way a classroom community is developed, nurtured, and sustained.

Students work together to create a learning contract that will establish classroom guidelines and interactions. The learning contract is student initiated and student drafted as a way to support communication and collaboration.

The activity promotes reflection, communication, and proactive feedback (as students share ideas for a desirable and optimal learning environment) and supports the development of a tool that can help promote dialogue, engagement, feedback loops, and active learning.

The activity works especially well at the start of a semester/school year. The activity is also beneficial when new groups and/or learning teams are formed for a particular course project or assignment.

### Recipe

Step 1: Introduce the activity. Explain how "House, Kitchen, and Table Rules" activities work.

Step 2: Clarify the purpose of an individual, group, or whole-class learning contract.

Step 3: Share examples of learning contracts that can be used as inspiration for the activity.

Step 4: Clarify expectations (individual, small group, whole class) and desired content (including length and detail) for the assigned learning contract.

Step 4: Provide time for students to draft and finalize learning contracts (recommended minimum 10–15 minutes).

- Offer support as needed.
- Share directional reminders, as applicable.

Step 5: Share drafts and discuss.

Step 6: Collect drafts for review and later feedback.

Step 7: Open discussion and reflection on the exercise (out loud or independent journaling).

Sample prompts:

- How has this activity changed the way you feel about our class?
- How has this activity changed the way you feel about learning?
- How has this activity changed the way you feel about collaboration?

## The Secret Sauce (Why It Works)

This **group** activity prompts students to **draft and create** guidelines and expectations that will both directly and indirectly influence and impact their learning experience. Students reflect on their values and their desires for an optimal learning experience. The activity both **empowers** students and holds students more **accountable** to each other and their learning experiences. Students simultaneously provide instructors valuable **feedback** on their desired learning experience. The activity promotes hands-on, **active learning** that requires students to do something (create a learning contract). Goals include increased **student awareness** of individual learning preferences as well as increased **dialogue** and **communication** to instructors regarding a desired student experience.

## Ingredients

- ☐ A template and/or list of recommended content to be addressed in a learning contract
- ☐ Clock/Timer (as applicable)

## Activity Prep

A template and/or list of recommended content to be addressed in a learning contract.

## Activity Adaptations/Toppings

Depending on the instructional goals and objectives, this activity can be used and adapted in a variety of ways. A few examples follow:

- Open discussion regarding the qualities of an optimal learning environment.
- Open discussion of individual strengths and weaknesses that might impact a classroom learning community and environment. Discussions might address time management, motivation, communication, collaboration, teamwork, and/or organizational skills (as examples).
- Open journaling, independent student writing to reflect on preferred learning environments.
- Students work in pairs or small groups to create learning contract templates.

## Activity Extensions

- Provide opportunities for students to discuss benefits and disadvantages of variations on clauses in an agreed-upon learning contract.
- Provide opportunities to discuss learning contracts either independently and/or in small groups with instructor.

## Portion Type and Size

Single (independent work), pairs, small group, or whole class

Time: Variable

- As few as five minutes
- No maximum length
- *Note*: The activity takes significantly less time when the instructor prepares contract templates for use and modification.

Online and/or face to face

## Web Resources

- Sample Learning Contract: https://uwaterloo.ca/centre-for-teaching-excellence/teaching-resources/teaching-tips/tips-students/self-directed-learning/self-directed-learning-learning-contracts
- Learning Contracts: https://strategiesforspecialinterventions.weebly.com/learning-contract.html
- Collect student responses and input via Google Forms (or other survey tool).

Sample Question: What guidelines and expectations would you like to see captured in our class contract?

## References

Barlow, R. M. (1974). An experiment with learning contracts. *The Journal of Higher Education, 45*(6), 441–449. DOI: 10.1080/00221546.1974.11776979

Kim, R., Olfman, L., Ryan, T., & Eryilmaz, E. (2014). Leveraging a personalized system to improve self-directed learning in online educational environments. *Computers & Education, 70*, 150–160.

Knowles, M. S. (1986). *Using learning contracts: Practical approaches to individualizing and structuring learning*. London: Jossey-Bass.

Lemieux, C. M. (2001). Learning contracts in the classroom: Tools for empowerment and accountability. *Social Work Education*, 20(2), 263–276. DOI: 10.1080/02615470120044347

University of Waterloo, Centre for Teaching Excellence. (n.d.). *Self-directed learning: Learning contracts*. https://uwaterloo.ca/centre-for-teaching-excellence/teaching-resources/teaching-tips/tips-students/self-directed-learning/self-directed-learning-learning-contracts

## I Tried This and This Is What I Learned

| DATE USED/LESSON TOPIC | REFLECTIONS/WHAT I MIGHT DO DIFFERENTLY NEXT TIME |
|---|---|
| | |
| | |
| | |

Have a "House, Kitchen, and Table Rules" activity adaptation to share?

Submit your tweaks and experiences here:

Survey Link: https://forms.gle/G7JS4RPADQK8ykp89

# My Sweet Spot (Getting to Know My Tastes)

**Sweet Treats/Desserts**

**Ice Breaker Title: My Sweet Spot (Getting to Know My Tastes) (Self-Assessments)**

Personality and aptitude survey activities to promote reflection and self-awareness

## Activity Description

"My Sweet Spot" and related "Getting to Know My Tastes" self-assessment activities are designed to support reflection and self-awareness. Students develop greater appreciation for personal strengths as well as the application of course concepts to real-world applications and future career paths.

In this activity, students complete free personality, values, and related self-assessments and reflect on results to better understand potential career opportunities that might be best suited for their skills, talents, and preferences.

"My Sweet Spot" and "Getting to Know My Tastes" activities offer opportunities for students to develop a deeper understanding of themselves and to connect course concepts to real-world contexts and associated career opportunities. The activities promote both reflection and application. Students explore how they might apply knowledge about themselves in and to actual, real-world situations.

The activity promotes forward-focused and career-related thinking, as well as reflective thinking and self-analysis. This activity is designed to support creative thinking and sustain increased student confidence associated with personal strengths and related career paths. Students will gain additional insights into their relative strengths and values, information which can help focus and optimize job search processes.

This activity works well as an introductory review warm-up at the conclusion of a unit (or at the mid- or endpoint of a semester).

## Recipe

Step 1: Define and explain "My Sweet Spot (Getting to Know My Tastes) (Self-Assessments)" activities.

Step 2: Introduce the activity. Clarify content focus and type of resource (e.g., paper-based assessment, digital assessment) to be used for the activity.

Step 3: Provide tips and reminders for how to complete the self-assessment.

- Answer truthfully.
- Reflect carefully before selecting a response.
- Review all question options.

Step 4: Share a link to suggested assessment (if applicable).

Step 5: Provide active work time for students to complete the self-assessment.

Step 6: Students reflect on results. Options include paired, small group, and/or whole-class discussions. Students might also reflect independently through written reflections.

- Offer support as needed.
- Share directional reminders about the activity, as applicable.

Sample prompts:

- Based on the results of the self-assessments, share an analysis of your relative strengths as well as areas with room for improvement. Consider both strengths and weaknesses in the context of your future work as a _____.
- Identify and summarize the results (areas of strength and areas of weakness) of the self-assessments and resources you completed and/or reviewed.

- How would you rate yourself on each of the assessment categories? Are you surprised by your results? Do you agree with the assessment results?
- Discuss the importance of a(n) ____________ mindset for a __[insert any relevant career/job]_____.
- Identify three to five specific steps you can (will) take in order to strengthen your __________ mindset and related skills.
- Evaluate how taking the identified steps might help you professionally in your work as a future ________.

Step 7: Open discussion and reflection on the exercise (out loud or independent journaling).

Sample prompts:

- How has this activity changed the way you feel about your preferred/desired career path?

Step 8: Facility an open discussion that critically analyzes the shared self-assessment.

- Encourage students to reflect on possible biases, flaws, and inaccuracies associated with the test design and/or results.

## The Secret Sauce (Why It Works)

This **interactive** activity breaks down course concepts into relatable, forward-focused activities that increase **relevance** for students. Students engage in **self-reflection** and develop greater **self-awareness** of personal strengths. The activity promotes hands-on, **active learning** that requires students to complete personal self-assessments associated with course and related career concepts. Goals include increased **student comfort** with a particular area of course content as well as increased **confidence** and **awareness** of associated career opportunities. The activity offers opportunities for **reflection** for both individuals and groups, **career-related awareness**, and **application**.

## Ingredients

- ☐ A free personality/career/values-related self-assessment
- ☐ Clock/Timer (as applicable)

## Activity Prep

A free self-assessment

- Paper-based or digital

## Activity Adaptations/Toppings

Depending on the instructional goals and objectives, this activity can be used and adapted in a variety of ways. A few examples follow:

- Introduce the activity using a passage (several paragraphs, a page of text) from a current reading, assigned book, or related news article. After reading the text, students brainstorm and generate lists of different types of careers and jobs that might be involved with the roles described in the readings.
- Introduce the activity with a discussion question/reflection prompt that explores the value of breaking down jobs into specific skills (both essential and helpful).

- Introduce the activity with a discussion question/reflection prompt that explores the benefits of applying course concepts to career applications.
- Introduce the activity using a current event/news article related to the lesson topic and from which students generate job profiles.
- Introduce the activity with a discussion question that explores the value of self-assessments to identify relative strengths.
- Use the activity as a collaborative learning exercise where one student is responsible for drafting a course-related scenario and another is tasked with identifying a variety of job opportunities related to such scenario.

## Activity Extensions

- Students conduct independent research and share career-related articles and resources. Students might post resources to a class bulletin board or gallery. A Padlet board, class Google Site, or Pinterest board are free options that work well.
- Students review job postings in fields of interest. Discuss associated job-specific skills (necessary/preferred).

### Example Self-Assessments

- Implicit Association Test. See: https://implicit.harvard.edu/implicit/takeatest.html
- TapRoot, Core Values Exercise. See: https://www.taproot.com/live-your-core-values-exercise-to-increase-your-success/
- CMU Values Exercise. See: https://www.cmu.edu/career/documents/career-guides/myCareerPathGuide2018-2019.pdf
- Core Values Discovery Process. See: https://scottjeffrey.com/personal-core-values/
- Entrepreneur Assessment Survey. See: https://cnx.org/contents/1ttgPM0x@4.3:bLnTnPz1@4/Entrepreneur-assessment-survey
- Career Assessment Matrix. See: https://career-intelligence.com/career-assessment-matrix/
- James Clear Core Values. See: https://jamesclear.com/core-values
- Mindtools. See: https://www.mindtools.com/
- How Creative Are You? See: https://www.kellogg.northwestern.edu/faculty/uzzi/ftp/page176.html
- How Creative Are You? Mindtools. See: https://www.mindtools.com/pages/article/creativity-quiz.htm
- Mindtools Reflection Quizzes. See: https://www.mindtools.com/pages/main/SelfTestsIndex.htm
- Jung Typology Test. See: http://www.humanmetrics.com/cgi-win/jtypes2.asp#questionnaire
- Keirsey Temperament Sorter. See: https://profile.keirsey.com/#/b2c/assessment/start
- O*NET Interest Profiler. See: https://www.mynextmove.org/explore/ip
- Myers-Brigg Test (describes one's preferred way of interesting with others). See: http://www.humanmetrics.com/cgi-win/jtypes2.asp. See also: https://www.16personalities.com/
- The Strong Interest Inventory. See: https://www.themyersbriggs.com/en-US/Products-and-Services/Strong
- Values Assessments. See: https://www.myplan.com/assess/values.php
- Leadership Skills, Self-Assessments. See: https://www.mindtools.com/pages/article/newLDR_50.htm
- VIA Character Skills Self-Assessment. See: https://www.viacharacter.org/

## Portion Type and Size

Single (independent work), pairs, small group, or whole class

Time: Variable

- As few as five minutes.
- No maximum length.
- Time will vary depending on the adopted approach to implementation.

Online and/or face to face

## Web Resources

- Jobs-Related Resources
  - Bureau of Labor Statistics. See: https://www.bls.gov/
  - Occupational Outlook Handbook. See: https://www.bls.gov/ooh/
  - Free Career Aptitude Tests. See: https://www.thebalancecareers.com/free-career-aptitude-tests-2059813
  - Career Assessment Matrix. See: https://career-intelligence.com/career-assessment-matrix/

## I Tried This and This Is What I Learned

| DATE USED/LESSON TOPIC | REFLECTIONS/WHAT I MIGHT DO DIFFERENTLY NEXT TIME |
|---|---|
| | |
| | |
| | |

Have a "My Sweet Spot" activity adaptation to share?

Submit your tweaks and experiences here:

Survey Link: https://forms.gle/G7JS4RPADQK8ykp89

# Odd Flavor Out

**Sweet Treats/Desserts**

**Ice Breaker Title: Odd Flavor Out**

"Which one doesn't belong" exercises as a tool to apply learning, distinguish concepts, and develop arguments

## Activity Description

"Odd Flavor Out" or "Which one doesn't belong" activities are valuable tools to promote critical thinking, reflection, and deeper analysis. In this activity, students review a grouping (e.g., concepts, topics, events,) and analyze the grouping for similarities and differences. Students are tasked with identifying (and developing an associated argument) one item in the group as an "off flavor" or distinguishable in some way (e.g., characteristics, use, content) from the other items in the group.

This activity offers opportunities for students to engage with complex topics in new ways. "Odd Flavor Out" activities present instructional opportunities for students to develop associated arguments in a low-stakes and stress-free environment.

This activity is designed to support and sustain increased student comfort and confidence when testing (and sharing) ideas, developing arguments, and interacting with complex concepts.

The activity works well with any grouping of related concepts.

This activity works well as review for a substantive lesson associated with prior course topics.

## Recipe

Step 1: Define and explain "Odd Flavor Out" activities.

Step 2: Introduce the activity. Clarify content focus and type of resource to be used for the activity.

Step 3: Create groups (if applicable).

Step 4: Share a link or copy of the resource (if applicable).

Step 5: Provide time for students to create original groupings (optional/if applicable).

Step 6: Share applicable prompt.

Step 7: Provide active work time for students to reflect and generate a response (along with an associated argument).

- Offer support as needed.
- Share directional reminders about the activity, as applicable.

Step 8: Collect and share responses. Discuss shared responses (in pairs, small groups, or as a whole class).

Step 9: Open discussion and reflection on the exercise (out loud or independent journaling).

Sample prompts:

- How has this activity changed the way you feel about the identified "odd flavor out"?
- How has this activity changed the way you feel about the related topic?
- How has this activity change the way you feel about argument construction?

Step 10: Provide time for students to reflect (with opportunities for journal writing) .

## The Secret Sauce (Why It Works)

This **interactive** activity breaks down complex material into **individual elements/components** that reduce **cognitive load** on students. Students draw on and **actively recall** prior learning and knowledge. The activity promotes hands-on, **active learning** that requires students to interact with a collection of related concepts/topics. The activity also provides opportunities for **communication, argument construction, critical thinking**, and **elaboration**. Goals include increased **student comfort** with a particular topic as well as increased **confidence** constructing, developing, and communicating arguments. The activity offers opportunities for **reflection** for both individuals and groups. The activity also offers opportunities for **formative assessment**.

## Ingredients

- ☐ A graphic or document with a collection or list of related concepts
- ☐ Clock/Timer (as applicable)

## Activity Prep

A graphic or document with a collection or list of related concepts.

Optional: Students create a grouping (list/collection/set of graphics) for this activity.

## Activity Adaptations/Toppings

Depending on the instructional goals and objectives, this activity can be used and adapted in a variety of ways. A few examples follow:

- Alternate Prompts
    - Which one must go?
    - Which one can go?
    - Which one can't go?
- Swaps
    - What item might be swapped for one of the listed items/ingredients?
- Introduce the activity with a discussion question/reflection prompt that explores the general concept/topic from which the images/groupings are derived.
- Introduce the activity with a discussion question/reflection prompt that explores the different ways topics/items might be grouped, distinguished, curated, etc.
- Introduce the activity using a current event/news article related to the lesson topic and from which students create "which one doesn't belong" groupings.
- Use the activity as a collaborative learning exercise where paired/grouped students create collections of related activities. Students then swap collections to complete the "which one doesn't belong" activity and related discussion.
- Students create an "Odd Flavor Out" collection on a course topic/theme of choice.
- Students create an "Odd Flavor Out" collection on an assigned course topic.
- Vary time permitted to work on grouping construction and/or related discussion.
- Vary number of items included in each grouping.

## Activity Extensions

- Provide opportunities for students to publicly share "Odd Flavor Out" graphics. Students might post graphics to a class bulletin board or gallery. A Padlet board, class Google Site, or Pinterest board are free options that work well.
- During the warm-up activity, students create original graphics (Canva, Google Slides, and Google Draw all work well) for use in "Odd Flavor Out" activities. Students swap graphics, with independent journaling (e.g., which one doesn't belong, which is most needed, what else might be added) assigned as independent work.

## Law-Based Examples

- **Judicial Opinions**

Share a collection of judicial opinions (three or more) for student review. Students select one which "doesn't belong" and share associated reasons in support of their selection.

- **Statutes**

Copyright Statutes, Patent Statutes, Trademark Statutes, Trade Secret Statutes

- **Illustrative Graphics**

Which one doesn't belong. See: https://drive.google.com/drive/folders/1rNZCaw0PJf4Mk0tVPckPaYlj1uJoLNez?usp=sharing

Samples:

## Communication Examples

- Writing Instruments
- Communication Devices

## History Examples

- Historical events (e.g., wars, treaty signings).
- Historical figures (e.g., presidents, Supreme Court justices).

## Physics Examples

- The Physics Classroom, Which One Doesn't Belong. See: https://www.physicsclassroom.com/Concept-Builders/Newtons-Laws/Which-One-Doesnt-Belong

## Geometric Patterns Examples

- Desmos Classroom, Tessellations. See: https://teacher.desmos.com/activitybuilder/custom/5f18e0f7403ce72e85172e09?collections=featured-collections%2C5e44be054273ab1a7f4e7471#preview/731fe2c1-9a35-4284-b891-1974cc767742

For more interactive math activities, see: https://teacher.desmos.com/

### Mathematics Examples

- Exponents, Parentheses, Square Roots, Logarithms

### Healthcare Examples

- Doctor, Nurse, Surgeon, Patient
- Stethoscope, Pulse Ox, Blood Pressure Cuff, Thermometer
- Otoscopes, Electrocardiographs, Sphygmomanometers, Ophthalmoscopes

### Culinary Examples

- Carrots, Radishes, Celery, Cabbage
- Pork, Chicken, Turkey, Ground Beef, Tofu
- Lettuce, Cabbage, Kale, Spinach
- Tomato, Pickles, Coleslaw, Bacon
- Pot, Pan, Dish, Spatula

### Veterinary Care

- Collar, Leash, Harness, Kibble

### Emergency Medicine Examples

- Bag Valve Mask, Bandage, Splint, Blanket

### Biology Examples

- Pipette, Cell Culture Shield, Computer, Patient

### Physical Education Examples

- Soccer Ball, Cleat, Net, Shin Guard

### Education Examples

- Teacher, Student, Physical Classroom, Textbooks

## Portion Type and Size

Single (independent work), pairs, small group, or whole class

Time: Variable

- As few as five minutes.
- No maximum length.
- Time will vary depending on the adopted approach to implementation.
- *Note*: The activity takes significantly less time when the instructor prepares a collection/grouping of related items in advance.

Online and/or face to face

## Web Resources

- Which One Doesn't Belong. See: https://wodb.ca/index.html

- Which One Doesn't Belong. See: http://www.meaningfulmathmoments.com/which-one-doesnt-belong-wodb.html
- Graphic Creation Tools
    - Canva. See: https://www.canva.com/

## I Tried This and This Is What I Learned

| DATE USED/LESSON TOPIC | REFLECTIONS/WHAT I MIGHT DO DIFFERENTLY NEXT TIME |
|---|---|
| | |
| | |
| | |

Have an "Odd Flavor Out" activity adaptation to share?

Submit your tweaks and experiences here:

Survey Link: https://forms.gle/G7JS4RPADQK8ykp89

## Temperature Checks: How Are You/We Doing?

**Sweet Treats/Desserts**

**Ice Breaker Title: Temperature Checks: How Are You/We Doing?**

Low-risk sharing and reflection to build trust and community

## Activity Description

"How Are You/We Doing?" exercises are intended to provide safe spaces for students to share in low-risk, nonpersonal ways. Conducting "How Are You/We Doing?" exercises provide opportunities to gage student well-being, stress, and mindset.

This activity is designed to support and sustain increased student comfort and confidence when interacting with a classroom community. The activity is also designed to provide insights into student and class mindset and overall well-being. The activity can provide helpful information that might inform pacing, time spent on review, and assigned work.

Students can share anonymously (e.g., polling software, individual submissions, chat, index cards) or out loud (e.g., round robin, by initial, by seating). Participation can be optional to respect student privacy.

## Recipe

Step 1: Share a prepared grid (either via a computer screen or in hard-copy format) of related images that reflect a range of emotions.

Step 2: Introduce the activity. Ask students to identify which of the presented images best captures how they are feeling at the start of class.

Sample prompts:

- How are you feeling about the pace of our class?
- How are you feeling about our course content?
- How are you feeling about our course assignments?

Step 3: Encourage students to share their reasoning. Remind students that elaboration and explanation are optional.

Step 4: Open discussion and reflection (out loud or independent journaling).

## The Secret Sauce (Why It Works)

The activity promotes classroom community and trust. Goals include increased **student comfort** and learning readiness. Goals also include heightened awareness of students' emotional states. The activity offers opportunities for **reflection** for both individuals and groups. This **low-stakes activity** can be used to break down complex material into **discrete components** that reduce **cognitive load** on students. Depending on the selected implementation, students might also draw on and **actively recall** prior learning and knowledge. The activity can also promote **active learning** that requires students to interact with provided images. The activity also offers opportunities for **formative assessment**.

## Ingredients

- ☐ A web-based or paper grid/template that conveys a variety of moods/emotional states and/or is related to a class learning objective or lesson topic
- ☐ Clock/Timer (as applicable)
- ☐ Templates for use: https://drive.google.com/drive/folders/1nvMSM23m-LAVbbJUUiip2AqjmzO3u9Yu

Illustrative Images

## Activity Prep

A web-based or paper grid/template that conveys a variety of moods/emotional states and/or is related to a class learning objective or lesson topic.

- Instructors can use pre-made templates. See: https://drive.google.com/drive/folders/1nvMSM23m-LAVbbJUUiip2Aqjmz03u9Yu
- Students might create grids/templates for use.

## Activity Adaptations/Toppings

Depending on the instructional goals and objectives, this activity can be used and adapted in a variety of ways.

- Instead of presenting as a "How are you/we doing?" reflection, modify questions to fit course content.
- Students view a template with different positions/jobs/career paths related to a course topic.
    - Prompt: Which position/job/career path is most interesting to you?
    - Prompt: What question would you ask if presented with an opportunity to interview someone in this position?
- Students view a template with characters from an assigned novel.
    - Prompt: Identify a character trait of any presented character.
    - Prompt: Which character do you most identify with and why?
- Students view a template with annotated diagrams (e.g., human anatomy).
    - Describe the function of any identified body part.
    - Identify the scientific name of any identified body part.
- Introduce the activity with a discussion question/reflection prompt that explores the various images in the presented grid.
- Introduce the activity with a discussion question related to the shared images and which promotes active recall.
    - Examples
        - Which image ____?
        - Order the images from ____.
        - Explain how each image ____.
        - Compare and contrast the images that ____.
- Introduce the activity using a template of images from a current event/news article related to the lesson topic. Students might select an image to research and/or write about further.
- Use the activity as a collaborative learning exercise where a group of students is responsible for finding images and creating a grid/template on an assigned topic. Depending on desired group size, additional roles can be developed. Student groups can share/present work products with the class.
- Students create grids that illustrate key vocabulary terms.
- Students (individually or in groups) create grids on an assigned theme or topic.

- Vary time permitted to find content and create grids.

## Activity Extensions

- Provide opportunities for students to publicly share original grids. Students might post grids to a class bulletin board or gallery. A Padlet board, class Google Site, or Pinterest board are free options that work well.
- If student research leads to sources used for grid/template generation, ask students to share resources in a class library (Google Docs, Google Sites, Padlet board). Source identification can be used as research reinforcement and library building.
    - Either individually, in pairs, in small groups, or as a whole-class exercise, students create an original grid that illustrates various tasks associated with an identified role or job
    - Sample templates. See: https://drive.google.com/drive/folders/1nvMSM23m-LAVbbJUUiip2Aqjmz03u9Yu

## Portion Type and Size

Pairs, small group, or whole class

Time: Variable

- As few as five minutes.
- No maximum length.
- Time will vary depending on the adopted approach to implementation.

Online and/or face to face

## Web Resources

- Templates for Use: https://drive.google.com/drive/folders/1nvMSM23m-LAVbbJUUiip2Aqjmz03u9Yu
- Additional web-based examples.
    - Sample Mood Scales. See: https://www.pinterest.com/trudywoo/mood-scales/
    - Sample Mood Scales. See: https://www.pinterest.com/jessicalyndon/mood-scale/

## I Tried This and This Is What I Learned

| DATE USED/LESSON TOPIC | REFLECTIONS/WHAT I MIGHT DO DIFFERENTLY NEXT TIME |
| --- | --- |
| | |
| | |
| | |

Have a "Temperature Checks: How Are You/We Doing?" activity adaptation to share?

Submit your tweaks and experiences here:

Survey Link: https://forms.gle/G7JS4RPADQK8ykp89

# To Culinary & Beyond (I'd Like to Be...)

**Sweet Treats/Desserts**

**Ice Breaker Title: To Culinary & Beyond (I'd Like to Be...)**

"To Culinary & Beyond (I'd Like to Be...)" activities as a tool to promote real-world applications of course concepts

## Activity Description

"To Culinary & Beyond (I'd Like to Be...)" activities are designed to support the application of course concepts to real-world applications and future career paths.

In this activity, students reflect on course learning to date and generate (with research, as applicable) a list of potential career opportunities.

Students share jobs of interest in writing, out loud, or via graphical illustrations.

"To Culinary & Beyond" activities offer opportunities for students to connect course concepts to real-world contexts and associated career opportunities.

The activity promotes forward-focused (career-related thinking) as well as reflective thinking and recall of past learning. This activity is designed to support creative thinking and sustain increased student confidence associated with mastery of course concepts and related career paths.

This activity works well as review at the conclusion of a unit (or at the mid- or endpoint of a semester).

## Recipe

Step 1: Define and explain "To Culinary & Beyond (I'd Like to Be...)" activities.

Step 2: Introduce the activity. Clarify content focus and type of resource to be used for the activity.

Step 3: Create groups (if applicable).

Step 4: Share a link to suggested software (if applicable).

Step 5: Explain the nature of the content/topic to focus on for purposes of this activity. Instructor might share a course unit or a specific course topic to help narrow student focus.

Sample prompts:

- What career options are related to these topics?
- What jobs might someone who is interested in these topics find especially appealing?
- Generate a list of possible jobs that rely on skills we developed when studying these concepts.
- What skills did we develop from our study of these topics?
- Brainstorm lists of skills students developed in connection with prior course study/assignments.

Step 6: Provide active work time for students to research related jobs and careers.

- Optional: Students review job-postings in fields of interest. Review posted skills (necessary/preferred).

Step 7: Students reflect and then identify (in writing, out loud, or via a recommended tool) a job of interest that draws on skills developed in connection with prior coursework.

Provide active work time for students to create and generate an original career sketch (content related) using an identified tool (recommended minimum five minutes).

- Options
  - Bitmoji for Careers. See: https://www.bitmoji.com/
  - Pencil and Paper Sketches
  - Written Reflections
- Offer support as needed.
- Share directional reminders about the activity, as applicable.

Step 8: Open discussion and reflection (out loud or independent journaling).

Sample prompts:

- How has this activity changed the way you feel about your preferred/desired career path?

Step 9: Share graphics/sketches (either out loud or on digital bulletin boards) (if applicable).

## The Secret Sauce (Why It Works)

This **interactive** activity breaks down course concepts into relatable, forward-focused activities that increase **relevance** for students. Students draw on and **actively recall** prior learning and knowledge and then **apply** that learning to explore potential career opportunities. The activity promotes hands-on, **active learning** that requires students to do something (create a personal sketch related to a job of interest) with course concepts. Goals include increased **student comfort** with a particular area of course content as well as increased **confidence** and **awareness** of associated career opportunities. The activity offers opportunities for **reflection** (both individual and group), **career-related awareness**, and **application**. The activity also offers opportunities for **formative assessment**.

## Ingredients

- ☐ An identified course topic
- ☐ Clock/Timer (as applicable)

## Activity Prep

An identified course topic.

Optional: Students reflect on course content to date and identify a topic for this activity.

## Activity Adaptations/Toppings

Depending on the instructional goals and objectives, this activity can be used and adapted in a variety of ways. A few examples follow:

- Conduct the activity using a passage (several paragraphs, a page of text) from a current reading, assigned book, or related news article. After reading the text, students brainstorm lists (or sketches) of the many different types of roles and jobs that might be associated with the reading.
- Introduce the activity with a discussion question/reflection prompt that explores the value of breaking down jobs into specific skills (both essential and helpful).
- Introduce the activity with a discussion question/reflection prompt that explores the benefits of applying course concepts to career applications.

- Introduce the activity using a current event/news article related to the lesson topic and from which students generate job profiles.
- Use the activity as a collaborative learning exercise where one student is responsible for posing a course-related scenario and another is tasked with identifying a variety of job options that are related to such scenario.
- Students create hypothetical job postings that might require knowledge and skills learned in a prior course unit or session.
- Students sketch course-related concepts, processes, and/or terms to make learning more visible.

Using Drawings for Formative Assessment. See: https://www.edutopia.org/article/using-drawings-formative-assessment

## Activity Extensions

Benefits of creating work for an audience are well-documented in research. Provide opportunities for students to publicly share original graphics. Students might post work to a class bulletin board or gallery. A Padlet board, class Google Site, or Pinterest board are free options that work well.

### Law-Based Examples

- Court-Related Career Opportunities
- Legal-Related Career Opportunities
- Civil Law Opportunities
- Criminal Law Opportunities
- Social Justice Careers

## Portion Type and Size

Single (independent work), pairs, small groups, or whole class

Time: Variable

- As few as five minutes.
- No maximum length.
- Time will vary depending on the adopted approach to implementation.

Online and/or face to face

## Web Resources

- Bitmoji. See: https://www.bitmoji.com/
- Pixton. See: https://www.pixton.com/
- Avatar Maker. See: https://avatarmaker.com/
- Google Slides/Google Draw
- Jobs-Related Resources
    - Bureau of Labor Statistics. See: https://www.bls.gov/
    - Occupational Outlook Handbook. See: https://www.bls.gov/ooh/
    - Free Career Aptitude Tests. See: https://www.thebalancecareers.com/free-career-aptitude-tests-2059813

- Using Drawings for Formative Assessment. See: https://www.edutopia.org/article/using-drawings-formative-assessment

## I Tried This and This Is What I Learned

| DATE USED/LESSON TOPIC | REFLECTIONS/WHAT I MIGHT DO DIFFERENTLY NEXT TIME |
|---|---|
| | |
| | |
| | |

Have a "To Culinary and Beyond: I'd Like to Be..." activity adaptation to share?

Submit your tweaks and experiences here:

Survey Link: https://forms.gle/G7JS4RPADQK8ykp89

# Half-Baked Activities: A Collection of 60-Second Content-Aligned Fill-Ins

No time to prep for a full ice breaker? Class momentum starting to melt? No problem! Grab and adapt a half-baked activity from the buffet. You might also look to these short, bite-sized activities as seasoning for an existing activity or for a mid-session snack break.

> "The more you know, the more you can create. There's no end to imagination in the kitchen."
>
> *Julia Child*

## Controversial Statements (Review and Discussion)

- Present a controversial statement related to a course or lesson objective. Open discussion for 60 seconds.

## A Daily Funny

Present a joke or comic related to course content.

## A Daily Grammar Faux Pas

Share an image (menu, sign, advertisement, communication) with an overlooked typo or grammatical error. Identify errors. Explore proofreading strategies.

Illustrative Resources:

- Scary Grammar Memes. See: https://www.bookbub.com/blog/scary-grammar-memes
- Fourteen Worst Typos Ever. See: https://blog.hubspot.com/marketing/14-worst-typos-ever

## Fact of the Day (Content Related)

Share an interesting, content-aligned fact that is selected for some identified characteristic (e.g., relevance, timeliness, historical significance).

## Word Origins

Explore origins and etymologies of key course terms.

## Trivia

Share an interesting, content-aligned trivia question that is selected for some identified characteristic (e.g., relevance, timeliness, historical significance).

## Controversial Statement Generator

Prompt students to generate a controversial statement related to a course or lesson objective. Open discussion for 60 seconds.

## Task Assignments/Rotations

Ask for volunteers and assign session tasks. Roles include timekeeper, notetaker, etc.

## Tell Me Anything!

Anonymous surveys/What do you want me to know?

## Can You Draw That for Me?

Students create quick draw visual representations or models of identified course concepts.

## Ask Me Anything

Open Q & A on any course-related topic.

## Note Swap and Review

Review a classmate's notes on a topic for 60 seconds.

## Study Strategy Swap and Share

Share a study strategy or tip that has worked well in the past week.

## "I Agree" Exercises

Share a collection of statements, assumptions, or cliches often associated with a course. Students vote (anonymously, out loud) on statements they agree or disagree with. Discuss results.

## What's Habit Got to Do with It?

- Introduce Habits of Mind. Identify one (instructor or student selected). Conduct a class discussion exploring the identified habit in connection with course assignments and topics.
- Resources
    - What are Habits of Mind? See: https://www.habitsofmindinstitute.org/what-are-habits-of-mind/
    - Integrating the 16 Habits of Mind. See: https://www.edutopia.org/blog/habits-of-mind-terrell-heick

## Podcast, Please

- Open class session with a short podcast. Students take notes, write reflections, and/or discuss in small groups or as a whole class before proceeding.
- Legal Podcasts. See: https://www.simplelegal.com/blog/20-best-legal-podcasts

## True/False

Instructor or student-generated true/false statements. Use for review and to build a question bank.

## It's My Understanding That...

Instructor- or student-generated "complete that thought" prompts. Introduce an exploratory hypothetical or partially constructed statement for students to complete.

## Students Score a Sample Assignment

Use for both past and upcoming assessment activities. Students compare/contrast with their own work.

## Student-Generated Exam/Review Questions

- True/False
- Multiple Choice
- Short Answer
- Essay

Resources

- How to Write Multiple-Choice Questions. See: https://testing.byu.edu/handbooks/14%20Rules%20for%20Writing%20Multiple-Choice%20Questions.pdf
- How to Write Good Short Answer Questions. See: https://sites.google.com/site/testwritingtutorial/short-answer-questions
- Suggestions for Writing True/False Questions. See: https://www.bristol.ac.uk/esu/media/e-learning/tutorials/writing_e-assessments/page_28.htm

## Name That Term

State or share a definition. Students respond with key terms.

## Acronym Generations

Students create acronyms or mnemonics to help review and/or memorize a course topic.

- Acronymify. See: http://acronymify.com/
- Generate Name Acronyms. See: https://www.nameacronym.net/

## Word Associations and Word Cloud Generation

Pick a prompt/phrase/concept that's relevant to weekly content. Students enter (into word cloud software) words they associate with it and then discuss.

## Set Game

- Daily Set Puzzles. See: https://www.setgame.com/welcome.
- Create original "Set"-themed cards using course terms, visuals, and/or concepts.

## What's Different?

Present two topics for consideration. Prompt students to brainstorm as many differences as possible.

## Song Lyrics, Name that Tune

- Draft original lyrics to describe a course concept.
- "Name that tune." Play/share lyrics from songs related to content.
- Students create playlists, identify songs related to content (e.g., lyrics, theme).

## Perfect Pairings: Music and Meals

After sharing a course topic or reading, prompt students to reflect on a song that would be a proper accompaniment for the topic or reading. Encourage students to consider characteristics such as mood, tone, and/or message. Provide time for students to reflect and share a song (artist, title, or specific lyrics) as well as their associated reasoning for the choice. Connections might be shared privately, anonymously, or out loud (whole class or small groups). Discuss.

## Error Identification

- Present statements on course concepts. Each statement should contain one or more substantive errors.
- Generate statements with grammatical errors and typos.
- Students identify as many errors as possible.

## In the News

Research recent news on a topic, post links to a Padlet board, then read and discuss in small groups.

## Design an Original Emoji

- Introduce a course topic. Design an emoji that either represents the topic and/or represents current feelings (e.g., comfort level, understanding, clarity) related to the topic.
    - "Anyone can create a new emoji. Here's an animated guide to doing it right". See: https://www.washingtonpost.com/graphics/2018/lifestyle/design-history-meditation-emoji-designer-explains-how-to-pitch-a-new-icon/?utm_term=.b943eef7ad80&itid=lk_interstitial_manual_6

## One Word

List and define one key term from last week's content. Draft a sample sentence.

## Name the Logical Error/Fallacy

- Review common logical errors and fallacies.

Logical Fallacies. See: https://owl.purdue.edu/owl/general_writing/academic_writing/logic_in_argumentative_writing/fallacies.html

Logical Fallacies. See: https://blog.hubspot.com/marketing/common-logical-fallacies

- Share a scenario or illustrative news article. Students identify associated logical error(s).

## Identify Errors in a Context-Substantive Sentence

Students draft a collection of three to five descriptive sentences aligned with a lesson topic. Drafted sentences include substantive (content-based) errors. Students swap sentences and work to identify errors.

## Feedback on Feedback

- Post a variety of feedback responses that one might receive in connection with a specific course assignment. Discuss. Share a sample assignment for student (individual or whole class) grading. Align with an assignment and rubric elements.
- As a class, develop generator feedback for use in specific assignments.
- Case Brief Generator and Discussion Board Feedback Generator Examples (top left of site). The Feedback Bank. See: https://www.thefeedbackbank.com/

## Uh-Oh, I've Got an Upset Stomach

Students identify a course topic or concept that they struggle with (in pairs, small groups, whole class, or individually). Discuss, swap, and/or share strategies and experiences.

## What's Inside That?

- Whole-class, small-group, individual exploration of "Open Middle Problems" (math exercises with a "closed" beginning and end and an "open" middle).
- Open Middle Problems. See: https://www.openmiddle.com/whats_open_middle/
- Submit original Open Middle Problems here: https://www.openmiddle.com/submit/
- Adapt for other disciplines.

Example: Create an original, unfinished sentence that includes concepts from a recent lesson. Share opening and closing parts of the sentence. Students reflect and work on middle parts of the sentence individually or in small groups. Students share original sentences (once complete) for discussion.

## Fermi Questions

- Whole-class or small-group exploration.
- Fermi Questions/Illustrative examples. See: https://navajomath.math.ksu.edu/wp-content/uploads/2015/03/fermi_questions_handouts_and_lesson_plan.pdf

- "30 Fermi Problems for Students and Teachers". See: https://www.innovativeteachingideas.com/blog/an-excellent-collection-of-fermi-problems-for-your-class
- Enrico Fermi, Fermi Questions in Everyday Life. See: http://www.math.lsa.umich.edu/WCMTC/Fermi-Questions-RCMC-Three-Levels.pdf

## Scavenger Hunts (Paper or Digital with Google Forms)

- Instructor or student created.
- Google Forms: Creating a Scavenger Hunt. See: https://behindmytechiewall.wordpress.com/2017/09/25/google-forms-creating-a-scavenger-hunt/
- Google Form Scavenger Hunt. See: https://passionatelycuriousssci.weebly.com/blog/google-form-scavenger-hunt
- Intellectual Property Scavenger Hunt Example:
  - Find and describe three examples of copyrights.
  - Find and describe three examples of patents.
  - Find and describe three examples of trademarks.
  - Find and describe three examples of trade secrets.

## Community Annotations

- Annotate complex text in individual, small-group, or whole-class settings.
- Tools: Hypothesis (https://web.hypothes.is/), Kami App (https://www.kamiapp.com/)
- Project examples
  - BookSnaps (Students snap and then annotate book passages of personal interest). See: https://twitter.com/booksnapsreal?lang=en
  - MathSnaps. See: https://makemathnotsuck.com/2017/03/24/mathsnaps/

## Worst Approach You Can Think Of/Worst Possible Outcome

- Present a problem to be solved/topic.
- Generate bad ways of solving it to later compare with alternatives.
- For an adaptation, consider "Bump in the Road" activities as described by Chapman and King (2012). Provides students an opportunity to pause, reflect, and share (in writing) a problem or question related to a specific course concept or skill (Chapman & King, 2012, p. 91). After writing a problem or question at the top of a piece of paper, students then pass their paper to classmates (an individual student or a group of students). The recipient student(s) then provide (again in writing) their recommendations to the problem (or an answer to the question). Each contributing student should initial their suggestions. Each contributing student helps the original drafter "overcome the bump in the road" relating to a particular concept or process skill (Chapman & King, 2012, p. 91).

In the online classroom, a discussion forum can be used for the same purpose and in a similar manner. Students can be grouped into pairs, teams, or participate as a class. In a dedicated discussion forum, students can post questions and peers can be required to respond to one or more questions throughout the week or module.

"Bump in the Road" Business Model Example. See: https://docs.google.com/document/d/13_RtCbNQMUZZknD27E4yToe1CMCYy53IrsRuQrYKjys/edit?usp=sharing

## Variation of Minute Paper

Pose questions related to an earlier class session. Students answer one or more questions in quick response format (can use polling software, Google Docs, surveys, index cards, paper). Sample questions: "What was the most important thing you learned during the class?" "What important questions remain unanswered?"

## Learning Transfer

- Students identify connections between course concepts and real-world applications. Four Square/Four Corners.
- Four corner templates break down a course concept into four characteristics or factors. Instructor or student generated. Each corner explores a different characteristic or theme associated with a course topic.
- Students add content to each template corner.
- Example: Analyze a particular software across at least four characteristics/factors. Corners might include cost, efficiency, privacy concerns, usability, accessibility.
- Example: Analyze a story for four craft elements. Examples might include plot, conflict, characterization, action, point of view, voice, etc.
- Self-checks for assignment submissions. Four corners might include rubric elements, format, grammar, references, etc.
- Four Corners Game. See: https://www.icebreakers.ws/small-group/four-corners.html

## 60-Second Debates/Mini Mock Trials

- Students construct an argument on an assigned topic. Argument must be delivered in 30 or 60 seconds.
- Limit response time to 30 or 60 seconds. Focus on brevity, clarity, conciseness, and delivery.
- "Short Activities and Exercises". See: https://noisyclassroom.com/oracy-ideas/short-activities-and-exercises/

## Pick-Up Sticks

- Assign colors (and associated actions) to course topics or content-aligned categories. Depending on color, students respond in unique ways.
  - Examples: If red, share a _____. If blue, identify a ____. If green, describe a ___.
  - Literary-based example when studying a novel:

    - If red, identify a character.
    - If blue, describe a conflict.
    - If green, describe a book theme.
    - If yellow, identify a line of dialogue that ___.

- Color/Topic Online Wheel Generator:
    - Wheel of Names. See: https://wheelofnames.com/
    - Picker Wheel. See: https://pickerwheel.com/
- Alterative application: Create wheels with vocabulary terms. Students provide definitions as terms are selected.
- Pick up Sticks. See: http://www.teambuildingsolutions.co.uk/activities/pick-up-sticks-icebreaker
- The Gratitude Game, Pick Up Sticks. See: https://teachbesideme.com/gratitude-game-pick-sticks/

## Fill in the Blank (Citations, Formatting)

Practice preferred citation/format style. Share partially complete citations with fill-in-the-blank options.

## Reflection through Critical Questioning

- Students generate a variety of question types and prompts to explore a topic from different critical perspectives and lenses.
- Example Resources
    - Questions for Critical Thinking. See: https://www.hunschool.org/resources/questions-for-critical-thinking
    - Critical Thinking Questions. See: https://www.weareteachers.com/critical-thinking-questions/
    - 48 Critical Thinking Questions for Any Content Area. See: https://www.teachthought.com/critical-thinking/48-critical-thinking-questions-any-content-area/
    - Types of Questions for Critical Thinking. See: https://www.teachthought.com/critical-thinking/types-of-questions-for-critical-thinking/
    - Question Stems Frame Around Bloom's Taxonomy. See: https://www.teachthought.com/critical-thinking/question-stems-blooms-taxonomy/
    - The Socratic Questioning Technique. See: https://www.intel.com/content/dam/www/program/education/us/en/documents/project-design/strategies/dep-question-socratic.pdf
- Curate and create a student-generated discussion prompt bank.

## Taking Stock: Let's Talk about Note-Taking

- Compare and contrast a variety of note-taking methods.
- Explore advantages of each method.

- Review digital tools to support strong note-taking.
- Students reflect on potential gaps/weaknesses in current practices and strategies for improvement.

## Labeled Diagram Fill-Ins

- What's missing?
- Sample use cases: Human anatomy, timelines
- Student completed and/or created and generated

## Critical Incident Questionnaire (CIQ)

Provide students the same five questions at different points throughout a course. Students respond then reflect on knowledge growth as a course progresses. See: http://www.stephenbrookfield.com/critical-incident-questionnaire"

## Graphic Organizer Templates

- Student-generated visual content
- Free digital tools:
    - Free Graphic Organizer Templates. See: https://www.hmhco.com/blog/free-graphic-organizer-templates
    - Graphic Organizer Software. See: https://creately.com/lp/graphic-organizer-software-k12/
    - Canva. See: https://www.canva.com/graphs/graphic-organizers/
    - Graphic Organizers. See: https://sites.google.com/view/freeudltechtoolkit/graphic-organizers
    - Bubbl.us. See: https://bubbl.us/
    - Popplet. See: https://www.popplet.com/

## Analogies

- Instructor or student generated
- Discuss:
    - How is one term/concept similar to another term/concept?
    - Identify similarities/differences across course topics or concepts.
    - Compare/contrast assignment expectations.
- Analogy and Analogical Reasoning. See: https://plato.stanford.edu/entries/reasoning-analogy/
- Problem Solving Exercise, Analogies. See: https://www.skillsconverged.com/FreeTrainingMaterials/tabid/258/articleType/ArticleView/articleId/744/Problem-Solving-Exercise-Analogies.aspx
- The Best Meeting Ice-Breaker to Break the Ice. See: https://tobyelwin.com/the-best-meeting-icebreaker-to-break-the-ice/

- How Do We Use Analogies in the Classroom?. See: https://k12teacherstaffdevelopment.com/tlb/how-do-we-use-analogies-in-the-classroom/

## Current Events Vocab Builder

Share a current events article. Students identify three-five key terms. Students add definitions to a collaborative document.

## Let's Get Goal Oriented

Craft a course-related SMART goal. How to Set SMART Goals. See: https://www.mindtools.com/pages/videos/smart-transcript.htm

## Name That Term

- Share flashcards with term definitions from a prior lesson.

## Word Match-Up

Create notecards with terms and definitions. Place cards face down. Students flip cards two at a time looking for matches.

## Mock Interviews

- Sixty-second interview question practice
- Two-minute mock interviews
- Discuss possible responses to sample interview questions.

## Career Tips/Databases

Explore career databases aligned with course concepts and topics.

## Presentation Skills

- Share quick tips and best practices for presentation preparation and delivery
- "Online Presentations and Assessment: Nurturing Student Comfort, Confidence, and Creativity". See: https://drive.google.com/file/d/1BfGA5BCqmTkBQgW2SG0eFxJZYn4nlYQH/view?usp=sharing

## Learning Strategies

- Practice activities and exercises that demonstrate evidence-based learning strategies.
- Active recall, spaced practice, retrieval practice, elaboration, etc.

## How Memory Works

- Self-paced module. Students complete over several days. Reclaiming Lost Learning and Winning the Battle against the Forgetting Curve. See: https://drive.google.com/file/d/1TqpQfNnR26iLTgxc3dkCVzZsogglmLiQ/view?usp=sharing

## Peer-Review Strategies and Tips

- Review best practices for providing peer review.
- Anti-Bias in Grading Checklists:
  - "Promoting Equity and Mitigating Bias in Grading Feedback". See: https://drive.google.com/file/d/1xoC95OUsHczO_zNoA0uXYIKZsKn-Wpsq/view?usp=sharing
  - Ant-Bias and Grading Checklists. See: https://sites.google.com/view/inclusive-unbiased-feedback/grading-checklists
  - Inclusive Feedback Resources. See: https://sites.google.com/view/inclusive-unbiased-feedback/additional-resources

## High-Five Check-In

Pose a question, identify a topic, and/or present a course term or concept. Prompt students to reflect and self-assess an emotional state or degree of understanding (e.g., scales of 1–5, 1–10). Use numerical scales, emoji scales, or any other visual scale. Can also use word scales (e.g., hot, cold, lukewarm). Responses can be shared privately, anonymously, and/or as a whole class.

**Business Model Canvas Example:** After working through each of the nine elements of the Business Model Canvas, provide students several minutes to reflect on their understanding of each element and how each element interacts with one another.

After students reflect, provide the following instructions:

- After naming one of the elements of the Business Model Canvas, say: "1, 2, 3, show me"
- Each student should respond by raising the appropriate number of fingers as an indication of their level of knowledge and understanding of the specific element.

Modify and adapt instruction based on student response.

In the online classroom, instructors can solicit responses via polling software, Google Surveys, etc.

"High-Five Assessment Tool". See: https://docs.google.com/document/d/12wl4rlTX4HGrUu1oD1cJkzXYtRiCPlEKw9flvx7Jo8g/edit?usp=sharing

## I've Seen That Pairing Before

- Post two letters (e.g., "ot").
- Students recall and generate course-related words using that combination of letters.

## Where Might We Use This Spice/Ingredient Again?

- Think of a concept or term we studied last week.
- Conduct research. Identify an example of this concept or term in practice.
- Reflect. Where might you utilize this term or concept again? Describe.

## Ooh, Can I Add a Dash of Salt (or Pepper)?

Students review a brief article that provides advice and strategies on a specific course topic. Students reflect and offer additional tips and strategies that might be added to the article.

- Example: "How to Read a Judicial Opinion" at https://pdfs.semanticscholar.org/f9cc/6a5600ae29cc0671cd5bcd78001aebc085bd.pdf
- Prompt: What additional recommendations and suggestions might you share?
- Kerr, O. S., & Washington, G. (2005). *How to read a judicial opinion: A guide for new law students.* https://pdfs.semanticscholar.org/f9cc/6a5600ae29cc0671cd5bcd78001aebc085bd.pdf

## Fresh from the Garden

Students share current event updates/articles associated with a course topic.

## Let's Introduce the Chefs in the Kitchen

Share a collection of personalization resources with students. These are helpful for students who are not comfortable sharing a personal picture online. Create original chef/class member graphics to build community.

- Bitmoji: https://www.bitmoji.com/
- Voki: https://voki.com/
- "Digital You: Tech Tools to Help You Create Amazing Avatars for the Online Classroom." See: http://www.codlearningtech.org/2018/03/01/digital-you-tech-tools-to-help-you-create-amazing-avatars-for-the-online-classroom/

## Test the Soup before Serving

- Utilize technology tools for formative assessment and as self-assessment resources for students.
- Formative Assessment Tech Tools. See: https://docs.google.com/presentation/d/1cUcPXxgbSiQDYILHy-29vu3q0buz882uAFnrAOQc5n0/edit?usp=sharing

## My Shopping Cart and List

List three concepts/terms you now feel are in your "shopping cart"; you understand them well and believe you can apply them. Explain why. List three concepts/terms that are on your shopping list and which you are still working to acquire (master). Explain the steps you are taking.

## Fill in the Blank/Make Our Own Recipe Cookbook

Using collaborative presentation software like Google Slides, prepare a template slide with pre-populated prompts for students to complete. Duplicate the slide with enough blank templates for each student in class to complete. Students select and complete a blank slide. Review presentations as a whole class.

## Quick, Clean Off the Counters

- Generate as many words as you can on a particular course topic in a defined period of time (e.g., 30, 60, 90 seconds).
- Write without thinking. Identify and document (e.g., write, share) as many words as possible on a presented course topic or concept.

## Strong Flavors, Strong Verbs

- Students write on a topic using as many strong verbs as possible.
- Alternatively, students randomly select one verb and one course topic from a prepared collection and draft original sentences.
- Alternatively, students craft application sentences using an assigned course term and a strong verb of choice.
    - Powerful Verbs. See: https://jerryjenkins.com/powerful-verbs/

## I Tried a New Spice

Students reflect and document a course concept or term they applied over the past week. Each student adds the term to a Google Slides deck, along with its meaning and the context in which it was applied. Review and discuss shared terms as a group.

## Select Today's Special

Students vote on questions/topics to explore as part of an opening discussion. See: Online Questions. See: https://onlinequestions.org/

## Yikes, That's Too Much ___

Students share anonymous feedback regarding the pacing of a course lesson or covered topic. Instructor presents an exercise, course topic, or course assignment for reflection and asks for anonymous student feedback. Instructor might also present a general question relating to assignment clarity, feedback quality, etc. Response options might include: "Too much too quickly," "Keep going," "We could use a bit more ___." Instructors can vary response options to best suit course needs.

- For an example of a "Stop, Slow, Go" activity, see: https://thoughtfulclassroom.com/wp-content/uploads/2019/12/TIP_2_TTA-Tools.pdf.

## Class Picture/Image Glossary

- Student generated visual glossary. Students select a key term aligned with a course topic and research free image sites (or create an original image) that illustrates the meaning of the term. After identifying an appropriate image, students draft an original, text-based definition to accompany the graphic.
- Visual glossaries can be hosted on a free public site (e.g., Google Sites) and can be curated over time.

## Take It to Twitter

- Identify real-world conversations and course-relevant accounts to follow.
- Students curate a list of accounts of interest.
- Curate tweets related to course topics and share as a resource for reflection and discussion.
- Example: Table of Authorities. See: https://docs.google.com/presentation/d/1SXbeMcdk6fA24bGgzlhC1tRrDdm9UA1i8mLtHJYKdbw/edit?usp=sharing

## Why Do We Even Talk about This in the Kitchen?

- Prompt students to reflect on a course topic or concept and explore why it is a part of the larger curriculum.

## Mindfulness in the Kitchen

- Five-minute mindfulness activities
    - Daily Mindfulness for Students, 6 Activities. See: https://www.ef.edu/blog/teacherzone/daily-mindfulness-for-students-6-activities/
    - Mindfulness Activities for Kids. See: https://www.waterford.org/resources/mindfulnes-activities-for-kids/
    - Mindfulness Activities in the Classroom. See: https://www.mentalup.co/blog/mindfulness-activities-in-the-classroom
    - Integrating Mindfulness in Classroom Curriculum. See: https://www.edutopia.org/blog/integrating-mindfulness-in-classroom-curriculum-giselle-shardlow

# Additional Pantry Readings and Resources


Baldomero Loor Ponce, J., Cedeño-Macías Mercedes, L., and Yahaira, R. (2020). https://www.researchgate.net/publication/342313072_The Advantages of Using Warm up Activities to Engage Students in the English Language Teaching and Learning Process: An Experience from GO Teacher Program, Warm Up Activities in English Language Lessons

Chapman, C., & King, R. (2012). *Differentiated assessment strategies: One tool doesn't fit all.* Corwin.

Cotter C., (2000). Better Language Teaching resource ebook. 2nd Edition, Japan.

Eberly Center for Teaching Excellence, Carnegie Mellon. (n.d.). *Make the most of the first day of class.* http://www.cmu.edu/teaching/designteach/teach/firstday.html

Eure, M. J., & Milner, J. O. (2004). *Opening salvos: The first five minutes of class.* https://files.eric.ed.gov/fulltext/ED489982.pdf#page=39

Gonzalez, J. (2016). A 4-Part System for Getting to Know Your Students. https://www.cultofpedagogy.com/relationship-building/

Guhlin, M. (2017). Grouping Tools for the Classroom. https://www.tcea.org/blog/grouping-tools/

Heritage, M. (2010). *Formative assessment and next-generation assessment systems: Are we losing an opportunity?* https://www.michigan.gov/documents/mde/formative_assessment_next_generation_heritage_338483_7.pdf

Honeycutt, B. (2019). *Three focusing activities to engage students in the first five minutes of class.* https://www.facultyfocus.com/articles/blended-flipped-learning/three-focusing-activities-engage-students-first-five-minutes-class/

Kris, D. F. (2021). *What kids need to know about their working memory.* https://intrepidednews.com/what-kids-need-to-know-about-their-working-memory-deborah-farmer-kris/

Lang, J. (2016). *Small changes in teaching: The first five minutes of class.* https://www.chronicle.com/article/Small-Changes-in-Teaching-The/234869

Marzano, R. J. (2006). *Classroom assessment & grading that work.* Association for Supervision and Curriculum Development.

Mather, K. (2020). *Why are we still forcing each other to play icebreaker games?* In the Know. https://www.intheknow.com/post/why-are-we-still-forcing-each-other-to-play-icebreaker-games/Miller, R., King, J., Mark, M., & Caracelli, V. (2016). The oral history of evaluation: the professional development of Robert Stake. *American Journal of Evaluation, 37*(2), 287–294. http://journals.sagepub.com/doi/10.1177/1098214015597314

Rosegard, E., & Wilson, J. (2013). *Capturing students' attention: An empirical study.* https://files.eric.ed.gov/fulltext/EJ1017063.pdf

Tutt, P. (2021). *5 metacognitive questions for students learning new material.* https://www.edutopia.org/article/5-metacognitive-questions-students-learning-new-material

University of Florida Center for Teaching Excellence. (n.d.). *First five minutes.* https://teach.ufl.edu/resource-library/first-five-minutes/

University of Washington Center for Teaching and Learning. (n.d.). *Teaching the first day of class.* https://teaching.washington.edu/topics/preparing-to-teach/teaching-the-first-day-of-class/

Walter, M. (2020). *The danger of team-building activities and ice-breakers.* https://medium.com/swlh/the-danger-of-team-building-activities-and-ice-breakers-5afd068070a9

William, D. (2018). *Embedded formative assessment*. Bloomington: Solution Tree Press.

Wright, D. L. (2012). *The most important day.* Teaching and Learning Center, University of Nebraska. https://www.honolulu.hawaii.edu/facdev/the-most-important-day/

(2016). *Formative Assessment Quotes.* http://www.sdcoe.net/lls/assessment/Documents/GettingSmarter/2016August/ScalingUp/7-2FAQuotes.pdf

"The thing about finishing a story is that finishing is really only the beginning."

***William Herring***